A POETICS OF COMPOSITION

CONTENTS

LIST OF PLATES

background). "Feast of the Boyars." Miniature of the seventeenth or eighteenth century.

11. Elements of direct perspective on the periphery of the painting. Abrupt foreshortening in the representation of the floor. "Execution of St. Matthew." German painting of the fifteenth century.

12. The laconic gestures and stressed three-dimensionality in the foreground of the painting contrast with the principles of representation in the background. Antonello da Messina's "St. Sebastian."

13. The Master of the Grossgmein Altar. "Madonna with Child and the Apostle Thomas." Fifteenth century. Several consecutively represented spatial layers each have their own framing in the form of an embrasure and their own perspective position.

14. Hans Schuchlin. "The Execution of St. Barbara." Fifteenth century. The background is represented as a picture within a picture.

15. "Collation." Illustration from an English psalmbook of the fourteenth century. The representation in the background is given as a picture within a picture.

16. The representation in the foreground (which in this instance is peripheral) is given as a picture within a picture. Displacement of the objects on the table is "toward the viewer." Illustration to a romance of the fourteenth century, *Three Ladies from Paris*.

17. Ornamentation of the background in the icon: the so-called icon hillocks. "The Entombment of Christ." Icon of the late fifteenth century.

18. Ornamentation of the background in the icon: the so-called icon hillocks. "Miracle of Archangel Michael in Chonae." Icon of the sixteenth century.

19. Ornamentation of garment folds in Medieval art. Detail of a mosaic of the Cathedral of Saint Mark in Venice.

20. Ornamentation of folds in Medieval painting. Detail of Andrey Rublev: "Trinity." Fifteenth century.

21. Heightening of conventionality (or of the symbolic nature) of the background of the representation. "Night Council in the Enemy Camp." Miniature from a chronicle of the sixteenth century. The details of the background receive a highly conventional treatment: night is represented as a scroll; dawn is represented as a rooster.

TRANSLATOR'S PREFACE

Boris Uspensky published *A Poetics of Composition* in 1970 as the first volume in a series entitled "Semiotic Studies in the Theory of Art." The announced aim of the series was to acquaint the reader with research of structuralist orientation in the theory of art, emphasizing formal study of structure as a means of content analysis. Literature, film, music, and painting were among the fields to be covered in the series. Two books have appeared, both treating literary problems: Lotman's *Structure of the Artistic Text*[1] and *A Poetics of Composition*, in which Uspensky explores a subject of current interest in literary studies—point of view in fiction—as a general problem in art theory.

Boris Uspensky, one of the younger members of the Russian structuralist group, was born in 1937. He graduated from the University of Moscow with a degree in General and Comparative Linguistics. His dissertation on structural typology of languages was published in 1965 and subsequently translated into English as *Principles of Structural Typology* (The Hague: Mouton, 1968). His doctoral dissertation was devoted to the sociological aspects of phonics, and specifically to the history of traditional Russian church pronunciation and its connection with the history of literary Russian.

In 1961 Uspensky studied at the University of Copenhagen at the *Institut for Lingvistik og Fonetik*, consulting with Louis Hjelmslev and Eli Fischer-Jørgensen. From 1963 to 1965, Uspensky's research at the Institute of African Languages of the Academy of Sciences of the USSR was

---

1. Iurii M. Lotman, *Struktura khudozhestvennogo teksta* [Structure of the poetic text] (Moscow, 1970). In German: *Die Struktur literarischer Texte* (Munich: Wilhelm Fink Verlag, 1972).

devoted to African linguistics. This led to the publication of the *Typology of African Languages* in 1966, of which he was the editor. Since 1965, Uspensky, now a staff member of Moscow University, has been conducting research at the Laboratory of Computational Linguistics and lecturing on the typology of languages (with special emphasis on language universals) and on the history of Russian literary language.

Uspensky's association with Structuralist semiotics dates from 1962, the year of the Moscow Symposium on Semiotic Analysis.[2] In the summer of the same year, Uspensky took part in a Siberian expedition for the study of the almost extinct language and culture of the Ket people. The expedition to the Yenisei River brought together a group of young scholars who subsequently contributed to the formation of the Russian school of structural semiotics, particularly after Yury Lotman joined the group in 1964.[3] Collaboration between Uspensky and the Moscow group, and Lotman, whose home university is in Tartu (Estonia), proved very productive. Since 1964, the Tartu Summer Symposia have become landmarks in the life of Russian Structuralism, and a special publication of the Tartu University, *Sēmeiōtika,* is now the main forum for Structuralist exchanges.[4] Research in semiotics, in many instances the result of group effort, appears in *Sēmeiōtika* under the following headings: "Myth"; "Folklore"; "Religion as Modelling Systems"; "Semiotics of Art"; "Poetics"; "Semantic Structures of Texts"; "Metrics"; "Nonlinguistic Communicative Systems"; "General Problems of Semiotic Description"; "Semiotics of Culture"; "Analysis of Texts"; and so forth.

A literary theoretician bred in the climate of contemporary Russian structural semiotics is concerned with methodology, broad interdisciplinary applications, and the relevance of linguistic theories. In his work —besides the genetic connection with linguistics in general and Saussurean linguistics in particular—Uspensky recognizes the influence of the Prague

2. *Simposium po strukturnomu izucheniiu znakovykh sistem* held in Moscow in 1962 may be considered the beginning of the Russian School of Structural Semiotics. For historical beginnings of Russian Structuralism see H. Günther, "Zur Strukturalismus-Diskussion in der sowjetischen Literaturwissenschaft," *Die Welt der Slaven* 14 (1969), 1–21; see also K. Eimermacher, "Entwicklung, Charakter und Probleme des sowjetischen Strukturalismus in der Literaturwissenschaft," *Texte des Sowjetischen literaturwissenschaftlichen Strukturalismus* (Munich: Wilhelm Fink Verlag, 1971), pp. 7–40. For a discussion of Structuralism and of the present work see also Stefan Żółkiewski, "Poétique de la composition," *Semiotica* 5 (The Hague, 1972), 3:2–24.

3. Among the participants in the expedition were V. V. Ivanov, V. N. Toporov, B. A. Uspensky, B. P. Korshunova (now Uspensky's wife), T. N. Moloshnaya, D. M. Segal, T. V. Tsivyan.

4. Summer Symposia were held at Kääriku, near Tartu, Estonia in 1964, 1966, 1968, and 1970.

School, and notably that of Jakobson, Trubetzkoy, and Bogatyrev.[5] In literary studies, his immediate predecessors are Bakhtin (and indirectly Voloshinov), and among the Russian literary theorists of the 1920s, Tynyanov and, to a certain extent, Zhirmunsky and Eikhenbaum.[6] As a semiotician, Uspensky recognizes the influence of the tradition of C. S. Peirce and Charles Morris.

In his research in semiotics Uspensky is concerned with describing different types of communicative processes, which, generally speaking, are part of the phenomenon of human culture. Specifically, his recent work comprises studies of the semiotic aspect of texts—the Russian Medieval icon, an individual style or styles, a type of human behavior, the poetic text, or the work of an individual author.[7] The "language" of those texts, and the internal system inscribed in the text by an author considered as an intentional carrier of a given communication, are of primary concern for Uspensky. This approach to the descriptive procedure may be characterized by the following statement defining the theoretical premises of Structuralism in general:

The methodological unity of the various structuralist schools lies in a common conception of structure and its manifestations: in this approach primary attention is given to distinguishing consistently between the level of observation and the level of constructs, or, in other words, between "parole" and "langue," "text" and "system," or "behavior" and "model." The aim in this approach is to take into account the multi-leveled character of structure, the concept of a hierarchy of levels; to apply the method of opposition in paradigmatics and the distributional method in syntagmatics; to construct minimal units from universal distinctive features; and to distinguish between synchrony and diachrony. Since structuralism operates constantly with sign systems, the problem of interaction between the object and subject of description is of vital importance; this problem is connected on the logical plane with the distinction between object language and metalanguage. At the same time, particular attention is given to discovering the interdependence between the results of the investigation and the metalanguage of the investigation. . . . Research in linguistic semantics, in which emphasis is placed on the search for structures that are isomorphic for natural languages and other sign systems, has been particularly fruitful. . . . An important achievement of struc-

5. Roman Jakobson and N. S. Trubetzkoy were among the founders of the Prague Circle; Petr Bogatyrev also contributed to and participated in the life of the circle.

6. M. Bakhtin as well as his collaborator V. N. Voloshinov initiated point of view studies in Russian literary criticism in the 1920s. Boris Eikhenbaum, Yury Tynianov, and, to a lesser degree, Viktor Zhirmunsky took part in the Russian Formalist movement.

7. See Selected Works by Uspensky.

turalism is to specify the concept of isomorphism and the hierarchy of systems with which human existence is connected.[8]

Uspensky presented his first study on point of view during the Summer Symposium at Kääriku (Estonia) in August 1966. His study was subsequently published under the title "Structure of the Artistic Text and the Typology of Composition." [9] At this stage Uspensky outlined the different levels of manifestation of point of view, but limited his analysis mainly to point of view on the phraseological level, to which Chapter Two of the *Poetics* is devoted. However, in his 1966 essay, Uspensky states clearly the two directions which a complete study in point of view should take: first, the investigation of points of view in one single work, and, second, the comparative study of the problem of point of view as it pertains to different arts. In the 1966 essay, Uspensky asserts more boldly than in the later work the final goal to which the study of point of view should lead. He states that in a single work, "In the transition from one point of view to another, from one manner of describing to another, there must be a harmony, an order, peculiar to the particular work, which eventually would allow us to define the inner rhythm of the work in question." [10] Structure is presented here as the product of descriptive activity or of the analytic act. In a single work of art, structures at which we may arrive in our analysis are manifold: "Different levels of description define different structures of one and the same work, and those structures need not correspond with each other. We may foresee, however, that there is some recurrent pattern in the relations between the different structures of one and the same work." [11]

On the other hand, in a comparative approach to the study of point of view as a compositional problem, "The analysis of the organization of the text in representational arts and in film will lead us to define a number of isomorphic principles and methods." [12] In the *Poetics*, the seventh and concluding chapter is devoted to a comparative study. Uspensky explores isomorphic structuring in painting and literature but does not undertake the comparison with film that he originally intended. Chapter Seven— possibly a chapter to read first—not only allows us to envisage the design which the particular process of analysis may offer, but reveals more clearly the nature of the component parts in the comparative context.

8. D. M. Segal and Iu. Senokosov, "Structuralizm," *Filosofskaia Entsiklopediia* (Moscow, 1970), 5:144–145.
9. Boris Uspenskii, "Struktura khudozhestvennogo teksta i tipologiia kompozitsii," *Tezisy dokladov vo vtoroi letnei shkole po vtorichnym modeliruiushchim sistemam* (Tartu, 1966), pp. 20–26.
10. Ibid., pp. 23–24.
11. Ibid., p. 25.
12. Ibid., p. 21.

The concept of point of view which Uspensky uses has been made familiar in Russian literary studies of the 1920s and 1930s; Uspensky writes in his introduction, "The beginnings of the study of point of view . . . were inaugurated by M. M. Bakhtin, V. N. Voloshinov (whose ideas were formed under the direct influence of Bakhtin). . . . In the present work we have tried to synthesize the findings of their research." [13]

Point of view as a functional unit of discourse has been defined by Uspensky in his 1966 essay with an example from Tolstoy. Here, Pierre, Natasha, and even minor characters may become potential "authors" describing a scene, and, consequently, the "carriers of the authorial point of view." This simplest concept of point of view, when extended to discourse in general, is shown to be a migrating phenomenon and a unit of a multitude of realizations. However, the attribution of the speech to an "author" is still of primary importance. Borrowing the concept of Bakhtin-Voloshinov, Uspensky approaches discourse from the "dialogical angle"—a subject belonging to the translinguistic level of speech—showing that to become dialogical, an expression must "acquire an author, a creator whose position it then expresses. Each expression in this sense has its own author, whom we hear in the utterance. . . . The dialogical attitudinizing also personifies the expression to which it reacts." [14]

On the other hand, the interaction of points of view becomes clearly manifest in the phenomenon of reported speech. Voloshinov shows the dynamic relation between different points of view as they collide in discourse:

Word comes into contact with word. The context of this inner speech is the locale in which another's utterance is received, comprehended, and evaluated, where, that is, the speaker's active orientation takes place. This active inner speech reception proceeds in two directions: first, the received utterance is framed within a context of factual commentary (coinciding in part with what is called the apperceptive background of the words) taking into account the situation (both internal and external), the visual signs of expression, and so on; second, a reply (*Gegenrede*) is prepared. Both the preparation of the reply (internal retort) and the factual commentary are organically fused in the unity of active reception, and these can be isolated only in abstract terms. Both lines of reception find their expression, are objectified, in the "auctorial" context surrounding the reported

13. M. Bakhtin, "Discourse Typology in Prose," in Matejka and Pomorska, eds., *Readings in Russian Poetics: Formalist and Structuralist Views* (Cambridge: MIT Press, 1971), pp. 176–197. See also V. N. Voloshinov, "Reported Speech," ibid.; and V. N. Vološinov, *Marxism and the Philosophy of Language*, translated by L. Matejka and I. R. Titunik (New York: Seminar Press, 1973).

14. M. Bakhtin, *Problemy poetiki Dostoevskogo* [Problems of poetics in Dostoevsky] (Moscow, 1963), p. 246. See also: M. Bakhtin, *Problems of Dostoevsky's Poetics* (Ann Arbor: Ardis Publs., 1973).

speech. Regardless of the functional orientation of the given context—whether a work of fiction, a polemical article, an attorney's summation, or the like—we clearly discern these two tendencies in it, that of commenting and that of retorting. Usually one of them is dominant. Between the reported speech and the reporting context, dynamic relations of high complexity and tension are in force.[15]

Uspensky's subtitle—*Typology of a Compositional Form*—suggests that his book may be understood as a rhetoric which describes and classifies the "attitudinizing conventions" (to borrow G. T. Wright's term)[16] of our speech acts. This rhetoric of means of expressing attitudes pertains not only to compositional forms in literature, and indeed to all linguistic activity, but to art forms in general.

A few words should be said about the present version of the book. The translation follows the 1970 text modified and corrected by the author, whose revision contains some fifty substantial additions to the text. I would like to thank Boris Andreevich Uspensky for carefully reading the translation and making valuable suggestions. I am also indebted to the faculty members of the Department of Rhetoric, University of California, Berkeley, for including my work in connection with this project as part of my doctoral program and, in particular, to Thomas Sloan for his support. I am grateful to Marvin Chachere, of the University of California Extension, for making possible my visit to Moscow. To Francis Whitfield I owe recognition for his scholarly advice.

VALENTINA ZAVARIN

15. Voloshinov, 1971, pp. 152–153. Reprinted from *Readings in Russian Poetics: Formalist and Structural Views*, Matejka and Pomorska, eds.; by permission of the M.I.T. Press, Cambridge, Massachusetts, 1971.
16. G. T. Wright, "The Faces of the Poet," *The Poet in the Poem* (Berkeley and Los Angeles: University of California Press, 1962), p. 5.

A NOTE ABOUT THE ENGLISH TRANSLATION

The English translation follows the author's revised copy of the 1970 edition. Transliteration in the footnote references follows the Library of Congress system, except that diacritical marks have been omitted. Spelling of Russian names in the text follows common English usage. Page numbers in parentheses following quoted passages in the text refer to the following Random House English translations: Fyodor Dostoevsky, *The Brothers Karamazov,* trans. Constance Garnett (Modern Library edition); Fyodor Dostoevsky, *The Possessed,* trans. Constance Garnett (Modern Library edition); Fyodor Dostoevsky, *The Idiot,* trans. Constance Garnett (Modern Library edition); Leo Tolstoy, *War and Peace,* trans. Constance Garnett (Modern Library edition). Other English translations are cited in the notes. In all instances original texts were consulted. French was retained as in the original Russian edition, and a more literal expression was used when necessary to bring out the point under discussion.

We are profoundly indebted to Josephine Miles for her comments. Meyer Schapiro had the generosity to give his valuable time and attention. We thank Robert Hughes for review of difficult problems. We are particularly indebted to Eugene Zavarin for thrice comparing the translation to the original. Our gratitude extends to all, but the responsibility for not carrying out to the full their valuable judgments for improving the manuscript must remain with us. Doris Ribera and Alexandra Sanders helped us in preparing the manuscript.

We wish to thank Seymour Chatman for first bringing to our attention the necessity for this translation, and Grant Barnes, of the University of California Press, for his cooperation. We owe a great debt to Boris Uspensky for carefully reviewing the English translation.

A selection from the present book appeared as *Prepublication* of the International Center of Semiotics and Linguistics, University of Urbino, Italy.

VALENTINA ZAVARIN *and* SUSAN WITTIG

ABBREVIATIONS

The following abbreviations have been adopted in the notes:

RANIION—Rossiiskaia Assotsiatsiia nauchno-issledovatel'skikh institutov obshchestvennykh nauk.

TODRL—Trudy otdela drevnei russkoi literatury Instituta russkoi literatury AN SSSR (Pushkinskii dom).

Uch. zap. TGU—Uchenye zapiski Tartuskogo gosudarstvennogo universiteta.

INTRODUCTION: POINT OF VIEW AS A COMPOSITIONAL PROBLEM

Point of View in Various Art Forms

The study of laws which govern patterns of composition and options in the formation of the work of art is one of the most vital problems of esthetic analysis. However, questions of composition have not yet been sufficiently developed. The structural approach to the work of art can offer many contributions in this field. Although the structure of the artistic work has been the subject of many recent discussions, the term "structure" itself remains to be defined. In most cases the word provides only a tenuous analogy to the kinds of structures recognized in the natural sciences, while the specific nature of this analogy remains unclear. There may be many approaches to the articulation of structure of a work of art. In this study we propose to consider one of them—an approach which is connected with the specification of the points of view from which the narration is conducted (or, in a work of pictorial art, the viewing position from which the image is constructed), and which aims at investigating the interrelations of these points of view in their various aspects.

Thus, this study focuses on the problem of point of view, a problem that is not only central to the composition of a work of art, but also a problem common to the various arts. Point of view pertains to any art immediately related to semantics (that is, arts concerned with the representation of some part of reality, set out as the *denotatum*), although it may be differently manifested in the various arts (literature, painting, film, theater).

The problem of point of view is directly related to those forms of art which by definition have two planes, a plane of expression and a plane of content (the representation and that which is represented); we shall call these the representational arts.[1] On the other hand, it is not immediately relevant, and may even be disregarded, in those forms of art that primarily involve syntactics, not semantics. (Abstract painting, nondescriptive music, architecture, and ornament are primarily connected with syntactics, architecture also with pragmatics.)

In painting, and in other visual arts, point of view is primarily connected with perspective.[2] Linear perspective, a normative concept in European painting since the Renaissance, assumes a single static point of view, a strictly fixed position from which the object is viewed. However, as many art historians have observed, linear perspective is almost never followed as an inviolable law; a number of great masters of the Renaissance and the post-Renaissance periods—among them the creators of the theory of perspective—deviated from it at different times.[3] Even more importantly, manuals on perspective recommended in certain cases that the rule be violated in order to achieve a higher degree of naturalness in representation.[4] When the artist deviates from a strict linear perspective, he uses plural visual positions, or points of view. A plurality of viewpoints is characteristic of medieval art, particularly in the complex phenomenon called inverse perspective.[5]

In visual art, the question of point of view (viewing position) is immediately concerned with foreshortening and illumination; it is also connected with the specific problem of combining the internal observer's point of view (located within the represented world) and the external observer's point of view (located outside the represented world), of differ-

1. Point of view may be related to the phenomenon of estrangement, one of the basic devices of artistic representation (see Chapter Seven for a discussion of this device). On estrangement and its significance, see V. Shklovskii, "Iskusstvo kak priem" [Art as device], in *Poetika. Sborniki po teorii poeticheskogo iazyka.* (Petrograd, 1919), p. 106, and also in his book *O teorii prozy* (Moscow-Leningrad, 1925). Shklovsky discusses the device only in terms of literature, but his suggestions can be generalized to all of the representational arts.

2. This observation is least important for sculpture. Without considering the question at length, however, we shall note that point of view is still relevant to the plastic arts.

3. Strict adherence to the law of direct or linear (geometric) perspective is characteristic particularly of the work of apprentices and of works of lower artistic value.

4. See N. A. Rynin, *Nachertatel'naia geometriia: Perspektiva* [Descriptive geometry: Perspective] (Petrograd, 1918), pp. 58, 70, 75–79.

5. See L. F. Zhegin, *Iazyk zhivopisnogo proizvedeniia,* [The language of a pictorial work] (Moscow, 1970). The introduction to this work contains a fairly complete bibliography of discussions of the problem. [See also L. F. Žegin, *The Language of a Pictorial Work: The Conventions of Ancient (Byzantine and Old Russian) Art,* trans, by Stephen Rudy (The Hague-Paris: Mouton, in press)—Trans.]

entiating the interpretation of figures depending on their semantic importance, and so forth.

In film, point of view is primarily connected with montage.[6] The use of multiple points of view is evident in the structuring of the film. The formal elements of the composition of the frame—the choice of background, of the foreshortening of the visual field, and of the various types of camera movements—are immediately dependent on point of view.

Point of view pertains also to the theater, although it is perhaps less important there than it is in other forms of representational art. What is specific to dramatic art in this respect becomes apparent when we consider the reader's perception of, let us say, a Shakespearian play as a literary work, outside of its dramatic performance, with the perception of the theater audience of that play. Discussing this problem, P. A. Florensky has written: "When, in *Hamlet*, Shakespeare shows the reader the theatrical presentation, the play within the play, he presents to us the world of this play within the play from the point of view of its audience: Claudius, the Queen, Hamlet, and so forth. For us as audience [as readers —B. U.] there is no great difficulty in imagining the world of the basic action of *Hamlet*, and within that, the world of the play within the play, separate and self-contained, independent of the world of the main play. But during the theatrical performance of *Hamlet*, we encounter insurmountable difficulties: the viewer in the theater inevitably sees the play within the play from *his own* point of view, and not from the point of view of the characters of the tragedy; he sees it with *his own* eyes, and not, for example, with the eyes of Claudius." [7]

The possibility of assuming different viewpoints, of identifying oneself with a character, of perceiving from his position, even temporarily, is far more restricted in the theater than in literature.[8] Nevertheless, we may consider that the problem of point of view may also be relevant in the theater, although perhaps to a lesser extent than in the other arts.

6. On montage, see works of S. M. Eizenshtein, *Izbrannye proizvedeniia* [Selected works] (Moscow, 1964–1970), vols. 1–6.
7. P. A. Florenskii, *Analiz prostranstvennosti v khudozhestvenno-izobrazitel'nykh proizvedeniiakh* [Spatial analysis in representational artistic works], in press. Compare, in this connection, M. Bakhtin's remarks about the necessary "monologue framing" in drama, in his book *Problemy poetiki Dostoevskogo* [Problems of poetics in Dostoevsky] (Moscow, 1963), pp. 22, 47. (The first edition of this book was published in 1929 under the title *Problemy tvorchestva Dostoevskogo* [Problems in the work of Dostoevsky].) [See also the French translation: *Problèmes de la poétique de Dostoïevski* (Lausanne, 1970). See M. Bakhtin, *Problems of Dostoevsky's Poetics* (Ann Arbor: Ardis Publs., in press)—Trans.]
8. On this basis P. A. Florensky arrives at the radical conclusion that theater is inferior to other arts.

For example, we may compare the contemporary theater, where the actor may freely turn his back to the audience, with the theater of the eighteenth and nineteenth centuries, where the actor was always required to face the audience. This convention was so strong that two actors who were holding a conversation tête-à-tête could never look at one another, but were obliged to look at the audience. (As a vestige of the old system, this convention may occasionally be encountered even today.)

The spatial restrictions that these conventions imposed upon the disposition of the characters on the stage were so important that they served as constraints for the whole structural arrangement of the *mise en scène* of the theater of the eighteenth and nineteenth centuries, and generated a chain of inevitable results. For example, an active role necessitated much use of the right hand; therefore, the actor who played an active role in the theater of the eighteenth century usually entered from the audience's right, while the actor who played a more passive role was placed at the left. The princess, for example, would stand on the left, while her rival, a slave girl (whose active role required more movement) would come on stage from the right. Thus, the actor who played a passive role would find himself in an advantageous position where he could remain relatively stationary and would not be obliged either to turn sideways or to turn his back to the audience; as a rule, therefore, this position was occupied by the actor who played a functionally significant part in the play. As a result of this convention, the on-stage distribution of characters in the eighteenth-century opera was also ordered according to fairly strict rules. The soloists, when standing in a row across the front of the stage, were lined up according to a descending hierarchy from the audience's left to right: the hero took the first position on the left, beside him the next character of importance, and so on.[9] However, this kind of frontal distribution in respect to the audience, which has been characteristic to some degree of theater since the seventeenth and eighteenth centuries, is not typical of the older forms of drama, because of the basically different position of the audience in respect to the stage.

The examples show that contemporary theater more often takes into account the point of view of the on-stage participants in the action, while in the eighteenth- and nineteenth-century theater most consideration was given to the audience's point of view. The two positions, of course, may be combined (as with the previously mentioned combination of the internal and external viewpoints in painting).

9. See A. A. Gvozdev, "Itogi i zadachi nauchnoi istorii teatra" [End results and aims of the history of the theater] in *Zadachi i metody izucheniia iskusstv* (Petrograd, 1924), p. 119; and E. Lert, *Mozart auf der Bühne* (Berlin, 1921).

Finally, the problem of point of view is particularly important to literature, and this topic will constitute the main subject of our study. In literature, as in film, we find a wide application of the montage technique; in literature, as in painting, there may be multiple points of view (internal and external in respect to the work); in literature and in drama, there are many similarities in terms of composition. Nevertheless, in spite of the similarities, literature has specific ways of solving the problem of point of view.

We are justified, then, in envisioning a general theory of composition studying the laws which govern the structural organization of the artistic text, and which are applicable to various arts. The terms *artistic* and *text* [*khudozhestvennyi, tekst*] are used here in their broad sense, which does not restrict them to arts whose medium is language. The first word, *khudozhestvennyi*, is understood in the same sense as the English word *artistic;* the word *text* has reference to any semantically organized sequence of signs. In general, the expression *artistic text,* like the phrase *artistic work,* may be used both in a narrow sense, when applied to literature only, and in a broad sense. We shall specify the particular use when it seems unclear by its context.

Furthermore, the *montage* (and here again we use the word in its general sense, not specifically limited to the art of the cinema, but as it applies to all the arts) may be conceived in terms of the generation of the artistic text (the synthesis): the *structure* of the artistic text should be regarded as the result of the reverse process, the analysis.[10]

It is assumed that the structure of the artistic text may be described by investigating various points of view (different authorial positions from which the narration or description is conducted) and by investigating the relations between these points of view (their concurrence and nonconcurrence and the possible shifts from one point of view to another, which in turn are connected with the study of the *function* of the different points of view in the text).

Possible Aspects of the Manifestation of
Points of View in Literature
The basic aim of the present study is to consider the typology of compositional options in literature as they pertain to point of view.[11] We are

10. A direct analogy can be made here with generative models (of synthesis) and analytic models, in contemporary linguistics.

11. The study of point of view in Russian letters was inaugurated by M. M. Bakhtin, V. N. Voloshinov (whose ideas were formed under the direct influence of Bakhtin), V. V. Vinogradov, and G. A. Gukovsky. These scholars have shown the relevance of the prob-

interested, then, in what types of point of view are possible, what kinds of relationships may occur among them, what their functions are, and so forth.[12] These problems will be observed on a general level, independently of any one particular author; although the work of some authors will be used consistently as illustrative material, the study of a particular work will not be the specific subject of our study.

The results of such a study, of course, depend in the first place upon how point of view is understood and defined. Indeed, several approaches are possible: we may consider point of view as an ideological and evaluative position; we may consider it as a spatial and temporal position of the one who produces the description of the events (that is, the narrator, whose position is fixed along spatial and temporal coordinates); we may study it with respect to perceptual characteristics; or we may study it in a purely linguistic sense (as, for example, it relates to such phenomena as quasi-direct discourse); and so forth. We will come to these approaches in our further discussions; specifically, we will distinguish in our analysis the basic semantic spheres in which viewpoint may generally be manifested, and the planes of investigation in terms of which point of view may be fixed. For our purpose, these planes will be designated as the plane of ideology, the plane of phraseology, the spatial and temporal plane, and the psychological plane.[13] Each will be the subject of a separate discussion in the first four chapters of the present study.

The proposed division into planes is characterized by a certain arbitrariness. The planes of analysis which have been outlined here generally cor-

lem of point of view for literature and have suggested some ways to approach its analysis. However, their considerations of the question were usually part of a much larger study, an investigation of the whole complex of problems associated with all of the works of a specific author; the analysis of point of view was not their specific aim, but was rather one of the instruments with which they approached the material at hand. Because their methods were designed to deal with larger questions in the whole of the literary material they studied, and because a thorough analysis of point of view was not immediately important to their investigation, their concept of point of view was not always carefully articulated, and the term sometimes took several meanings simultaneously. In this study, I have often referred to these scholars. I have drawn generalizations from the combined results of their critical analysis and have attempted to complement their work. In addition, I have attempted to bring out the significance of point of view in achieving different compositional tasks in the work of art. Wherever possible I have shown connections between literature and other forms of art.

12. In this connection, and in addition to the works of the Russian critics cited above, see K. Friedemann, *Die Rolle des Erzählers in der Epik* (Leipzig, 1910); and also the investigations of American literary critics who continue to develop the ideas of Henry James: N. Friedman, "Point of View in Fiction, The Development of a Critical Concept," *PMLA* 70 (1955): 1160–1184; see also the bibliography of Friedman's article.

13. Gukovsky suggests that distinctions may be made between the psychological, ideological, and geographical points of view. G. A. Gukovskii, *Realizm Gogolia* [Realism in Gogol] (Moscow, 1959), p. 200.

respond to different possible manifestations of point of view, and although these planes appear to be fundamental in our approach, the possibility of discovering some new plane which is beyond our schema is by no means excluded; it is also possible, of course, to detail these particular planes in ways other than those we have presented. Our enumeration of planes is not exhaustive, nor does it pretend to be absolute. A degree of arbitrariness seems almost unavoidable here.

We may consider further that different approaches to the articulation of points of view in an artistic work (that is, different planes of investigation of point of view) correspond to different levels of analysis of the structure of a work. In other words, different approaches to the articulation and the fixing of the points of view of an artistic work correspond to different methods of describing the work's structure; thus, on the different levels of description, there may be articulated various structures of the same work, structures which do not necessarily concur with one another. We shall illustrate some instances of the nonconcurrence of structures on different levels of a single work in Chapter Five.

Our study will focus on literary works, but will also include such borderline phenomena as material from newspapers, jokes and anecdotes, and so on. Two kinds of parallels will be made throughout. On the one hand, we shall draw parallels throughout the study with painting and other forms of representational art. Some generalizations and attempts to establish common compositional patterns will be made in the concluding chapter. On the other hand, we shall emphasize the relationship between literature and the practice of everyday speech: throughout the discussion we will stress the analogies between works of artistic literature and the everyday practice of story-telling and conversation.

If the parallels between the arts bear witness to the universality of the laws of composition, then the connection between literature and ordinary speech testifies to the naturalness of those laws—a fact which may in its turn shed light on the evolution of some principles of composition.

Furthermore, whenever we refer to the juxtaposition of viewpoints, we will try to offer examples which illustrate those juxtapositions within a single sentence, to demonstrate that the sentence as a minimal object of analysis may have a special compositional organization.

Our thesis will be illustrated, in terms of the aims outlined above, with references to various authors, mainly to Tolstoy and Dostoevsky. We will try, however, to exemplify different compositional devices with the same work, in order to demonstrate the great variety of principles of composition that may coexist in a single work. Tolstoy's *War and Peace* serves this purpose.

1 | POINT OF VIEW ON THE IDEOLOGICAL PLANE

We will look first of all at the most basic aspect of point of view, which may be manifested on the level which we may designate as ideological or evaluative (understanding by "evaluation" a general system of viewing the world conceptually). This level is least accessible to formalization, for its analysis relies, to a degree, on intuitive understanding. We will therefore be concerned in our analysis primarily with the compositional aspect of point of view on this level. We are interested in this problem: whose point of view does the author assume when he evaluates and perceives ideologically the world which he describes.[1] This point of view, either concealed or openly acknowledged, may belong to the author himself; or it may be the normative system of the narrator, as distinct from that of the author (and perhaps in conflict with the author's norm); or it may belong to one of the characters. Various ideological points of view may be involved in the composition of a text. When we speak of the system of ideas that shape the work, we are speaking about the deep compositional structure, as opposed to the surface compositional structure which may be traced on the psychological, spatio-temporal, or phraseological levels.

From the viewpoint of compositional possibilities, the simplest case (and for us, the least interesting) occurs when ideological evaluation is carried out from a single, dominating point of view.[2] This single view-

---

1. Compare the analysis of point of view manifested in particular aspects of English Victorian poetry in K. Smidt's "Point of View in Victorian Poetry," *English Studies* 38 (1957): 1–12.
2. In Bakhtin's terms, this is an instance of monologue structure. M. Bakhtin, *Problemy poetiki Dostoevskogo* [Problems of poetics in Dostoevsky] (Moscow, 1963).

point will subordinate all others in the work; if some other point of view should emerge, nonconcurrent with the dominant one (if, for example, some facts should be judged from the point of view of one of the characters), this judgment will in turn be reevaluated from the more dominant position, and the evaluating *subject* (the character), together with his system of ideas, will become the *object,* evaluated from the more general viewpoint.

In other cases, we may observe definite changes in the author's position on the ideological plane; consequently, we may speak about the presence of multiple evaluative views. In a work, for example, when character X is evaluated from the position of character Y, and vice versa, the different evaluative (ideological) positions may be organically incorporated in the authorial text, entering with one another into various relationships. These cases are compositionally more complex and will therefore be of more interest to us.

As an example, let us turn to Lermontov's *A Hero of Our Times.* It is not difficult to see that the events and the people which constitute the object of this narrative are presented here according to several completely different world views. In other words, there are several ideological viewpoints which together form a fairly complex network of relationships.

The main character, Pechorin, is revealed to us not only in terms of his own evaluative system, but also in terms of the author's (narrator's) evaluative system, and from the point of view of one of the characters, the veteran Captain, Maxim Maximych; other characters, Grushnitsky, for example, are presented from Pechorin's and a number of other characters' viewpoints. Characters' views may blend or stand in opposition: Maxim Maximych functions as a vehicle for the world view of the common people, naive and simple, an ideological position which is opposed to that of Pechorin but essentially coincides with that of the Caucasian people (for example, Bela).[3] Pechorin's system of values has much in common with the values of his friend Doctor Verner, and in most situations the ideological positions of the two characters are virtually identical. Further, in the evaluative system of Maxim Maximych, Pechorin and Grushnitsky resemble each other, while in the system of Pechorin himself, Grushnitsky's position is opposite to his; and so forth. Within the narrative these different evaluative systems assume definite relationships to each other, forming a complex design of oppositions and identifications: some points

3. Iurii M. Lotman, "O probleme znachenii vo vtorichnykh modeliruiushchikh sistemakh" [Concerning the problem of meaning in the secondary modeling systems], *Trudy po znakovym sistemam,* II (Uch. Zap. TGU, vyp. 181) (Tartu, 1965), pp. 31-32.

of view concur, their identity being established through a third point of view; some concur in some situations (their opposition being neutralized in this case) but diverge in others; some may be contrasted as opposing viewpoints (again from some third point of view); and so forth. The system of interrelations thus established may be considered as the compositional structure of the particular literary work on the corresponding level.

A Hero of Our Times seems to represent a rather elementary case, a case where the work is divided into separate sections, each of which is narrated by one of the heroes and thus presented from a single point of view; in the novel as a whole, a common theme intersects and unites the subject matter of each section.[4] However, it is not difficult to imagine a more complex instance, where a similar interlacing of various viewpoints takes place in a work, not separated into sections, but representing a single unified narration.

If the various viewpoints are not subordinated, but are presented as essentially equal ideological voices, we have a polyphonic narration. The concept of polyphony was introduced into the study of literature by Mikhail Bakhtin, who has also demonstrated that the clearest example of polyphonic structuring is found in the works of Dostoevsky.[5] For the purposes of our discussion of point of view, polyphony may be defined in terms of the following basic requirements:

(a) Polyphony occurs when several independent points of view are present within the work. The term polyphonic, that is, "many-voiced," is self-explanatory.

(b) The points of view in a polyphonic work must belong directly to characters who participate in the narrated events (in the action). In other words, there must be no abstract ideological position outside of the personalities of the characters.[6]

(c) When studying polyphony, we take into consideration points of view manifested on the plane of ideology only. They become manifest primarily in the manner in which characters (vehicles for the ideological positions) evaluate the world around them.

Dostoevsky's work may serve as an example of a polyphonic work; Bakhtin writes: "To Dostoevsky it is not important what any of his characters are in this world; he is primarily interested in what the world is to the characters, and what each character is to himself." And further about Dostoevsky, Bakhtin writes: "The elements of which the image of a person

4. Wilkie Collins' *The Moonstone* provides an even more clear-cut example of this kind of compositional organization.
5. Bakhtin, 1963.
6. Ibid., pp. 105, 128, 130–131.

is composed are not features of his character and of his everyday surround-ings—but the *significance* of those features for *his own self*, for his self-consciousness." [7]

Polyphony, as has been exemplified by Bakhtin in the work of Dostoevsky, is an instance of the manifestation of multiple points of view on the ideological plane.[8]

Author, Narrator, and Character as Possible Vehicles of Ideological Viewpoint. The Function of the Character as a Vehicle of Ideological Point of View in a Work

In our discussion of point of view on the ideological plane, it is essential to distinguish between evaluations made from abstract positions (by definition external to the work[9]), and those which are made from the po-sition of a character who is directly represented in the work. In either case, one or more different ideological positions are possible in the same work; or there may be alternation between the point of view of a particu-lar character and the abstract authorial point of view.

It is important to clarify one point: when we speak about the authorial point of view, here and elsewhere, we refer not to the author's world view in general, independent of his work, but only to the viewpoint which he adopts for the organization of the narrative in a particular work. Further-more, the author may deliberately speak in a voice other than his own (cf. such stylized monologues as the *skaz*); he may, within one work, change his point of view several times; and he may adopt multiple positions; that is, he may view and evaluate from several points of view simultaneously.

When ideological evaluation in a work belongs to a particular charac-ter, he may be either the central character or a secondary, even an in-cidental character. The first case is obvious enough: in general, the main character in a literary work can be either the object of evaluation (like Onegin, in Pushkin's *Eugene Onegin*, or Bazarov, in Turgenev's *Fathers*

7. Ibid., pp. 110–113, 55, 30. The self-awareness that is so characteristic of Dostoev-sky's characters (see Bakhtin, pp. 64–67 and 103) seems not so much a feature of po-lyphony as a specific feature of Dostoevsky's work.

8. The conflict between different ideological (evaluative) points of view often appears in such specific genres as the anecdote. The analysis of the anecdote on this level, gen-erally speaking, may prove fruitful, inasmuch as it may be considered a relatively simple object of study—composed of the elements of complex compositional structure. Conse-quently, it may be considered in some sense an analytically convenient model of the artistic work.

9. Such a judgment, as we have already pointed out, is impossible in a polyphonic work.

and Sons), or its vehicle (as is Alyosha in *The Brothers Karamazov,* or Chatsky, in Griboyedov's *Woe from Wit*).

However, the second case is also common: a secondary or minor figure only incidentally related to the action may serve as the vehicle for the authorial point of view. Such a device appears frequently in film narrative, where the character whose evaluative distancing frames the narrative—that is, the particular spectator for whom, so to speak, the action is performed—is presented within the scene itself, as an accidental bystander on the periphery of the events.[10] And turning to painting, we might also recall in this connection the old masters who sometimes placed their own portraits next to the frame, that is, on the periphery of the depicted scene.[11]

In both of these cases, the person from whose point of view reality is "distanced" (essentially, the viewer of the scene), is present inside the work as an incidental character, on the periphery of the action. With respect to literature, we might refer here to the works of neoclassicism. The *raisonneur,* like the chorus in Greek drama, usually participated little in the action; he served two functions, playing the role of a participant and of a spectator who perceives and evaluates the action.[12]

We have been speaking about general cases in which a character in a given work (either the main character or some minor figure) serves as a

10. In one Italian film, *Seduced and Abandoned,* produced by Pietro Germi, a large part of the action is framed from the estranged evaluative viewpoint of one of the minor characters, a naive aide of the police sergeant, who stands around through much of the film, gaping at the action.

11. For example, see Dürer's *Feast of the Rosary* (Plate 2), where the artist has represented himself in the crowd on the right side of the painting; or see Botticelli's *The Adoration of the Magi* (Plate 1), in which exactly the same phenomenon may be observed. Here, the artist is present as a spectator who perceives the depicted world—and this spectator himself is within the picture.

12. Moreover, it seems to have been obligatory that there be only one ideological point of view; thus, to the unities which are characteristic of the neoclassical drama (unities of place, time, and action), we may add the unity of the ideological position. Yury Lotman has clearly articulated this aspect of neoclassical art: "It was characteristic of Russian poetry of the pre-Pushkin period that all expressions of subjective-objective relationships converge in a single focus in the text. In the art of the eighteenth century, which we have traditionally defined as "classical," this single focus extended beyond the author's personality and coincided with the concept of truth in the voice of which the artistic text was speaking. It was the relationship between truth and the represented world that constituted the artistic point of view. The stability and unambiguousness of these relationships, their striving towards and gathering within a common center, corresponded to the concepts of eternity, unity, and the stability of truth. Truth was conceived as being single and immutable, but hierarchically structured—revealing itself at the same time in different degrees to each individual consciousness." Iurii M. Lotman, "Khudozhestvennaia struktura 'Evgeniia Onegina'" [The poetic structure of Pushkin's *Eugene Onegin*], *Trudy po russkoi i slavianskoi filologii,* IX (Uch. zap. TGU, vyp. 184) (Tartu, 1966), pp. 7–8.

vehicle for the ideological evaluation, not about a situation in which the whole action is presented in the form of perceptions or evaluations of a particular character. A character may not even take part in the action (this is true particularly when he plays an incidental role in the narrative), and therefore he cannot evaluate the described events as they happen; what we witness as readers is distinct from what the character sees.[13] In this case, when we say that the work is structured from the point of view of a certain character, we mean that if this particular character had participated in the action, he would have evaluated (judged) the events just as it is done by the author of the work.

Generally, it is possible to distinguish between actual and potential carriers of the ideological point of view. The author's or the narrator's point of view may in some cases be explicitly presented in the work (when an author or a narrator conducts his narration in his own voice), while in other cases it may be discovered only by a process of a special analysis. A character who functions as the vehicle of the ideological point of view may in one instance actually be portrayed as perceiving and evaluating the action which is described; in other cases the character's presence is only potential, and the action is presented as if from the point of view of that character.

In this respect the work of G. K. Chesterton is of interest. Almost always in Chesterton's works the person from whose ideological viewpoint the world is evaluated is presented as a character in the novel.[14] In other words, in almost all of Chesterton's works, there is a character who might have written the book (a character whose world view is reflected in the book). It might be said that the world of Chesterton is potentially represented from within.

Here we have touched on the distinction between the internal and external points of view, but only in terms of ideological evaluation; we shall examine it on other levels of point of view at a later time, and will make some generalizations concerning it in Chapter Seven.

Special Means of Expression of the Ideological Point of View

As we said earlier, the manifestation of point of view on the level of ideology is least accessible to formal study. We shall exemplify, however, some specific means available to the author to express the evalu-

13. Later in the discussion we will interpret this particular construction as an instance of the nonconcurrence of the ideological and the spatial-temporal levels.

14. This observation was made by N. L. Trauberg in her lecture on Chesterton during the Second Summer School on Secondary Modeling Systems, Kääriku, 1966.

ative point of view. One of these is the use, in folklore, of fixed epithets, words which do not depend upon their particular context and which testify primarily to the author's attitude toward the object he is describing. For example:

Tut sobaka Kalin tsar' govoril Il'e da takovy slova:
Ai ty staryia kazak da Il'ia Muromets!
Da sluzhi-tko ty sobake tsariu Kalinu.

[Then the pagan dog Tsar Kalin spoke to Ilya these words:
"Hey, you old cossack—you, Ilya Muromets!
Now serve me, dog Tsar Kalin!"][15]

Some instances of fixed epithets in texts of a later period are especially interesting. Here, for example, a nineteenth-century author is writing an historical account about the Vygovtsian Old Believers, in *The Proceedings of the Kievan Theological Academy*—he speaks, naturally, from the position of the official orthodox church:

Po smerti predvoditelia Andreia vse vygovtsy . . . pristupili k Simionu Dionis'evichu i stali umoliat' ego—da budet vmesto brata svoego Daniilu pomoshchnikom v dele mnimo-tserkovnogo predstoiatel'stva.

[After the death of their leader Andrey, all the Vygovtsians . . . approached Simion Dionisyevich and begged him to take Andrey's place as helper to Daniel in the matter of their pseudo-ecclesiastical service.[16]]

Thus, the author conveys the request of the Vygovtsians, but puts in their mouths the epithet "pseudo," which corresponds not to their ideological viewpoint, but to his own. Such use of a fixed epithet is characteristic of folklore narrative.

In this connection, we should also note the writing of the initial letter in the word *Bog* (God), which in the Pre-Revolutionary Russian orthography is written with a capital letter in all instances, regardless of the nature of the text (whether it be atheistic, sectarian, or pagan). Similarly, the word *Bog* appears in Old Slavic texts in an abbreviated form *bg* with a tilde of abbreviation over it, the way *nomina sacra* were generally written, even when a pagan god, and not the Christian God is meant.

Although the fixed epithet may appear within the direct speech of a character, it does not belong to the speech characteristics of the speaker; rather, it manifests the evaluative position of the author. These special

---

15. *Onezhskie Byliny* [Onega Byliny], collected by A. O. Gilferding. *Sbornik Otdeleniia russkogo iazyka i slovesnosti Imp. Akademii Nauk,* LIX–LXI (1894), no. 75.

16. *Trudy Kievskoi Dukhovnoi akademii* (February, 1866), p. 230.

means of expressing the ideological point of view, however, are naturally small in number.

Although it is common for the ideological point of view to be expressed through the use of certain speech (stylistic) characteristics (that is, by phraseological means), the ideological point of view cannot be reduced to characterizations of this kind.

Some scholars who dispute the theories of Bakhtin which assert the polyphonic character of Dostoevsky's works, have proposed that the work of Dostoevsky is "strikingly uniform." [17] The very possibility of such differences of opinion is a result of the fact that scholars have examined the problem of point of view (that is, the compositional structure of the work) in its various aspects. Generally speaking, the occurrence of different ideological points of view in Dostoevsky's works is unquestionable, as Bakhtin has convincingly shown; however, this diversity of ideological positions is almost never reflected in phraseological characteristics. Dostoevsky's characters (as critics have often pointed out) all speak in a uniform manner; they all speak for the most part the same language as the author himself or the narrator.

When the differences in ideological points of view are expressed by phraseological means, we must concern ourselves with the relationship between the two levels, ideological and phraseological.

The Relationship Between the Ideological and Phraseological Levels

Different phraseological features—that is, the strictly linguistic means of expressing a point of view—may serve two functions. First, they may characterize the person to whom the particular stylistic feature belongs; thus, the world view of a character (or of the author himself) may be defined through stylistic analysis of his speech. Second, phraseological means may indicate concretely whose point of view the author has adopted for his narration. For example, the use of quasi-direct speech (in the authorial text) may indicate quite definitely the author's use of the point of view of a certain character.

In the first instance of this particular phenomenon, we are talking about the level of ideological evaluation, in other words the expression of a definite ideological position (point of view) by means of phraseological characteristics. In the second case, we are dealing with the phraseological plane, and with the expression of phraseological points of view (this plane will be discussed in the next chapter).

17. See G. Voloshin, "Prostranstvo i vremia u Dostoevskogo" [Space and time in the works of Dostoevsky], *Slavia* 12 (1933): 1–2, 171.

The definition of a particular ideological point of view by means of phraseology may take place in any art form which uses language as its medium. In literature, in theater, and in film, speech (or stylistic) features may serve to characterize the position of the speaking person, and the ideological plane is common to all of these art forms. The second case is, however, peculiar to literature, and the phraseological plane is limited to this art form.

With the aid of speech characteristics (and, in particular, stylistic characteristics) the author may refer to a more or less concrete individual or social position.[18] But he may also use speech characteristics to refer to some ideological position or world view.[19] As an example we may use Lotman's discussion of Pushkin's *Eugene Onegin,* in which he shows that stylistic analysis allows us to distinguish in this work two thematic planes, each of which corresponds to a specific ideological position: the "prosaic," or the level of everyday life; and the "romantic" (or, more precisely, the "nonromantic" and the "romantic").[20] As another example we may refer to Vinogradov's analysis of *The Life of Avvakum,* in which two levels are singled out: the "biblical" and the "everyday" ("nonbiblical").[21] In both of these examples, the two thematic levels are shown to run parallel and their interaction is manifest throughout the work: in *Eugene Onegin* this parallelism is used to bring the romantic level down to the level of everyday life; in *The Life of Avvakum* it is used to raise the everyday level to the biblical.

18. In this regard, it is interesting to study the headings of newspaper columns to see from whose point of view they are constructed: from an intellectual's point of view, from the point of view of a gallant soldier, of an old worker, of a retired man, and so on. Such an investigation might indicate some of the characteristics of life in a given society.

Also interesting are different announcements about smoking rules in restaurants: "We do not smoke here," "No Smoking!" "Smoking Is Forbidden," and their connections to the different points of view indicated in them (the point of view of an impersonal administration, of the police, of the maitre d'hotel, and so on).

19. The relationship between world view and style may be illustrated by examples of the struggle after the Russian Revolution over words associated with reactionary ideology—and similarly, during the reign of Paul I, Paul I's struggle against the use of words which symbolized for him the revolution. See A. M. Selishchev, *Iazyk revoliutsionnoi epokhi* [The language of the revolutionary period] (Moscow, 1928); and V. V. Vinogradov, *Ocherki po istorii russkogo literaturnogo iazyka, XVII–XIX* [Essays in the history of Russian literary language] (Moscow, 1938), pp. 193–194. Compare in connection with this problem different socially conditioned tabus.

20. See Lotman, 1966, p. 13.

21. See V. V. Vinogradov, "O zadachakh stilistiki: Nabliudenia nad stilem Zhitiia protopopa Avvakuma" [Stylistic problems: observations on the style of *The Life of the Archpriest Avvakum*], *Russkaia rech'*, ed. L. V. Shcherba (Petrograd, 1923), 1:211–214.

2 | POINT OF VIEW ON THE PHRASEOLOGICAL PLANE

That the differentiation of points of view in a literary work may be manifested not only on the plane of ideology but on the phraseological plane as well (and even more so, perhaps), is especially apparent in those cases where the author uses different diction to describe different characters or where he makes use of one form or another of reported or substituted speech in his description. For example, within the same work the author may first describe one character from the point of view of another character, then he may use his own point of view (that is, he may speak in his own voice), then he may resort to the point of view of a third person who is neither the author nor an immediate participant in the action, and so forth. In many cases the plane of phraseology (or the plane of speech characteristics) may be the only plane in the work on which we can detect changes in the authorial position.

Theoretically the generation of a narrative may be conceived from this perspective in the following way. Let us assume that an event to be described takes place before a number of witnesses, among whom may be the author, the characters (the immediate participants in the event), and some other, detached spectators. Each of the observers may offer his own description of the events; presumably these versions would be presented in the form of direct discourse (in the first person). We would then expect these monologues to be distinct in their particular speech characteristics; however, the facts described by the various people—who may be in different relations to each other and may describe each other—would coincide, intersect, and complement each other in specific ways.

Theoretically, the author, constructing his narrative, may use first one and then another of these various narrations. These narrations, originally assumed to be in direct discourse, may merge and be transposed into authorial speech. Within the authorial speech the shifting from one point of view to another is expressed in different uses of forms of someone else's speech.

As a simple example of possibilities in the choice of position, let us assume that a narration has begun. A character has been described (apparently from the point of view of an observer); he is in a room, and the author wants to say that the character's wife, Natasha, is now entering the room. The author may say: (a) *"Voshla Natasha, ego zhena"* (Entered Natasha, his wife), (b) *"Voshla Natasha"* (Entered Natasha), (c) *"Natasha voshla"* (Natasha entered).

In the first instance, we have the usual description by an author or by an outside observer. In the second example, however, we change to narrated monologue, or the phraseological point of view of the husband. As readers, as outsiders, we could not know who Natasha is; the point of view which the author intends us to adopt is an internal point of view belonging to the perceiving character, the husband of Natasha. Finally, the syntactical organization of the third example suggests that it corresponds neither to the perceptions of the husband, nor to the perceptions of an abstract, detached observer; rather, it seems that Natasha's own point of view is used in this case.

Here, we are taking into account the functional sentence perspective, that is, the correlation between what is "given" and what is "new" in the organization of a sentence.[1] In the sentence "Entered Natasha," "entered" functions as the given, taking on the role of the logical subject of the sentence: the word "Natasha" functions as the new information, serving as the logical predicate. The functional construction, therefore, corresponds to the sequence of perceptions of an observer (the husband) located in the room, who perceives first that someone has entered the room, and then sees that this "someone" is Natasha.

However, in the sentence "Natasha entered," the given information is expressed by the word "Natasha," and the new information is expressed by the word "entered." The sentence is constructed, therefore, from the point of view of a person for whom the given fact is that Natasha's behavior is being described, while the new information is that she did the *entering,* and not something else. Such a structure appears when Natasha's own point of view is used to narrate the event.

1. [In the terminology of the Prague school the functional sentence perspective or actual division of the sentence distinguishes the given information (the basis or *theme* of the sentence) from the new information (the nucleus or *rhema* of the sentence). Functional syntax has been the subject of discussion in the works of V. Mathesius and J. Firbas.—Trans.]

The shift from one point of view to another is a common phenomenon within authorial narration, though it is often inconspicuous, almost as if it were being surreptitiously introduced into the narrative; in a later discussion we will present specific examples of this technique.

The most elementary case of authorial speech is when only one point of view is used. This point of view does not have to belong, phraseologically, to the author himself; the author may make use of someone else's speech (reported speech), conducting the narrative not in his own voice, but in the voice of some narrator who can be defined by specific phraseological characteristics. (In this case, the author and the narrator do not coincide.) If this point of view does not belong to a direct participant in the narrated action, we have a stylized narration, or the purest form of *skaz*.[2] The classic examples are Gogol's "The Overcoat," or the short stories of Leskov.[3] This technique is also well illustrated by the short stories of such recent authors as Zoshchenko.

In other cases, the phraseological point of view of the author (the narrator) concurs with the point of view of one participant in the narrative (for the compositional design of the narration, it is essential to determine in this instance whether the character who serves as the vehicle for the authorial point of view is a main or a secondary character): this can be a narration either in the first person (*Icherzählung*), or in the third person. But the essential characteristic for this case is that only one

2. Concerning *skaz*, see B. M. Eikhenbaum, "Kak sdelana 'Shinel' " [How "The Overcoat" was made], *Poetika. Sborniki po teorii poeticheskogo iazyka* (Petrograd, 1919); "Leskov i sovremennaia proza" [Leskov and contemporary prose] in his book: *B. M. Eikhenbaum, Literatura* (Leningrad, 1927); V. V. Vinogradov, "Problema skaza v stilistike" [Problems of *skaz* in stylistics], *Poetika: Vremennik otdela slovesnykh iskusstv*, I (Leningrad, 1926); M. Bakhtin, *Problema poetiki Dostoevskogo* [Problems of poetics in Dostoevsky], (Moscow, 1963), pp. 255–257. As Bakhtin and Vinogradov have noted, Eikhenbaum was the first to bring up the problem of stylized monologue or *skaz*, although he thought of it only as a form which imitated oral speech. It might have been more useful to define the *specifica* of *skaz*, however, in terms of reported speech.

3. Compare the analysis by Eikhenbaum in the work cited above. Leskov's comment is interesting here: "The training of an author's voice consists in his learning how to control the voice and the language of his character and never to drop from the alto to the bass. In my own work, I have tried to develop this skill, and I have managed, I think, to make my priests speak spiritually; my nihilists, nihilistically; my peasants like peasants; and those among them who are social climbers and buffoons have been made to speak pretentiously. As for me, I speak in my literary writings the language of the ancient tales, the speech of the people and of the church. . . . each of us—my characters and myself—has his own personal voice. Each voice has been trained correctly (or at least conscientiously). I have not invented the language that appears on many pages of my work—the people's language, vulgar or fanciful—I have overheard it among the peasants, the half-educated, the gabs, the fools in Christ, and the sanctimonious." See A. I. Faresov, *Protiv techenii* (St. Petersburg, 1904), pp. 273–274.

character functions as the vehicle for the author's point of view in the whole work.

However, we are more interested in those narratives in which several points of view are present—that is, where a distinct shift in the authorial position can be traced.

Subsequently, we shall consider various manifestations of plural points of view on the level of phraseology. But before we turn to these manifestations in all their variety, we will attempt to show the possibilities of changes in point of view in deliberately restricted material.

It is to our advantage to choose the simplest material possible as a model in which we may illustrate interplay between various phraseological points of view. The use of personal names and appellations within the authorial text fits these requirements. Our special concern will be to emphasize the similarity of structures in the artistic text to those used in everyday speech.

NAMING AS A PROBLEM POINT OF VIEW

Naming in Ordinary Speech, Magazine Writings,
and Epistolary Prose

The change of the authorial position as formally expressed by the use of elements of reported speech (specifically, in the act of naming) occurs not only in literary texts but also in everyday story-telling and indeed in ordinary speech where the same compositional devices are in operation as in a literary work. Any speaker constructing a narration may change his position and assume in sequence the point of view of one or another of the participants in the action, or even of characters who do not take part in the action.

Let us take a simple example from the practice of everyday conversation by assuming that X talks with Y about Z. Z's family name is Ivanov, and his given name and patronymic are Vladimir Petrovich. But when X speaks to Z, he is accustomed to calling him by his nickname, Volodya, and Y in talking to Z calls him Vladimir. When Z thinks about himself he uses the name Vova, a nickname his family gave him when he was a child. So, in a conversation between X and Y about Z, X may give Z one of several possible names:

(a) X may call Z by the nickname "Volodya." In this case, he speaks from his own personal point of view.

(b) X may call Z "Vladimir." Here, he adopts someone else's (Y's) point of view on Z. It is as if he had assumed the point of view of his interlocutor.

(c) X may call Z by the nickname "Vova." The point of view he has adopted here is that of still another person (namely, that of Z), for "Vova" is a name which neither the speaker nor the interlocutor ever used in direct intercourse with Z.

(d) X may speak about Z respectfully as "Vladimir Petrovich," in spite of the fact that both X and Y, in personal contact with Z, address him by one of the forms of the given name. In this case, it is as if X has adopted the point of view of some abstract detached observer who is neither a participant nor the subject of the conversation, and whose place is unspecified. This case is rather common. A simpler variation of this case occurs when both interlocutors in direct address use the same appellation for Z, the familiar form "Volodya," for example. While aware of each other's way of referring to Z, they may adopt in speaking to each other the more formal "Vladimir Petrovich."

(e) X may refer to Z by his last name, "Ivanov," even though both X and Y are close acquaintances of Z. In this case, the point of view of a detached observer, an outsider to the conversation, is even more pronounced than in the previous case.

All of these examples are common in everyday speech.[4] The adoption of one or another point of view in naming a person here serves an essentially stylistic function and is directly conditioned by the attitude towards the person referred to.[5]

This use of names to express attitudes is characteristic of journalistic writing. We may recall the well-known case of the different naming of Napoleon Bonaparte by the Paris press during Napoleon's march on Paris in 1815 before assuming power for The Hundred Days. The first account by the press described Napoleon's arrival in France from the island of Elba: "The Corsican monster has landed in the Gulf of Jouan." The second announced, "The cannibal advances toward Grasse"; the third reported, "The usurper entered Grenoble"; the fourth, "Bonaparte

4. The reader might observe these five categories of naming, which are common in conversational speech, in his own speech and in the speech of his acquaintances. All of these uses of personal names depend not only upon the situation but also upon the individual qualities of the speakers. For a more detailed account of the use of personal names as a criterion of individual characteristics, see B. A. Uspenskii, "Personologicheskie problemy v lingvisticheskom aspekte" [Personological problems from a linguistic point of view] *Tezisy dokladov vo Vtoroi letnei shkole po vtorichnym modeliruiushchim sistemam* (Tartu, 1966), pp. 8–9.

5. Consider, for example, the distinct irony in the reference to "Vova" (case c)—and the emphasized respect in the use of the name "Vladimir Petrovich" (case d).

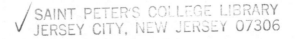

occupied Lyon"; the fifth, "Napoleon approaches Fontainebleau"; and finally, the sixth, "His Imperial Majesty is expected today in his faithful Paris." [6]

Those devices to express attitudes are typical of magazine writing and feuilleton in general: the author's attitude toward his hero is manifested primarily in his way of naming the hero (various forms of proper names are characteristic in this respect), and changes in the hero are marked by changes in the author's way of naming him.

We may note the difference in attitude (with respect to the person about whom one speaks) manifested in the placing of initials before or after the last name, for example. Compare "A. D. Ivanov" with "Ivanov, A. D." The latter use is indicative in Russian of a much more official attitude toward a given person.

The memoirs of Ilya Ehrenburg, which in general carry evident marks of magazine style, provide examples of this use of personal names.[7] When Ehrenburg introduces a new character to the reader, he usually identifies him according to his occupation or his position, and gives his last name and initials—simulating the introduction of the character to the reader. Immediately after this introduction, however, Ehrenburg shifts to his own point of view of closer acquaintance with the character and begins to call him by his first name and patronymic. The reader can only guess that the name and patronymic belong to the same person as the initials which preceded the surname in the previous sentence. Ehrenburg writes, for example:

In May, a co-worker from *Izvestia*, S. A. Raevsky, came unexpectedly to see me. . . . Stefan Arkadievich told me . . .

I went to our consul, V. S. Dovgalevsky. . . . Valerian Savelievich knew France very well.

V. A. Antonov-Ovseenko found me, . . . I had known Vladimir Aleksandrovich since the years before the Revolution.[8]

This device, simulating first the process of introduction and then that of acquaintance, places the reader in the author's own position.

A distinction between several points of view may be clearly shown when different forms of address (representing different points of view)

---

6. E. Tarle, *Napoleon* (Moscow, 1941), p. 348. In this particular case it happens that the change in naming is related to the distance of the named object from those who name him; we may note in this respect the change in size of an object in a perspective experiment, which depends upon its distance from the position of the observer.

7. See I. Erenburg, *Liudi, gody, zhizn'* [People, years, life] (Moscow, 1961–1966).

8. Ibid., Book 3, 4, pp. 331, 555, *passim*.

collide in a single sentence. Here is an example of early Russian epistolary form, the conventional opening of a petition addressed to a lord:

Gosudariu Borisu Ivanovichu b'et chelom tvoei gosudarevy arzamaskiia votchiny sela Eksheni poslednii sirota tvoi krest'ianinets Tereshko Osipov.	[My Lord Boris Ivanovich, Tereshko Osipov, the last and humblest peasant of the village Eksheni, of thy Lordship's ancestral estate of Arzamas, humbly beseeches thee.][9]

Here, the points of view of two different people, the sender and the
receiver of the petition, are juxtaposed in one sentence. The name of
the receiver of the petition, the lord ("My Lord Boris Ivanovich"), is
presented respectfully, from the point of view of the sender, the peasant;
the name of the sender, the peasant, Terenty Osipov, is presented dis-
paragingly ("Tereshko Osipov") in a diminutive form, as if from the point
of view of the addressee.

The juxtaposition of the point of view of the sender and the receiver
by means of specific forms of address appears to be a required ceremony
in petitions of the time, where it may be observed throughout entire
texts:

a ia, kholop, tvoi chelovechenka, u tebia, gosudaria, novoi, ne otpisat' k tebe, gosudariu, o takom dele ne posmel.	[but I, thy unworthy servant, newly come into thy service, my lord, did not dare fail to write to thee, my lord, about a matter of such gravity.][10]

What is particularly characteristic of the two preceding examples is the
form used to designate the sender of the message. Functionally, these
forms are a conventional, polite etiquette: the exaltation of the addressee
increases in proportion to the self-abasement of the sender. Similar
devices for the formulation of polite expression are known in many other
languages, as, for example, in Chinese.[11]

9. From the petitions to the boyar B. I. Morozov, in *Trudy Istoriko-arkheologicheskogo instituta Akademii nauk SSSR*, vol. VIII, vyp. 2 (*Khoziaistvo krupnogo feodala-krepostnika XVII v.*), Part I, Leningrad, 1933. See under No. 26.

10. Ibid., see under No. 152.

11. See K. Erberg, "O formakh rechevoi kommunikatsii" [Concerning the forms of speech communication], *Iazyk i literatura*, III (Leningrad, 1929), p. 172. In Russian diminutives of the sort may be extended to apply to any noun relating to a particular petitioner generating a kind of "agreement in diminution" among the things pertaining to him. In the preceding examples we have observed the use of the diminutive for "peasant" (*krest'ianinets*) and "unworthy servant" (*kholop, tvoi, chelovechenka*). Directly associated with this is the use of diminutive forms in expressions of politeness and forms of requests in contemporary Russian colloquial speech (a meaning of diminution, in the proper sense of the word, cannot, of course be applied here): "U menia k vam

Another example of the same juxtaposition of the points of view of the sender and receiver is apparent at the beginning of this letter written to Ivan the Terrible by a member of his bodyguard, the oprichnik Vasily Grigorievich Gryaznoy-Ilyin, from a Crimean captivity:

Gosudariu tsariu i velikomu kniaziu Ivanu Vasil'evichiu vsea Rusii bednyi kholop tvoi polonianik Vasiuk Griaznoi plachettsia.	[To my Lord, the Tsar and the Great Prince of all Russia, Ivan Vasilyevich: thy poor servant, the captive Vasyuk Gryaznoy earnestly entreats thee.][12]

As in the previous examples, we may observe not only the characteristic diminutive form of the name of the sender (the diminutive "Vasyuk" derived from "Vasily"), but also the use of the personal pronoun "thy" (in Russian the familiar form of the second person pronoun), indicating that the statement is constructed from the point of view of the addressee of the petition, Ivan the Terrible.

Of course these conventional forms of address are not only defined in relation to a situation, but also reflect absolute social norms of a class society. (For example, the use of the full name and patronymic ending in "ich," as in "Ivan Ivanovich," was, in Russia of the sixteenth to eighteenth centuries, an honorary form to which not all men were entitled.) For our purpose, however, the forms of address in their relative aspect—when conditioned by the place in the communication process—are of greater interest. Thus, in Old Russia when a member of the high aristocracy addressed someone who held an even higher social position (for instance, a prince addressing the tsar), he would write just as would a serf in addressing his master,[13] or a teacher addressing the father of his students.[14]

---

del'tse," "Daite, pozhaluista, vilochku," "Naleite shchets," "Ia proidu peshochkom?" etc. [Literally (all nouns appear in diminutive form in Russian): "I have some *business* to discuss with you," "Please hand me the *fork*," "Pour me some *soup*," "Shouldn't I go by *foot?*"] See L. A. Bulakhovskii, *Istoricheskii kommentarii k russkomu literaturnomu iazyku* [Historical commentary on Russian literary language] (Kiev, 1950), p. 151.

12. See *Poslaniia Ivana Groznogo* [Letters of Ivan the Terrible] (Moscow-Leningrad, 1951), p. 566.

13. Bulakhovskii, 1950, p. 149.

14. See D. L. Mordovtsev, *O russkikh shkol'nykh knigakh XVII v.* [Russian school books of the seventeenth century] (Saratov, 1856), p. 25. Such forms of address were accepted until the eighteenth century, when they were prohibited by a special decree of Peter the Great, Dec. 20, 1701. "O pisanii liudiam vsiakogo zvaniia polnykh imen svoikh s prozvaniiami vo vsiakikh bumagakh chastnykh i v sudebnye mesta podavaemykh" [To people of all ranks, concerning the writing of their own full names with surnames in all papers, privately submitted or submitted in courts]. See A. A. Dement'ev, "Maksimko, Timoshka, and others," *Russkaia rech'* (1969), no. 2, p. 95.

We may conclude that, although the social positions of sender and receiver are important, the choice of a form of address in the preceding examples is primarily the result of the conventions of the epistolary style. The change in points of view as a device is prescribed here by the requirements of etiquette accepted in written address.

It would be wrong to consider this device archaic or to attribute it solely to the *specifica* of an outmoded epistolary style, for a similar collision of points of view of sender and receiver can be found in contemporary usage. Consider, for example, the form common in dedications of books and paintings, or in inscriptions on gifts ("To my dear Berta Yakovlevna from her Ilyusha Blazunov"), or different types of declarations, or inscriptions on envelopes, and so forth. The completeness of the name and the placing of the first name and patronymic before or after the last name are indicative of the relations between the addressor and the addressee (for example, "To Andrey Petrovich Ivanov from Sergeev, N. N.").[15]

Here again, in a single phrase, we see the interplay of juxtaposed points of view.[16]

Naming as a Problem of Point of View in Literature

We have exemplified the use of different points of view in everyday speech, in epistolary prose, and in magazine writing manifested in the choice of appellations. In the construction of literary works similar devices are in operation, and we will now turn to a consideration of them.

In a literary work, one character may be called by several different names or designated by a variety of titles. Frequently, different names are attributed to one and the same person in a single sentence or in closely connected passages in the text, like "Pierre" and "Count Bezuhov" in the next examples from *War and Peace*.

In spite of Count Bezuhov's enormous wealth, Pierre ever since he had inherited it, and had been, as people said, in receipt of an annual income of five hundred thousand, had felt much less rich than when he had been receiving an allowance of ten thousand from his father (p. 345).

15. See above concerning the significance of style in the choice of this position.
16. A curious and to some extent paradoxical device of the latter use of someone else's point of view in epistolary writing can be found in the letter of the mother of the playwright A. V. Sukhovo-Kobylin to her daughter, in which she constantly refers to her son as "brother"; she thus uses the viewpoint of her addressee. See letter dated June, 1856 in *Trudy Publichnoi biblioteki SSSR im. Lenina*, vyp. III (Moscow, 1934), pp. 204–206.

At the conclusion of the sitting, the Grand Master spoke with ill-will and irony to Bezuhov of his hasty temper; and observed that it was not love of virtue alone, but a passion for strife, that had guided him in the discussion.

Pierre made him no reply (p. 402).

His face [Fyodor Pavlovich Karamazov's] was covered with blood, but he was conscious and listened greedily to Dmitri's cries. He was still fancying that Grushenka really was somewhere in the house. Dmitri Fyodorovich looked at him with hatred as he went out (p. 167).

It seems clear that several points of view are used in each text—that is, the author designates the same character from several different positions. Specifically, he may be using the points of view of various characters in the work, each of whom stands in a different relationship to the character who is being named.

If we know how different people habitually refer to one particular character (this is easy enough to establish by an analysis of corresponding dialogue), then it may be possible formally to define whose viewpoint the author has assumed at any one moment in the narrative. For example, in Dostoevsky's *The Brothers Karamazov*, different characters refer to Dmitri Fyodorovich Karamazov in the following ways:[17]

(a) He is called "Dmitri Karamazov" by the prosecutor in court, and he occasionally refers to himself by the same name;

(b) Alyosha and Ivan call him "brother Dmitri" or "brother Dmitri Fyodorovich," both in direct communication with him or when they speak about him;

(c) his father, Grushenka, Alyosha, and Ivan address him as either "Dmitri" or "Mitya";

(d) he is nicknamed "Mitenka" by the townspeople who gossip about him (for example, Rakitin, a seminary student, and the spectators during the trial);

(e) he is sometimes called "Dmitri Fyodorovich," a name which is neutral and impersonal in the narrative because it is not used by any one particular character.

In the authorial narration the author might refer to D. F. Karamazov by any of the enumerated names, except, perhaps, for "Mitenka." It seems, then, that in his descriptions of this character's actions, the author may change his position and assume the points of view characteristic of one or another participant in the action. At the beginning of the novel, and often in the beginning of a new chapter, the author uses the name

17. We are now considering those speeches of the characters which are in the form of direct discourse.

"Dmitri Fyodorovich," adopting the viewpoint of an objective observer;[18] only after the reader has become more closely acquainted with the character does the author allow himself to refer to him as "Mitya." [19] Moreover, in the beginning of the work, when Dostoevsky uses the nickname "Mitya" for the first time, immediately after Dmitri Fyodorovich Karamazov has appeared before the reader, he encloses the name in quotation marks, as if to emphasize that he is not speaking from his own point of view. As the novel progresses, Dostoevsky continues to refer to Dmitri, in the authorial text, from the point of view of Alyosha (a point of view which he often borrows) as "brother Dmitri," or from the point of view of some abstract person who is relatively well acquainted with Dmitri as "Mitya."

Illustrations: Analysis of the Naming of Napoleon in Tolstoy's War and Peace

In the context of our discussion of the use of personal names and titles as an aspect of the problem of point of view, we may examine the different appellations of Napoleon Bonaparte in *War and Peace*, both in the speech of the characters, and in authorial speech.[20] Analysis limited to the problem of naming may allow us to specify some compositional patterns pertaining to the organization of the work as a whole.

The attitude of Russian society toward Napoleon as reflected in the use of his name is a theme which continues through the whole novel. The change in the appellation reflects the corresponding change in the attitude of the society toward Napoleon himself. Those changes form one of the plot lines of the novel. We will briefly outline the basic stages in this development.

In the year 1805, in the salon of Anna Pavlovna Scherer, Napoleon is generally called "Buonaparte" (the non-French origin of the word is emphasized by this spelling):

"And what do you think of this latest farce *du sacre de Milan?*" said Anna Pavlovna. *"Et la nouvelle comédie des peuples de Gênes et de Lucques, qui viennent présenter leurs voeux à M. Buonaparte assis sur un trône, et exauçant les voeux des nations! . . . On dirait, que le monde entier a perdu la tête"* (p. 13).

18. Here we have a direct analogy with the ritual of introduction and the transition to informal naming in everyday speech.

19. For more details concerning this device, see the sections devoted to frames in the artistic work, and typological analogy to the representational arts in Chapter Seven.

20. For other remarks in this connection see V. V. Vinogradov, "O iazyke Tolstogo" [Concerning the language of Tolstoy] in *"L. N. Tolstoi,"* Part I, *Literaturnoe nasledstvo,* vol. 35–36 (Moscow, 1939).

Prince Andrey, however, calls him "Bonaparte" (without the *u*):

"Bonaparte said so," observed Prince Andrey (p. 14).

Pierre is the only one in the whole group who refers to him constantly as "Napoleon":[21]

"The execution of the duc d'Enghien," said Monsieur Pierre, "was a political necessity, and I consider it a proof of greatness of soul that Napoleon did not hesitate to take the whole responsibility of it upon himself" (p. 14).

Later, after the French have taken Vienna, Bilibin, the Russian ambassador, remarks significantly about Napoleon's name in response to Andrey:

"But what an extraordinary genius!" cried Prince Andrey suddenly, . . . "And what luck the man has!"
"Buonaparte?" said Bilibin interrogatively, puckering up his forehead and so intimating that a *mot* was coming. "Buonaparte?" he said, with special stress on the *u*. "I think, though, now that he is dictating laws to Austria from Schönbrunn, *il faut lui faire grâce de l'u.* I shall certainly adopt the innovation, and call him Bonaparte *tout court*" (p. 139).

Sometime later, in a conversation between Prince Dolgorukov, Prince Andrey, and Boris Drubetskoy, we again encounter the problem of Napoleon's name. Napoleon has sent a letter to Alexander, the Tsar, and the court has difficulty deciding how to address him in their answer:

"They couldn't think how to address an answer to him. If not 'consul,' and of course not 'emperor,' it should be 'general' Bonaparte, it seemed to me."

"But between not recognizing him as emperor and calling him General Bonaparte, there's a difference," said Bolkonsky.

"That's just the point," Dolgorukov interrupted quickly, laughing. "You know Bilibin, he's a very clever fellow; he suggested addressing it 'To the Usurper and Enemy of the Human Race.'" Dolgorukov chuckled merrily.

"And nothing more?" observed Bolkonsky.

"But still it was Bilibin who found the suitable form of address in earnest. He's both shrewd and witty."

"How was it?"

"To the Chief of the French Government: *au chef du gouvernement*

21. There is only one exception: when Pierre first begins to speak of him, he calls him "Bonaparte" once (p. 14).

français," Dolgorukov said seriously and with satisfaction. "That was the right thing, wasn't it?" (p. 228).

We hear Bilibin's joking phrase again, in a letter he writes to Prince Andrey after the battle of Austerlitz:

"The enemy of the human race," as you know, is attacking the Prussians. The Prussians are our faithful allies, who have only deceived us three times in three years. We stand up for them. But it occurs that the enemy of the human race pays no attention to our fine speeches, and in his uncivil and savage way flings himself upon the Prussians without giving them time to finish the parade that they had begun (p. 341).

Later, after Napoleon's successes, the Russian and French emperors are to meet at Tilsit, and we overhear at that time the following conversation between Boris Drubetskoy and a general:

"Je voudrais voir le grand homme," he [Boris] said, meaning Napoleon, whom he had hitherto, like every one else, always spoken of as Bonaparte.
    "Vous parlez de Buonaparte?" the general said to him, smiling.
    Boris looked inquiringly at his general, and immediately saw that this was a playful test.
    "Mon prince, je parle de l'empereur Napoléon," he replied. With a smile the general clapped him on the shoulder.
    "You will get on," said he (pp. 373–374).

With the alliance of the French and the Russians, Bonaparte officially became "le grand homme" and "Napoleon" which he had been earlier (and actually had now ceased to be) for Prince Andrey and Pierre. For Nikolay Rostov, however, the new appellation of "Napoleon" adopted by the official circles after the "change of feeling" is incomprehensible, for his point of view is that of the army, in opposition to that of headquarters (pp. 374–375).[22]

Shortly afterward, we learn from a letter that Princess Marya writes to Julie Karagin that:

"It seems that Bleak Hills [the Bolkonsky estate] is now the only spot on the terrestrial glob where he [Buonaparte] is not recognized as a great man—still less as Emperor of France" (p. 448).

Tolstoy makes us the witnesses of the gradual change in attitude toward Napoleon in Russian society up to 1812;[23] a similar change is portrayed during the events of the year 1812. Consider the author's presentation of the opinion of high society at the beginning of the year 1812:

22. See V. V. Vinogradov, 1939, p. 158.
23. See further, *War and Peace,* p. 660.

They admitted that a war with such a genius as Bonaparte (they called him Bonaparte again now) did undoubtedly call for the profoundest tactical considerations (p. 592).

The changes in the authorial position, achieved by using first one designation for Napoleon and then another, are functional in the novel. Such changes in the designation of Napoleon may occur in the same sentence or in close proximity in the text. For example:

In 1809 the amity between the two sovereigns of the world, as Napoleon and Alexander used to be called, had become so close that when Napoleon declared war that year with Austria, a Russian corps crossed the frontier to co-operate with their old enemy Bonaparte against their old ally, the Austrian Emperor (p. 384).

Often, the sudden change in the naming of Napoleon is a clear indication of a shift from one point of view to another. For example:

Both Emperors dismounted from their horses and took each other by the hands. Napoleon's face wore an unpleasantly hypocritical smile. Alexander was saying something to him with a cordial expression.

. . . Rostov watched every movement of the Emperor Alexander and of Bonaparte, and never took his eyes off them (pp. 379–380).

The description of the encounter of the two sovereigns at Tilsit is presented at first from an impersonal, detached point of view, and then from the point of view of Rostov.[24]

The description of a conversation between Napoleon and Lavrushka, a Cossack soldier, is similarly structured: "But when Napoleon asked him whether the Russians expected to conquer Bonaparte or not . . ." (p. 664). A sudden change of point of view—in this particular instance the change from the French to the Russian point of view (specifically to the point of view of the Cossack Lavrushka)—is a typical case of the intrusion of quasi-direct discourse. And a few lines further: "The interpreter translated these words to Napoleon . . . and Bonaparte smiled" (p. 664). The point of view here changes from that of the interpreter (or of a detached observer) to the point of view of the Cossack Lavrushka.

We may note also the following characteristic sentence, where the point of view of Russian society as a whole, rather than that of some particular person, is made manifest by means of a peculiarly Russian designation of Napoleon:

What the political thermometer indicated at that *soirée* was something as follows: All the European rulers and generals may do their utmost to

24. Compare this with typologically similar camera movements in film.

flatter "Bonaparty" . . . but our opinion in regard to "Bonaparty" can undergo no change (p. 334).

This change in authorial position, the transitions to the point of view of the participants in the action, is not always obvious. It may be guessed, however, as in the quotation which we have just seen. Let us recall, for example, the encounter between Napoleon and Prince Andrey, lying wounded on the field of Austerlitz:

He . . . did not see the men who, judging from the voices and the thud of hoofs, had ridden up to him and stopped.
They were Napoleon and two adjutants escorting him. Bonaparte, making a tour of the field of battle . . . (p. 265).

We may suspect a transition from the point of view of a detached observer (who uses the name "Napoleon") to the point of view of Prince Andrey (who would use the name "Bonaparte" because it corresponds to his changed attitude toward Napoleon at this moment of the narrative).[25]

A similar change in naming Napoleon occurs in a later passage, in the internal monologue of Prince Andrey: "The best of them [of the Russian generals] is Bagration—Napoleon himself admitted it. And Bonaparte himself! I remember his fatuous and self-satisfied face on the field of Austerlitz" (p. 601). While Prince Andrey speaks about Napoleon's action of evaluating Bagration, he calls him "Napoleon," as people in general call him at that point in the narrative; but recalling the time of the battle of Austerlitz when Napoleon was referred to as "Bonaparte," Prince Andrey speaks about him as "Bonaparte."

In this connection we can consider what change would be produced by the substitution of one of the names used to designate Napoleon for another. Compare, for example, the description of the distribution of the army in Part II, Chapter XIV (p. 151): "If Kutuzov were to determine to remain at Krems, Napoleon's army of a hundred and fifty thousand men would cut him off from all communications," writes Tolstoy. We may assume that the appellation "Napoleon" indicates that this sentence is an objective discussion of the strategic possibilities by the author and not by Kutuzov. But if the name "Bonaparte" had been substituted into this sentence, we would read the sentence as a reflexion by Kutuzov from Kutuzov's point of view.

Thus, in the course of the narrative, we become witnesses to the changes in the names used by the Russian society to designate Napoleon. At the

25. See further the narrated monologue of Prince Andrey (p. 266): "He knew it was Napoleon—his hero—but at that moment Napoleon seemed to him such a small, insignificant creature."

beginning of the novel, especially in Parts I through III, he is consistently called "Bonaparte"; in Parts IX–XI, however, this name is seldom used by anyone, with the exception of minor characters like the Cossack Lavrushka and Makar Alekseevich; after Part XI, this name is never used by any of the characters.[26] Against this general pattern exceptions become more noticeable: Pierre, as we have already pointed out, uses the name "Napoleon" at a time when all of the other characters refer to him as "Bonaparte"; similarly Count Rastopchin uses the name "Bonaparte" when all of the other characters are calling him "Napoleon" (pp. 508, 701).

Corresponding to the change in the naming of Napoleon in the speech of the characters, there is a change in the authorial speech. In Parts I–III of *War and Peace,* in the majority of instances, the author calls Napoleon "Bonaparte";[27] in the authorial speech of Parts IV–VIII, "Bonaparte" and "Napoleon" are used equally; in Parts IX–XI the name "Bonaparte" appears only in isolated instances, and in Parts XII–Epilogue it is never used. Thus, the author adopts attitudes toward Napoleon which correspond to the attitudes of the society he describes.

THE CORRELATION BETWEEN THE SPEECH OF THE AUTHOR AND THE SPEECH OF THE CHARACTERS IN THE TEXT

Change in the authorial point of view becomes evident in the intrusion within the authorial text of elements of someone else's speech—that is, elements of speech characteristic of one or another character. The inclusion of elements of someone else's speech is a basic device of expressing changes of point of view on the level of phraseology. It is by no means limited to the use of personal names alone.

The subject of our present discussion will be the different possible ways of reporting someone else's speech—the combination of someone else's speech and the authorial speech proper—and in particular the problem of quasi-direct discourse.[28] We shall consider in turn the "contaminations"

26. There is one exception, however—the passage where Denisov is reminiscing about the old days (p. 1089). We may conjecture that retrospection justifies the choice of names here.

27. If we exclude however, those instances of the use in authorial speech of Pierre's viewpoint and the situations in which Napoleon's utterances are used, the uses of the name "Napoleon" in the authorial text in the first three parts of *War and Peace* may be reduced to a few examples.

28. The basic study in problems of the use of reported speech may be found in V. N. Voloshinov, *Marksizm i filosofiia iazyka. Osnovnye problemy sotsiologicheskogo*

of the authorial text ("authorial speech") and of the text of another speaker ("someone else's speech"): first, the modification of the authorial text under the influence of speech which does not belong to the author himself—that is, someone else's speech; and second, the reverse case: the modification of a text belonging to a character under the influence of authorial reworking—that is, authorial speech.

Here and in subsequent passages, we use the word "author" to mean the person to whom belongs the whole text that we are examining. This person may be the author of a work or anyone who speaks and whose utterance forms the object of our investigation (and in whose speech may be observed elements of someone else's speech).

In this sense, we may oppose "one's own" speech (authorial speech) to "somone else's" speech.

THE INFLUENCE OF SOMEONE ELSE'S SPEECH
ON AUTHORIAL SPEECH

Most Clear-Cut Cases of the Use of Reported Speech
The use of someone else's speech (or reported speech) is common and takes several forms. We will begin with the simplest of these.

An analysis of *War and Peace* clearly indicates that Tolstoy often made deliberate use of someone else's speech, by marking it in the text, as a rule, by italics (that is, if the text is not in another language). The italics in the following examples are Tolstoy's:

Anna Pavlovna had been coughing for the last few days: she had an attack of *la grippe,* as she said—*grippe* was then a new word only used by a few people (p. 1).

"Leave off, Boris, you're such a diplomatist" (the word *diplomatist* was much in use among the children in the special sense they attached to the word) (p. 39).

In a discussion between Pierre and Prince Andrey we read:

"You have everything, everything before you. And *you* . . ."
He did not say *why you,* but his tone showed . . . (p. 23).

"And after all, really. . ."—But he did not say *why really* (p. 23).

Tolstoy also italicizes those instances when elements of reported speech intrude not into the authorial text, but into the speech of one of the

---

metoda v nauke o iazyke [Marxism and the philosophy of language: Basic problems of the sociological method in the science of language] (Leningrad, 1929). [In English translation: V. N. Voloshinov, *Marxism and the Philosophy of Language,* trans. by L. Matejka, I. R. Titunik, (New York and London: Seminar Press, 1973)].

characters. Here is an example from a conversation between Natasha and Boris Drubetskoy:

"Boris, come here," she said. . . . "I've something I want to tell you." "What is the *something?*" he inquired (p. 37).

In other words, when Tolstoy uses someone else's speech sporadically, he seems to feel it necessary to emphasize that these words belong to another speaker, that they are "borrowed" for the moment from someone else's speech. This technique is found both in the authorial text and in the text which belongs to the characters.

The Combination of Different Points of View in a Complex Sentence. Quasi-Direct Discourse

More complex cases of the use of someone else's speech are represented by the various forms of "quasi-direct discourse." [29] The combination of several points of view is possible not only in a whole work, but also within a single sentence; this is especially characteristic of oral speech, where the speaker may inadvertently assume the point of view of the person about whom he speaks.

A classic example of such an instance is Ossip's statement in Gogol's play, *The Inspector General.* Ossip says to his master: "The innkeeper said that I shall not give you anything to eat until you pay what you owe [*"Traktirshchik skazal, chto ne dam vam est', poka ne zaplatite za prezhnee"*].[30] Here, two utterances belonging to two different people—to Ossip, the "author" of the whole sentence, and to the innkeeper—are combined. Although both utterances are united within a single sentence, each has retained its own grammatical features.

Here is another example of the same device in *War and Peace:*

29. Equivalent terms for *nesobstvenno-priamaia rech'* in other European languages are: *seemingly indirect style* (English); *die uneigentliche directe Rede* (German), and in part, *die erlebte Rede; le style indirect libre* (French); *estilo indirecto libro* (Spanish); and *mowa pozornie zależna* (Polish). [Voloshinov exemplifies "le style indirect libre" in French: "Il protesta: son père la haïssait!" In direct discourse this would be: "Il protesta et s'écria: 'Mon père te haït!'" and in indirect discourse: "Il protesta et s'écria que son père la haïssait." Voloshinov, 1929, Chapter Four. In the English translation of Voloshinov's work—"Reported Speech," trans. Matejka and Titunik, in *Readings in Russian Poetics: Formalist and Structuralist Views* (Cambridge: MIT Press, 1971)—the term *quasi-direct discourse* is used for *nesobstvenno-priamaia rech;* the same term has been adopted for the present translation. See Voloshinov, 1973, p. 1–11.—Trans.]

30. A. I. Peshkovskii, *Russkii sintaksis v nauchnom osveshchenii* [Russian syntax from a scientific point of view] 5 (Moscow, 1935), p. 429. This example is cited in Voloshinov, 1929, p. 148, note 2. [See Voloshinov, 1973, p. 126.—Trans.]

"His majesty drew his [the French ambassador's] attention to the grenadier division and their parade march," pursued the general; "and it seems the ambassador took no notice and it seems he ventured to remark that we in France do not pay attention to such trivial matters" (pp. 508–509).

Both of these instances are neither direct nor indirect discourse. If they were direct discourse, then in both examples the conjunction "that" would have been omitted (the innkeeper said, "I will not give you anything to eat"; the ambassador ventured to remark, "We in France . . ."). If they were instances of indirect discourse there would be grammatical agreement in person between the subject of the main clause and the subject of the subordinate clause (the innkeeper said that he would not give us anything to eat; the ambassador ventured to remark that they in France . . .).

These examples are neither direct nor indirect discourse, but quasi-direct discourse, a synthesis of both phenomena. They combine speeches belonging to two different authors: to the speaker himself, and to the person about whom he speaks. In other words, we can observe in the author's speech a shifting of point of view.

It has been conjectured that quasi-direct discourse is a new phenomenon in Russian, having been brought into the language under the influence of French.[31] This view can be refuted, however, by examples from Russian chronicles, the Ipatev chronicle of the year 6454, for instance:

Reche zhe im" Ol'ga, iako iaz" uzhe mstila esm' muzha svoego.	[Olga said to them that I have already avenged my husband.][32]

And also, by examples from folklore:

Govorit Staver syn Godinovich.— Chto ia s toboi svaechkoi ne igryval!	[Says Staver son of Godinovich:— That I did not play on you with my big stick!][33]

31. See L. A. Bulakhovskii, *Russkii literaturnyi iazyk pervoi poloviny XIX Veka* [Russian literary language in the first half of the nineteenth century], II (Kiev, 1948), p. 444.

32. See A. I. Molotkov, *Slozhnye sintaksicheskie konstruktsii dlia peredachi chuzhoi rechi v drevnerusskom iazyke po pamiatnikam pis'mennosti XI–XVII stoletii* [Complex syntactical structures for the transmission of reported speech in Old Russian as manifested in the writings of the eleventh through the seventeenth centuries] (dissertation), (Leningrad, 1952), p. 21; includes other examples. In addition, see D. S. Likhachev, *Chelovek v literature Drevnei Rusi* [Man in the literature of Old Russia] (Moscow, 1970), p. 134.

33. *Pesni, sobrannye P. N. Rybnikovym* [Songs, collected by P. N. Rybnikov] vol. I–III (Moscow, 1909–1910), no. 30.

We can speculate that the phenomenon of quasi-direct discourse is completely natural in language with developed forms of hypotaxis being
conditioned by the shift in the authorial position that is characteristic
of ordinary speech.

The quotations discussed above are examples of how two different
points of view and, consequently, the texts of two different speakers, are
united in a single complex sentence.[34]

Such instances are relatively simple, however, because the boundaries
of both texts, each belonging to a different author, are well-defined. Thus,
in each of the examples quoted we could enclose some words within
quotation marks and consider them to be the product of accidental speech
interference—that is, a phenomenon relating to *parole,* and not to
langue:[35] "The innkeeper said that 'I will not give you anything to
eat . . .'"; and "the ambassador . . . ventured to remark that 'we in
France . . .'"[36]

These two cases are related to the examples of italicized borrowed
speech in Tolstoy, for both have clear-cut boundaries, and it is easy to
enclose the borrowed portion of the phrase within quotation marks. The
italics which Tolstoy uses to emphasize the elements of the borrowed
text are, indeed, functionally equivalent to quotation marks.

Our discussion here has followed that of V. N. Voloshinov, in contrast
to that of the group of critics who combine such phenomena as narrated
monologue and other techniques of reporting "someone else's speech"
within the term "quasi-direct discourse." We have used the term in its
narrow sense: to designate a phenomenon midway between direct speech
and indirect speech, a phenomenon that permits transposition (by specific
operations) into both direct speech and indirect speech.

These operations may be described generally as follows: in order to
transpose quasi-direct discourse into direct discourse, the appropriate
material is enclosed within quotation marks and conjunctions are
omitted; to transpose quasi-direct discourse into indirect discourse, all
grammatical forms must be coordinated.[37]

34. Later we shall discuss the combination of different points of view in a simple sentence.

35. Concerning the distinction between *langue* and *parole* which is accepted in contemporary linguistics, see F. de Saussure, *Cours de linguistique générale.*

36. Quotation marks belong to the written language. In oral speech, their function
may be served by such Russian particles as *mol, de,* or *deskat',* or by a simple pause, or
by a change of intonation or of pitch. Corresponding elements may be found in other
languages.

37. In Russia, verbs in indirect discourse agree with the noun in the main clause
in person, gender, and number; in the Romance and Germanic languages, there must be

The Combination of Points of View in Simple Sentences.
The Intergration of the Speaker's and Listener's Points of View

Now we will examine the combination of points of view within the limits of a simple sentence. Although we could also have placed in this category the cases of intermittent use of someone else's speech in the passages by Tolstoy cited above, in this section we are concerned with a more organic fusion of elements of "someone else's" speech and "one's own" speech in one sentence.

Let us turn to an example from *War and Peace*:

Prince Vasily, who still filled the same important position, constituted the connecting link between the two circles. He used to visit *ma bonne amie* Anna Pavlovna and was also seen *dans le salon diplomatique de ma fille* (p. 660).

The important feature here is the twice-used first-person pronoun *ma* (my) in a text in which the narrative is conducted in the third person. This use of the first-person pronoun clearly indicates that the point of view of Prince Vasily himself intrudes into the text.

In Dostoevsky's *The Gambler,* we find a passage where the hero addresses the girl, Polina: "In your place, I would definitely take an Englishman for a husband." "*Ia by, na vashem meste, nepremenno vyshla zamuzh za anglichanina.*"

In the Russian text, the speaker, a man, adopts the point of view of his woman interlocutor grammatically, through the use of the feminine form of the verb (and against all the rules of Russian grammar). He has "put himself into her place" as he speaks to her, and this becomes manifest linguistically. If this phrase were taken out of its context, it could only be attributed [in Russian] to a woman speaker.

---

the additional agreement of tense (*consecutio temporum*). Languages may thus be distinguished according to the degree of similarity of meaning between direct discourse and its expression in indirect discourse; in Russian, however, the correspondence between direct and indirect discourse may only be approximated. Let us take, for example, the phrase in direct discourse *khot' by poest'* [literally: would that I might eat!]; the phrase is translated into indirect speech as *on skazal, chto zhelal by poest'* [literally: he said that he wanted to eat.] The phrase *"kak khorosho!"* [meaning: well done!] is translated into indirect speech as *on skazal, chto eto ochen' khorosho* [literally: he said that it had been done very well], or *on vostorzhenno skazal, chto eto khorosho* [literally: he said enthusiastically that it had been done well]. The conversion from one form into another cannot always be reversed—that is, we cannot move easily from a phrase in indirect discourse back to the initial phrase in direct discourse. In Latin, however, as well as in many other languages, the conversion of direct discourse into indirect discourse, and vice versa, may be accomplished without altering the meaning. See S. I. Sobolevskii, *Grammatika latinskogo iazyka* [The grammar of the Latin language] (Moscow, 1948), Part I, p. 347 ff.; see also V. N. Voloshinov, 1929, p. 151 and p. 166 ff. [For this discussion see also Voloshinov, 1971, p. 161. Voloshinov, 1973, pp. 128–129.—Trans.]

We can see that in one simple sentence we have two points of view—elements of two spheres of speech: of the speaker and of the listener. What takes place here is the internal integration of the two.

Moreover, the reported speech here is incorporated more organically into the text, and it is not so easy to distinguish the borrowed elements from the authorial context as it was in the examples we discussed earlier, for the boundaries of the reported speech are not clear.[38] Moreover, it is completely impossible to transpose the sentence into indirect discourse by predetermined rules. Therefore, this sentence and others like it do not represent cases of quasi-direct discourse in the narrow sense of the term that we have adopted here: the points of view in this sentence are bound together much more tightly.

The combination of different points of view—in particular, the point of view of the speaker and the listener—are often encountered in oral speech. We have, for example, the widespread use in contemporary speech: *Ubeditel'no vas proshu* [literally: "I beg you convincingly"]. In fact, it is only the listener, and not the speaker, who can correctly evaluate whether the request is "convincing" or "not convincing." Thus the speaker has, as it were, adopted the listener's evaluation and assumed his point of view. The same thing is true of the phrase: *Vy menia, konechno, izvinite* [literally: "You will, of course, forgive me"].

A similar transposition of the point of view from the speaker to his interlocutor occurs in the following sentence, recorded during a confrontation between an angry student and a porter who was demanding an identification card. The student said: *"Chego pristaete. Ne vidite razve chelovek speshit?"* [literally: "What do you want? Can't you see that someone's in a hurry?"] With the word "someone" the student refers to himself, hoping that the porter will identify with him and recognize that he is indeed in a hurry. By referring to himself in the third person, the student puts himself in the position of the porter, in order to prompt him to what he feels is the correct point of view. The same is true of a speaker who refers to himself through the use of the indefinite personal form—for example, when the giver says: *"Beri, poka daiut"* [literally: "Take it while they offer it"]. In this case, the speaker adopts the position of the interlocutor, speaking about himself from the listener's point of view, deliberately using an impersonal third-person plural form.

The special uses of elements of someone else's speech described above

---

38. In this case it is more difficult to transpose reported speech back into direct speech if we read the passage aloud, trying to distinguish someone else's direct speech through intonation. In the previous instances of quasi-direct speech, however, the translation into direct speech through intonation was possible.

may be found primarily in colloquial style. This is not accidental, because the process we have described here exemplifies one of the typical ways a language evolves or words change in meaning. Consider, for example, the evolution of the word *navernoe,* which, until the first third of this century, meant "surely, certainly." Now, however, the same word is used to mean "probably" and even "possibly"—a meaning almost opposite that which it had earlier. The change in the use of this word represents a shift from the point of view of the speaker to that of the listener. As a rule, colloquial style is more progressive in terms of linguistic change: evolutionary processes usually occur here first, before they have affected the other levels of the language.[39] We can understand, then, why the phenomena of quasi-direct discourse and of the different uses of someone else's speech in general are prevalent in colloquial style.

A related instance of the use of someone else's speech may be observed when we say to a child: *"Kakie my krasivye!"* [literally: "How pretty we are!"] We speak not only from our own point of view, but also from the point of view of the listening child; we are putting our own words, so to speak, into the child's mouth. The points of view of the speaker and of the listener are combined here in order to convey a sense of cooperation and oneness which is characteristic of our relationship to small children.[40]

In general, speaking with a small child (especially one who has not yet learned to talk) we tend to adopt his point of view, and this shift of position is manifested first of all on the plane of phraseology; in many linguistic situations such behavior is normative. Indeed, we speak many phrases using a child's voice and with his intonation, as if we were prompting him in what to say. We might say, for example, *"Idi ko mne na ruchki"* [approximately: "Come into mommy's arms"], using the diminutive form [*ruchki* rather than *ruki*]. In this case we use the point of view of the child, expressed phraseologically, and not our own point of view. Characteristically, in the presence of a child we often name another adult from the point of view of the child: husband and wife, for example, often call each other "Daddy" and "Mommy."

Maximum Concentration of Different Points of View

The combination of different points of view in a single word is a paradoxical occurrence which belongs characteristically to *parole* rather than

---

39. See concerning this problem: B. Uspensky, "Les problèmes sémiotiques du style à la lumière de la linguistique," *Information sur les sciences sociales* 7, No. 1 (1968): 137–138.

40. The same tone may be noted in the traditional command of a policeman to lawbreakers: *"Grazhdane, davaite ne budem"* [literally: "Citizens, let's not do it!"].

to *langue* (that is, it is usually connected with improvisation during the creation of a text rather than being an instance of the norm). This phenomenon may also be found in literature.

An example of the integration of two points of view in a single word occurs in Dostoevsky's *Notes from the House of the Dead*, in a chapter entitled "Akulka's Husband." Shishkov, a man who has been condemned for the murder of his wife, is relating the story of the killing: *"Kak tilisnu* [a coined word] *(ee) po gorlu nozhom"* ["So I slit her throat with a knife!"]. Zielinsky, commenting on this passage, asks: "Is there a correspondence between the articulatory movements in pronouncing the word *tilisnut'* and the movement of a knife slipping over the human body and penetrating it? No, there is not: the articulation of this word best corresponds to the contortion of the facial muscles which is instinctively brought about by the nervous pain one would feel in imagining a knife slipping over one's skin (and not penetrating the body): the lips are pulled up in a grimace; the throat is pinched; the teeth grit; at such a moment the only sounds that can be produced are consonants *t, l,* and *s,* and the vowel *i.* Furthermore, the choice of these particular letters, rather than the consonants *d, r,* and *z* was dictated also by a certain onomatopoeic quality they have." [41] What is important to our discussion, however, is that the criminal, the man who produced the pain, simulates the feeling of pain when pronouncing the word. Thus he assumes simultaneously the position of his victim (of the acted upon) and his own position (of the actor). Accordingly, there is a fusion here, in the same word, of the

41. F. F. Zelinskii, "Vil'gel'm Vundt i psikhologiia iazyka: zhesty i zvuki" [Wilhelm Wundt and the psychology of language: gestures and sounds] in *Iz zhizni idei*, 3rd ed. (St. Petersburg, 1911), 2:185–186. Also see V. Shklovskii, "O poezii i zaumnom iazyke" [About poetry and beyond the rational language], *Poetika. Sborniki po teorii poeticheskogo iazyka* (Petrograd, 1919), pp. 16–17. And M. V. Panov, *Russkaia fonetika* [Russian phonetics] (Moscow, 1967), p. 162, note 2.

In general, about the psycho-physiological conditioning of the meaning of different sounds, see the items of G. N. Ivanova-Luk'ianova, E. V. Orlova, and M. V. Panov in the collection *Razvitie fonetiki sovremennogo russkogo iazyka* [*The development of phonetics in contemporary Russian*], (Moscow, 1966); A. Shtern, "Ob'ektivnoe izuchenie sub'-ektivnykh otsenok zvukov rechi" [The objective study of subjective evaluations of sounds in speech], *Voprosy porozhdeniia rechi i obucheniia iazyku* (Moscow, 1967); E. Sapir, "A Study in Phonetic Symbolism," *Journal of Experimental Psychology* 3 (1929), 225–239; S. S. Newman, "Further Experiment in Phonetic Symbolism," *American Journal of Psychology* 45 (1933), 55–75; G. Bonfante "Pozitsiia neolingvistiki" [The position of neo-linguistics] in B. A. Zvegintsev, *Istoriia iazykoznaniia XIX–XX vekov v ocherkakh i izvlecheniiakh*, Part I (Moscow, 1964), p. 35.

About the special use of these meanings in poetry see M. V. Panov, "O vospriiatii zvukov" in the above collection, also G. A. Gukovskii, *Pushkin i russkie romantiki* [Pushkin and the Russian Romantics], 2nd ed. (Moscow, 1965), p. 61; also in Tynianov and others.

points of view of both imagined participants in the action: the *agens* and the *patiens*.

A similar conjunction of two points of view in the same element of speech is frequently encountered in mimicry, intonation, gesture, facial expression, and other paralinguistic phenomena that accompany speech. For example, when we pose a question, knowing that the answer will be in the affirmative, the intonation signalling the interrogative is accompanied by a nod of the head which signals affirmation. In the same way, a man who relates how he beat his opponent may, while describing his blows, simultaneously imitate his victim's face, distorted in pain (the same situation may be encountered in pantomime). Or a man, seeing a cat creeping along, may pronounce the phrase, "the cat moves so silently," in a cautious whisper, indicating that he has momentarily assumed the point of view of the object he describes.

In visual art a similar device is characteristic of Japanese drawing. In the representation of a bird, for example, the artist expresses the swift flight of the bird by means of quick, supple strokes of the brush.[42] In other words, the artist involves the observer and makes him a co-participant in the creative process by calling attention to his artistic gestures. At the same time he combines in his drawing his own feelings and the characteristics which he perceives in the object he represents.

THE INFLUENCE OF AUTHORIAL SPEECH
ON SOMEONE ELSE'S SPEECH

Less Obvious Cases: Narrated Monologue

The preceding discussion has presented instances of authorial speech modified under the influence of reported speech—or, to put it differently, by instances of the author's voice to some degree imitating someone else's voice. There are, however, cases in which someone else's speech (namely, the speech of a character) imitates the authorial speech. It acquires signs of the authorial influence and changes under this influence.

The author's reworking of someone else's speech is evident in cases when the feelings and thoughts of a character are made known to us in a form which seems to imitate the manner of that character, while references to this character are in the third person.

Here, for example, is Tolstoy's description of Petya Rostov, when he goes to the Kremlin to see Alexander I:

42. In this connection see L. Nikitin, "Ideograficheskii izobrazitel'nyi metod v iaponskoi zhivopisi" [Ideographic techniques of representation in Japanese painting], vyp. 1 (Moscow, 1924), p. 214.

he had gained a seat on the cannon, from which he hoped to see the Tsar, who was to walk back. Petya thought no more now of presenting his petition. If only he could see Him, he would think himself lucky! (p. 629).

Here we have, clearly, the speech of Petya himself, formally presented in the voice of the author. The syntax of the last sentence and the capitalization of the third-person pronoun which refers to Alexander I stress the identification between the author and his character.[43]

If we substitute first-person pronouns for the third-person pronouns referring to Petya, we will have a simple instance of direct discourse.[44] Thus, the substitution of pronouns is functionally analogous to the operation of enclosing certain portions of the text within quotation marks in our earlier examples of quasi-direct discourse. Both operations lead to the same end: the performance of either of them on indirect discourse gives us direct discourse.

In this way is formed a particular kind of narration called "narrated monologue."[45] In many instances this kind of narration may be correctly considered either as the result of the author's influence on the character's speech, or as the result of the influence of the character's speech on the authorial text. The substitution of pronouns alone may not be sufficient to transpose the text from authorial speech to the direct discourse of the character: the character's words may have been significantly reworked by the author or colored by the author's intonation. In this case, the point of view of the author and the point of view of the character are inseparably merged in the text; as a result, while we perceive the feelings of the character from his own point of view, we are constantly listening to the "intonations" of the author.[46]

Narrated monologue—which may be formally presented in the third

43. See also the analysis of a passage from Pushkin's poem *The Prisoner of the Caucasus* in Voloshinov, 1929, p. 164. [An English translation of this discussion may be found in Matejka and Pomorska, eds., *Readings in Russian Poetics*, p. 173—Trans.]

44. See Voloshinov, 1929, p. 164; cf. B. V. Tomashevskii, *Stilistika i stikhoslozhenie* [*Stylistics and poetics*] (Leningrad, 1959), p. 288.

45. We will not consider separately those instances of interior monologue where the monologue may be separated into two voices. See the examples from Tolstoy in V. V. Vinogradov, "O iazyke Tolstogo" [Concerning the language of Tolstoy] in *L. N. Tolstoi*, Part I, *Literaturnoe nasledstvo*, vol. 35-36, p. 186.

46. Voloshinov, pp. 156-157 [Uspensky refers here to the following passage, where Voloshinov analyzes Pushkin's "Bronze Horseman" and discusses the "impressionistic variant" of indirect discourse, which is used primarily "for reporting the internal speech, thoughts, and experiences of a character. It treats the speech to be reported very freely, it abbreviates it, often only highlighting its themes and dominants, and therefore it may be termed the impressionistic variant. Auctorial intonation easily and freely ripples over its fluid structure." Matejka and Pomorska, eds., *Readings in Russian Poetics*, p. 166.]

or first person—usually carries more traces of the author's reworking than the character's direct discourse. The character's individual manner, which appears unmediated in his own direct speech, is often eliminated by the author in the narrated monologue, and is substituted by the author's own style of speech. It is as if the author here performed the function of an editor reworking the discourse of a particular character.

The difference between the two modes may be interpreted as follows: direct discourse (dialogue) of a character represents an objective fact which is heard by the author, who assumes the position of a reporter faithfully recording what he hears; narrated monologue, on the other hand, reflects thoughts and meditations of the hero, and here the author concentrates on their essence, and not on their form.

Similar instances of the reworking of direct speech by the author appear frequently—both in fiction and in everyday storytelling—in order to communicate what was taking place in the consciousness of the character. Often the author makes reference to a conventional interior monologue which did not in fact happen but which might have taken place.

Here, for example, in *War and Peace,* is a description which is carried out from the point of view of Princess Marya. Then we observe a shift to the point of view of the little nephew Nikolay Bolkonsky and then back to the point of view of the princess:

However often she told herself that she must not let herself lose her temper, when teaching her nephew, almost every time she sat down with a pointer showing him the French alphabet, she so longed to hasten, to make easy the process of transferring her knowledge to the child, who was by now always afraid his auntie would be angry the next moment, that at the slightest inattention she was quivering in nervous haste and vexation, she raised her voice and sometimes pulled him by his little hand and stood him in the corner (p. 504).

At the beginning of the passage, the point of view of the princess is used, then the point of view of the boy, and finally the point of view of an abstract author-narrator. In cases like this, point of view may be attributed to a character not so much by the phraseological particularities of the expression as by the interpretation of the character's consciousness. Nevertheless, it seems convenient to classify these cases as expressions of point of view on the phraseological plane by arguing—as did V. N. Voloshinov—that they derive from a potential internal monologue (carried out in the character's own voice), which is then translated into authorial speech.

*More Obvious Cases: The Influence of the Author
on the Direct Discourse of the Characters*

The influence of an author's speech on the speech of a character is even stronger when the author speaks on behalf of his character. Voloshinov defines this phenomenon as "substituted direct discourse," and offers as an illustration of it the following passage from Pushkin's *The Prisoner of the Caucasus*:[47]

The Cossacks, leaning on their pikes, gaze over the dark rushing river at the weapons of the villain, blurred in the darkness, floating past them. . . . What are you thinking, Cossack? Are you recalling battles of bygone years? . . . Farewell, free frontier villages, paternal home, the quiet Don, and war, and pretty girls. The unseen enemy has reached the bank, an arrow leaves the quiver—takes flight—and down the Cossack falls from the bloodied rampart.

In his analysis of the passage, Voloshinov observes that Pushkin "stands in for his hero, says in his stead what the hero might or should have said, says what the given occasion calls for. Pushkin bids farewell to the Cossack's homeland for him (naturally, something the Cossack himself could not have done)." [48] Judging from this example, the author's reworking of someone else's speech may occur not only within the context of authorial speech but also when the character's speech is in the form of direct discourse.

We may turn to another example. In *The Life of the Archpriest Avvakum,* as demonstrated by Vinogradov, the text is built to a large degree upon a series of parallels with biblical motifs, and biblical text often intrudes into the speech of the characters.[49] Not only does Avvakum use biblical citations in his own speech (a fact which could be explained by his ecclesiastic education), but other characters in his narration are also made to speak biblical language. Avvakum's enemy, a Cossack chieftain named Pashkov, speaks in the words of Judas (Matt. 27:4), for example:

And Pashkov sat him down on a chair and, leaning on his sword, he came to his right mind, and beginning to weep, he said, "I have

47. Voloshinov, 1929, p. 163. What takes place here is the characteristic dialogue of the author and his character, what Voloshinov calls "talking in another's stead."
48. Ibid.
49. See V. V. Vinogradov, "O zadachakh stilistiki. Nabliudeniia nad stilem *Zhitiia protopopa Avvakuma*" [Stylistic problems: observations on the style of *The Life of the Archpriest Avvakum*], *Russkaia rech'*, ed. L. V. Shcherba (Petrograd, 1923), 1: pp. 211–214.

sinned, accursed that I am, I have betrayed innocent blood, I flogged the archpriest unjustly, God will punish me."

Nikodemus, the cellarer, speaks in the words of the prodigal son (Luke 15:21):

And he fell before me and clasped my chain and said, "Forgive me, for God's sake! forgive, I have sinned against heaven and in thy sight. I have insulted thee, and for this God hath punished me." [50]

Thus the author Avvakum speaks for his characters—not in the context of authorial speech, in this case, but in the direct discourse of the characters.[51]

In other cases, the author's reworking of the direct discourse of the characters is not so evident, although it may still be manifest. A change in the degree of the author's influence on reported speech (in this case, on the direct discourse of the characters) is indicative of a shift in the authorial position (point of view) during the course of the narrative. For an illustration of this phenomenon we may turn to an analysis of the positions which Tolstoy assumes in transmitting the direct discourse of the characters in *War and Peace*—and primarily in transmitting French spoken in direct discourse.

Some Questions of Authorial Transmission of Direct Discourse in War and Peace

The author's reworking of the direct speech of the characters (the influence of the authorial speech on that of a character) occurs in the transmission of direct speech in *War and Peace*. Tolstoy in various cases adopts several essentially different positions in respect to the direct speech of one character.

---

50. Ibid. Critics' attempts to prove the historicity of some New Testament figures by arguing that their language goes back to the Old Testament models are hardly convincing. See, for example, the unsuccessful attempt in the book by I. A. Lentsman, *Sravnivaia Evangeliia* [Comparing the Gospels] (Moscow, 1967), pp. 44–45.

51. This combining of New Testament events with the events of his personal life is characteristic of Avvakum. Not only is Avvakum's life paralleled by events taken from the New Testament, but the New Testament events are influenced by Avvakum's biography. In the retelling of the apocryphal Gospel of Nikodemus in his "Conversation about the cross addressed to the unfaithful," Avvakum relates that Christ was dragged before the high priests Annas and Caiaphas. This event does not occur in the Gospel of Nikodemus but resembles what has taken place in Avvakum's own life, where Annas and Caiaphas are frequently associated with the patriarch Nikon, to whom he was opposed. See N. S. Demkova, "Neizvestnye i neizdannye teksty iz sochinenii protopopa Avvakuma" [Unknown and unpublished texts of the writings of the Archpriest Avvakum], *Novonaidennye i neopublikovannye proizvedeniia drevnerusskoi literatury*, (TORDL, XXI) (Moscow-Leningrad, 1965), p. 214. [The English translations in the text have been adapted from *Medieval Russia's Epic, Chronicles, and Tales*, ed. Serge A. Zenkovsky (New York, 1963), pp. 346, 360—Trans.]

One of the positions assumed by the author of *War and Peace* is that of an objective observer who hears what the characters are saying to one another and whose aim is to record everything that he hears with the utmost precision. In this case we may observe Tolstoy's scrupulousness and almost pedantic attention to the transmission of the phonetic peculiarities of the characters (for example, Denisov's slurring of the consonant *r*, the phonetic irregularities in the speech of the naval officer at the Slobodsky palace, and many other examples),[52] as well as his general attention to modes of speaking. The faithful transmission of the French speech of the characters in *War and Peace* may be explained by the same objective attention.

Objective direct transmission is only one of the positions that the author assumes, however, for in other instances his attitude toward the speech of the characters is essentially different, and his position may be compared to that of an editor, filtering everything that he hears and reworking in definite ways the direct speech of the characters.[53]

An examination of the use of French in direct discourse in *War and Peace* indicates that the reporting of a character's speech in either French or Russian is not always dependent upon what language that particular character, at that moment, is assumed actually to have spoken (in the imagination of the author). The rendition of speech in one language or another has purely functional aims, directly related to the problem of the authorial point of view.

French speech (that is, speech which the author imagines to have been pronounced in French) may be given in Russian—directly translated or freely retold—or in French, just as it was supposedly spoken. This authorial reworking of direct discourse is paradoxically juxtaposed to the scrupulously accurate reporting of the speech of the characters elsewhere in the novel.

Actually, both the French characters and the Russian aristocracy use both languages in the novel, expressing themselves in Russian, or in a mixture of French and Russian. For example, Napoleon addresses Prince Andrey (when he is wounded at Austerlitz) or the Cossack Lavrushka, a captive, in Russian; he speaks Russian with General Balashev and even with his French generals. In many instances, Napoleon begins speaking in French and later changes either to Russian or to a mixture of Russian and French.

52. See *War and Peace*, pp. 156 ff. 632. For other examples see Vinogradov, 1939, pp. 202–204.

53. The two possibilities (the author's direct transmission of a character's speech and his reworking of direct speech) may be interpreted as synchronic and diachronic positions. We shall return to this problem at a later point in the discussion.

Sometimes Napoleon's adjutants speak French while he answers them in Russian, or they speak Russian and he responds in French:

"Sire, le Prince . . ." began the adjutant. "Asks for reinforcements?" said Napoleon, with a wrathful gesture (p. 749).

Or:

"Our fire is mowing them down in whole rows, but they stand firm," said the adjutant.

"Ils en veulent encore!" said Napoleon in his husky voice (p. 761).

Taken out of their context, these passages could be understood only in one way: that Napoleon and his adjutants spoke to one another in different languages, as bilingual people do.

Other French characters in the novel speak in exactly the same way—now in Russian, now in French: the Viscount Mortemart, whom we meet at Anna Pavlovna Scherer's soirée (p. 8), Murat (p. 574), Davoust (p. 576), and so forth.

Similarly, the French speech of the Russian aristocracy may be given by the author, not in French, but in Russian, even though Tolstoy may specifically indicate that the conversation occurred in French.

For example:

The princess came in. . . .
   "Why is it, I often wonder," she began in French as always . . . (p. 20).

The dialogue is then given in Russian, not in French. And in another instance:

She met Prince Vasily in that playful tone so often adopted by chatty and lively persons. . . . "Well, anyway, we shall take advantage of you to the utmost now we have got you, dear prince," said the little princess, in French, of course, to Prince Vasily (p. 201).

Prince Dolgorukov . . . addressed Prince Andrey in French.
   "Well, my dear fellow, what a battle we have won!" (pp. 227–228).

The rest of the dialogue is also given in Russian.

"Wherever you are, there is vice and wickedness," said Pierre to his wife. "Anatole, come along, I want a word with you," he said in French (p. 555).

Later in the same episode we hear:

"Did you promise Countess Rostov to marry her? Did you try to elope with her?" "My dear fellow," answered Anatole, in French (as was the whole conversation), "I don't consider myself bound to answer questions put to me in that tone" (pp. 555–556).

Princess Marya felt and appreciated this tone. "I am very, very grateful to you," she said to him in French (p. 686).

In other cases, the French speech of Pierre, Anatole Kuragin, Princess Marya, the wife of Andrey, and Count Dolgorukov is presented directly in French.

With even more attention to detail, when Tolstoy transmits French discourse in Russian, he points out the particularities and idiosyncrasies of the pronunciation of specific French words, even though they are given in Russian. In the following example, Ellen supposedly pronounces the word "lover" in French. Tolstoy, having transmitted the word in Russian, still carefully notes how it was pronounced in French:

"If you won't answer, I'll tell you . . ." Ellen went on. "You believe everything you're told. You were told . . . ," Ellen laughed, "that Dolohov was my lover," she said in French, with her coarse plainness of speech, uttering the word "lover" (p. 291).[54]

In another instance, Tolstoy calls attention to the misuse of French by a German doctor—the speech is actually given in Russian. The German doctor and another physician, Lorrain, are discussing Count Bezuhov's chances for recovery from a stroke:

The German doctor went up to Lorrain.
"Can he drag himself out till tomorrow morning?" asked the doctor, in his vile French (pp. 61–62).

Here, Tolstoy offers in incorrect Russian [*"Eshche, mozhet, dotianetsia do zavtrashnego utra?"*] the sentence which was supposed to have been said in incorrect French by the German doctor. In this instance, with incorrect French transmitted by incorrect Russian, the incorrectness becomes the invariant element.

Consider the dialogue between Napoleon and the captive Cossack Lavrushka:

Napoleon bade him ride at his side and began questioning him.
"Are you a Cossack?" [*"Vy kazak?"*]
"Yes; a Cossack, your honour" (p. 663).

In this episode Napoleon appears to be speaking the same language as Lavrushka; however, Napoleon uses the polite form of the second-person

---

54. Later in the same scene, in the transmission of Ellen's direct speech, the word *lover* occurs again, and Tolstoy finds it necessary to add, in parentheses, the French equivalent, as if underlining its actual pronunciation: ". . . it is a rare wife who with a husband like you wouldn't have taken lovers (*des amants*)" (p. 291).

pronoun [*vy*], while a Russian officer, speaking Russian to Lavrushka, would have naturally used the familiar form [*ty*]. This would seem to indicate that the phrase is a literal translation from the French. Another example demonstrates a similar use:

"You're a scoundrel and a villain; and I don't know what prevents me from permitting myself the pleasure of braining you with this," said Pierre, expressing himself so artificially because he was speaking French (p. 556).

Here, just as in the previous instance, the French speech of a character appears in the text translated into its Russian equivalent, but the Russian text represents Pierre's speech so literally that it preserves some formal characteristics of French, unnatural in Russian.

Thus, a French utterance may be transmitted in *War and Peace* either directly in French, in Russian, or in mixed Russian and French. We may assume, therefore, that the large number of cases in which Russians speak mixed Russian and French are not necessarily products of Tolstoy's desire to represent the speech of the characters realistically; they may instead be the products of some special compositional intentions.

It follows, then, that when direct discourse in *War and Peace* is presented in Russian (or in a mixture of Russian and French)—and is not accompanied by any indication from the author as to how it was spoken —we cannot be sure in what language it was originally supposed to have been uttered. In those instances where the speech is given in French, we may assume that it was supposed to have been uttered in French. We can say, then, that the opposition between French and Russian may be neutralized in *War and Peace,* with the French appearing to be the marked term in this opposition.

A comment written by Tolstoy demonstrates his concern for this matter: "Why, in my work, do both the Russian and French characters speak partly in Russian and partly in French? The complaint that characters speak and write in French in a Russian book is similar to the complaint that a man might make if he were looking at a portrait and happened to notice some black spots (or shadows) which are not there in reality. The painter is not guilty just because some people think that a shadow on a face in a painting is a black spot: the painter is guilty only if the shadows are in the wrong places and are crudely executed. . . . Although I cannot deny that some of the shadows I have made may appear to be crude and unrealistic, I only wanted those who laugh at the fact that Napoleon speaks sometimes in French, sometimes in Russian, to know that they are like a man who looks at a portrait and does not see a face with lights and shadows, but sees only a black spot under its nose." [55]

Thus, the French language is necessary to the author of *War and Peace* not so much because it corresponds to the real world described in the work, but as a technical device of representation.[56]

Tolstoy needed French speech along with other idiosyncratic speech characteristics to convey a sense of how a character speaks, to transmit to the reader a key to the individual style of a speaker. Later in the text, however, after the reader has formed an impression of a character's general manner, the author becomes less pedantic in transmitting direct discourse.

A similar statement may be made about Denisov's slurring. Tolstoy represents this particular idiosyncracy (although with little consistency) in the first and second editions of *War and Peace*, substituting *g* for *r* in the words he pronounces. It is completely eliminated in the third edition of 1873, however—the same edition in which all of the French speech is replaced by Russian. It seems hardly accidental that these two changes occur together: we may conjecture that the presentation of Denisov's idiosyncratic habit is functionally analogous to the use of French speech in *War and Peace,* and that the presentation of Denisov's slurring in the two earlier editions is inconsistent for the same reason that the presentation of French speech is inconsistent. The author feels a need not so much to transmit the phonetic specificity of each of Denisov's phrases as to convey a general impression of the manner of his speech, and to remind the reader of the distinctive features from time to time.[57]

INTERNAL AND EXTERNAL AUTHORIAL POSITIONS

Thus, in the transmission of the French language, of Denisov's slurring, and of all kinds of irregularities in the speech of the characters

55. Vinogradov, 1939, p. 202.

56. In the Gospels, Christ's words are in some instances transmitted in translation and in other instances directly in Aramaic, followed by a translation of the words (for example, Mark 5:41, 15:34, and others), or even without a translation ("Amen, I say to thee. . . ." "Amen" is an Aramaic word which means "truthfully.").

57. In this connection, it would seem that the wrong approach has been taken in the Jubilee edition of *War and Peace*, edited by G. A. Volkov and M. A. Tsyavlovsky. There, the French speech is retained, just as it was in the original and second editions of *War and Peace*, but Denisov's speech defect is not represented, at it was in Tolstoy's third edition. (See the commentary to the ninth volume of this edition.) This approach seems inconsistent precisely because the speech habits and the use of the French language are functionally analogous. Tolstoy has not made reference everywhere to Denisov's accent, to be sure, but this does not provide a valid reason for this editorial omission. Such modifications might have been applied, with equal justification, to the French speech.

in *War and Peace*, we can observe two different positions which the author may take. When foreign and irregular speech is represented naturalistically, the author stresses the distance between the speaking character and the describing observer. In other words, there is a special emphasis on the nonconcurrence or dissociation of the speaking character and the observer who notes the "strangeness" in the speaker.

The differences between the transmission of French speech by Tolstoy and by Pushkin illustrate our point. Tomashevsky notes: "Pushkin, who in his personal life was required to use French both in speaking and in writing more often than Tolstoy, is not anxious to reproduce foreign language in the discourse of his characters." [58] Besides the obvious differences in the stylistic devices of both writers, the difference in the rendition of French speech is due to the fact that in the Russia of Pushkin's time French was not a marked linguistic phenomenon. It was so much a part of everyday speech that it was not necessary to call special attention to it. Tolstoy, on the other hand, while describing the same period as Pushkin, describes it from a later vantage point when the use of French was at least to some extent already marked in the speech of the Russian society.[59]

It is characteristic that when Pushkin finds it necessary to call attention to French, for instance, when he needs to juxtapose French and Russian in the discourse of the characters, he reports a French conversation in a documentary fashion, and in these cases, the French speech is definitely marked. Look, for example, at the dialogue conducted in Russian and in French in Pushkin's *Dubrovsky*, between Dubrovsky (who is pretending to be a Frenchman named "Deforges") and the Russian landowner Anton Pafnutyich Spitsin. "Deforges" speaks French, while Spitsin speaks a mixed French and Russian:

Anton Pafnutyich began to circle round the young Frenchman, clearing his throat and coughing, and at last he turned to him and addressed him:
"Hm! Hm! Couldn't I spend the night in your room, *mossoo*, because you see . . ."
"*Que désire monsieur?*" asked Deforges, with a polite bow.
"Ah! What a pity, *mossoo*, that you have not yet learnt Russian. *Je vais moa chez vous coucher.* Do you understand?"
"*Monsieur, très volontiers,*" replied Deforges, "*veuillez donner des ordres en conséquence.*"

58. See B. V. Tomashevskii, "Voprosy iazyka v tvorchestve Pushkina" [Questions of language in the work of Pushkin], *Stikh i iazyk* (Moscow-Leningrad, 1959), p. 437.
59. The controversy that took place at the time of the publication of *War and Peace* forced Tolstoy to eliminate French speech entirely from the third and fourth editions of the novel, and to replace it with Russian equivalents.

Anton Pafnutyich, well satisfied with his knowledge of the French language, went off at once to make the necessary arrangements.[60]

In those cases where the author reproduces foreign or irregular speech naturalistically, he adopts the position of an uninvolved observer (in other words, he takes a deliberately external point of view in respect to the person described). The writer emphasizes those features which would simply go unnoticed for someone at all close to or acquainted with the person. In this case the author reproduces external particularities.

However, in instances where the same writer concentrates not on the external particularities of speech, but on its essence—not on the "how" but on the "what"—and where he accordingly translates the idiosyncratic features of speech into a neutral phraseology, the phraseological points of view of the describer and the described (the character who speaks at the time) approach each other. The concentration on the essence rather than on the form reaches its ultimate point in narrated monologue, where the speech of the character interlocks with the authorial speech. Indeed, we have already noted that narrated monologue is typically detached from the *specifica* of the expression. We may consider this case an instance of internal point of view.

The less differentiation there is between the phraseology of the described (the character) and the describing (author or narrator), the closer are their phraseological points of view. The two opposite poles are: the faithful representation of the *specifica* of the character's speech (the case of maximum differentiation), and the narrated monologue (the case of minimal differentiation).

The naturalistic representation of distinctive features of speech is often used by the author to convey to the reader a general sense of the style which is characteristic of the person described. But as the reader becomes more closely acquainted with the character, the author no longer needs to stress the distinctive qualities of his manner of speech. For example, in "The Captain's Daughter," [61] when Pushkin describes the general of the fort of Orenburg, who is a native German, he reports to us that the general has a German accent when he speaks Russian—and we hear this accent reproduced in direct discourse by the substitution of voiceless consonants for voiced consonants, especially if these are in the initial position.[62] Later, however, the reproduction of the accent ceases,

60. This translation is from *The Poems, Prose, and Plays of Pushkin,* ed. Avrahm Yarmolinsky (New York, 1936), p. 837.—Trans.
61. This has been noted in Tomashevsky, 1959, pp. 439–440.
62. "*Pozhe moi!*—skazal on.—*Tavno li, kazhetsia, Andrei Petrovich byl esche tvoikh let, a teper' vot ush kakoi y nego molotets! Akh, fremia! fremia!*"

and the speech of the general is transmitted in normal Russian. It is as if we have entered the described world and are now perceiving it from within, not from without; as a result of this shift in position, we no longer hear the general's accent. In the same way, we are struck by the speech irregularity of a person we do not know, but we can forget about it when we become more closely acquainted with him.

Thus, at first the reader is given the impressions of a detached observer from a point of view external to the speaking character. This point of view may be replaced thereafter, either at times or once and for all, by an internal viewpoint. It is as if the reader has become acquainted with the manner of speech, and may now turn his attention away from the external features of expression in order to concentrate on its essence.[63]

Until now, we have been analyzing cases where, during the transmission of the direct speech of the character, the author takes up a position either external or internal to that of the speaker. These positions may alternate in the course of the narrative.

Or they may be synthetically combined within the text, and manifested almost simultaneously in the speech of the described character—in that case, the point of view of the describer (the author) loses all definiteness and becomes unreal.

For an illustration of this phenomenon, we may turn again to the French speech in *War and Peace*. Commonly during the transmission of French discourse in Russian occasional words are given in French. For example, Napoleon asks: "Is it true that *Moscou* is called *Moscou la sainte?* How many churches are there in *Moscou?*" (p. 582). The single word *Moscou* refers to Napoleon's consciousness, because for him Moscow is *Moscou*. Tolstoy feels it necessary to show the actual pronunciation of this particular word from Napoleon's position, while all the other words of the same sentence are given in Russian from a different position.[64]

Sentences of this kind may be viewed as the result of the synthesis (an indivisible combination) of the French phrase as it was supposed to have been pronounced and the Russian translation of it. In other cases, a spoken French phrase and its Russian equivalent present a juxtaposition, rather than a synthesis. When transmitting French speech in Russian, Tolstoy sometimes duplicates some phrases in the direct discourse by their French equivalent. In the speech of Napoleon, French and Russian phrases are set side by side:

63. We will treat this question in more detail in our discussion of the frame of the artistic text.
64. The resultant effect is similar to the effect which takes place in bilingualism, where elements from two different languages are combined.

"Ah, he's alive!" said Napoleon. "Pick up this young man, *ce jeune homme,* and carry him to an ambulance!" (p. 266).
"*Et vous, jeune homme?* And you, young man," he said to him, "how are you feeling?" (p. 267).

"You have not two hundred thousand troops, while I have three times as many. I give you my word of honor . . . I give you *ma parole d'honneur,*" said Napoleon, forgetting that his word of honor could carry no weight (pp. 580–581).

The same juxtaposition occurs in the discourse of Alexander I:

Rostov saw the tears in the Tsar's eyes, and heard him say in French to Tchartorizhsky, as he rode off: "What an awful thing war is, what an awful thing! *Quelle terrible chose que la guerre!*" (p. 232).

And in the speech of the freemason, Count Villarsky:

"One more question, count," he said, "to which I beg you, not as a future mason, but as an honest man (*galant homme*) to answer me in all sincerity" (p. 324).[65]

Here, the author has fused the sentence as it was supposed to have been pronounced with its translation. The position Tolstoy has adopted here is that of a translator who finds it necessary to include in his translation fragments of the original text, in order to refer the reader from time to time to the actual context in which the phrase was spoken.

The sentences obtained as a result of this combination of different authorial positions cannot be taken for a reproduction of real speech, of course; and they clearly do not claim to have a direct correspondence with reality. Rather, the device of including fragments of the original text is used to refer to the general conditions surrounding the utterance of the sentence or to the individual consciousness of the speaker.

Similar examples when words and phrases are duplicated by a translation for the purpose of making reference to an individual perception occur in *War and Peace* not only in the transmission of direct discourse but in the authorial speech as well:

The following day Napoleon drove on ahead of the army, reached the Niemen, put on a Polish uniform in order to inspect the crossing of the river, and rode out on the river bank.
When he saw the Cossacks posted on the further bank and the expanse of the steppes (*les Steppes*)—in the midst of which, far away, was *Moscou la ville sainte,* capital of an empire, like the Scythian empire invaded by

---

65. French speech in direct discourse is transmitted in several ways in *War and Peace*: either directly in French; translated into Russian; in a text of mixed French and Russian; and by means of the duplication of the expression in Russian and in French.

Alexander of Macedon—Napoleon surprised the diplomatists and contravened all rules of strategy by ordering an immediate advance (p. 567).

The French words which intersperse the Russian text obviously refer to the individual consciousness of Napoleon. Where Tolstoy uses a French translation immediately following a Russian word, he seems to make reference to the perceptual system of Napoleon himself. These words represent elements of someone else's speech—of narrated monologue inserted in the authorial text.[66] What we have here, then, is essentially a translation of the authorial text into the individual language of the character.

The opposite situation is also possible: the speech of an individual character (using elements of reported speech) may be followed by a translation into the language of objective description.

But the countess would not agree to the count's going; for several days he had had a bad leg. It was decided that the count must not go, but that if Luisa Ivanovna (*Madame Schoss*) would go with them, the young ladies might go to Madame Melyukov's (p. 488).

The emperor wore the uniform of the Preobrazhensky regiment, white elkskin breeches and high boots and a star which Rostov did not recognize (it was the *légion d'honneur*) (p. 379).

In both cases, the speech of an individual perception is translated into the authorial speech.

This particular device is exemplified by the description of the hunting scene at the Rostov estate, Otradnoe. The description is executed simultaneously from two points of view—from the viewpoint of the hunters, which is internal to the described action, and from the neutral viewpoint of a side observer, external in relation to the described action. The description of the hunt is in a special hunter's vocabulary, but the special expressions are also translated each time into a neutral language. This technique is like the presentation of French speech when it is followed by a translation into Russian.

Another harrier . . . arched its back, darted headlong to the steps, and lifting its flag (tail) rubbed itself against Nikolay's legs (p. 458).

The wolf . . . gave one bound and a second, and waving its pole (tail) disappeared into the bushes. . . . all the pack flew across the open ground toward the very spot where the wolf had gone to cover (found refuge) (pp. 463–464).

66. Concerning the function of parentheses in the authorial speech in Tolstoy, see Vinogradov, 1939, p. 179.

The wolf stole a glance at Karay, . . . and, tucking his pole (tail) further between his legs, he quickened his pace (p. 466).

And now the fox was beginning to wind in circles between them, making the circles more and more rapidly, and sweeping its bushy brush (tail) around it (p. 468).

[Nikolay] said that he would give a rouble to any one who would bring a hare to earth (kill) (p. 470).

The hunters' expressions here carry a function similar to that of the French speech in *War and Peace*. Both cases illustrate the alternation of authorial positions, which may be interpreted as an alternation of an internal and an external point of view.

3 | POINT OF VIEW ON THE SPATIAL AND TEMPORAL PLANES

In some cases, the point of view of the narrator may be more or less clearly specified in space or in time, and we may be able to guess the position, defined in spatial or temporal coordinates, from which the narration is conducted. In particular instances, for example, the narrator's position in a literary work may concur with the position of a character, as though he were carrying out the narration from the point where the character is standing.

Using somewhat different terminology, we might also speak of the spatial or temporal perspective adopted in the construction of the narrative; the analogy with perspective representation in painting is more than a metaphor in this case.

Perspective in general is a system for the representation of three- or four-dimensional space by means of artistic devices, specific to the particular art form. The reference point in the system of linear perspective is the position of the person who does the description.

In visual art we speak about the transferral of real, multidimensional space onto the two-dimensional surface of a painting; the key orientation point here is the position of the artist. In literature, the same is achieved by the verbally-established spatial and temporal relations of the describing subject (the author) to the described event.

We will look first at examples of the fixing of the authorial point of view registered in three-dimensional space, and then turn to examples of its temporal definition.

SPACE

THE CONCURRENCE OF THE SPATIAL POSITION OF
THE NARRATOR AND A CHARACTER

We have already suggested that in a literary work the positions of the narrator (or the observer) and a specific character may or may not concur. The first alternative, the subject of our immediate discussion, is encountered frequently: the narrator seems to be "attached" to the character, either temporarily or for the entire narrative and thus holds the same spacial position as the character. For example, if the character enters a room, the narrator describes the room; if the character goes out into the street, the narrator describes the street. Furthermore, the author may merge with the character, assuming, for the moment, his ideological, phraseological and psychological systems; consequently, the point of view adopted by the author will manifest itself on all corresponding planes.

In other instances, however, the author accompanies the character but does not merge with him; then the authorial description is not limited to the subjective view of the character but is "suprapersonal." In such cases the positions of the author and character correspond on the spatial plane, but diverge on the planes of ideology, phraseology, and so forth. As long as the author accompanies the character but does not become embodied in him, he can portray the particular character; he could not do this if they shared one perceptual system.[1]

Instances of the spatial attachment of the author to one of the characters in a literary work are common. For example, in a large part of the narration of Dostoevsky's *The Possessed,* the author (the narrator) spatially follows Stavrogin, although he does not describe the events from Stavrogin's point of view.[2] In *The Brothers Karamazov,* the narrator becomes Alyosha's and Mitya's invisible companion for long periods of time. Sometimes the author motivates the description of a certain event by following a character; however, he may not describe the event from that character's point of view. In *War and Peace,* for example, we, as readers, accompany Pierre to the battle of Borodino and become eye-witnesses to the battle. However, Pierre only brings us there, and having

1. In some cases a similar description may be defined as having been received through a combination of several points of view—for example, through both the psychological point of view of a particular character and the point of view of a narrator, invisibly present beside the character. For a further discussion, see Chapter Five.

2. For illustration and an analysis of this point, see Chapter Five.

reached the battlefield we are not necessarily bound to him; we may leave him and assume different spatial positions.

Sometimes the position of a narrator may only be relatively defined: he may be attached not to one particular character, but to a group of characters. Still, we can pinpoint his spatial location. Let us look at a scene from *War and Peace* which takes place at the Rostovs' one evening. The young people—Natasha, Sonya, and Nikolay—are gathered in the sitting room, reminiscing about their childhood. The description here is not carried out from one particular character's viewpoint:

In the middle of their talk in the divan-room, Dimmler came into the room, and went up to the harp that stood in the corner. He took off the cloth-case, and the harp gave a jarring sound. "Edward Karlitch, do, please, play my favourite nocturne of M. Field," said the voice of the old countess from the drawing-room (p. 486).

In answer to the countess' request, Mr. Dimmler plays the harp:

"Natasha! now it's your turn. Sing me something," the voice of the countess was heard (p. 487).

If Tolstoy had simply told us that "the countess spoke from the drawing room," the narrator's location would not be as precisely defined as it is in this passage. Nevertheless, the phrase "the countess spoke from the drawing room" is entirely possible and would easily fit into the text, since only a paragraph later Tolstoy writes: "Count Ilya Andreevich listened to her [Natasha's] singing from his study, where he was talking to Mitenka" (p. 487). Here, the author shifts from his earlier spatial position, which was clearly defined and concrete, to an undefined spatial position, a position from which he is privileged to see and to know what is going on not only in one room, but throughout the house, and in other places as well.

If, on the other hand, the author had relied on the perceptions of Natasha, Sonya, and Nikolay, he would have said that "they heard the voice of the countess." In this case Tolstoy would have used their psychological point of view (a position which is, generally speaking, typical of his style elsewhere).[3] This is not what the author does, however; he chooses instead to describe the scene through some observer who is invisibly present in the room and who describes whatever he sees.

THE NONCONCURRENCE OF THE SPATIAL POSITION OF THE AUTHOR AND A CHARACTER

We have examined instances where the point of view from which the narrative is told concurs with the spatial location of one of the char-

3. Chapter Four presents an extended discussion of the psychological point of view.

acters or of a group of characters. In other cases, however, even though the observer's spatial position may be just as precisely defined, his position does not correspond to that of any of the participants in the action. Several forms of this kind of narration will be examined presently.

The Sequential Survey

Sometimes the narrator's viewpoint moves sequentially from one character to another and from one detail to another, and the reader is given the task of piecing together the separate descriptions into one coherent picture. The movement of the author's point of view here is similar to those camera movements in film that provide a sequential survey of a particular scene.

The battle scene in Gogol's *Taras Bulba* provides an illustration of this particular construction. Out of the general mass of combatants, the author focuses with his camera first on one pair of single warriors and then another. The movement of the author's camera is not arbitrary, however. It follows one character until he is defeated; when he is killed, it moves to the victor and remains with him until his defeat, and so on. The author's point of view passes, like a trophy, from the defeated to the victorious.

The authorial description here is not at all impersonal, for the author stands close to the fighters, continually shifting from one to another. This shifting depends on physical contact between the characters: the author's camera is not arbitrary in its movement on the battlefield, and the situation is rather like a relay race, where the point of view, like a baton, is passed from one character to another. Thus, in a sense, the spatial attachment of the narrator to one character is still preserved here, for his spatial position is limited by the location of a character.

In other instances, the movements of the author's point of view are not dependent on a character's movement. For example, in the following description of a dinner party at the Rostovs' in *War and Peace*:

The count peeped from behind the crystal of the decanters and fruit-dishes at his wife and her high cap with blue ribbons, and zealously poured out wine for his neighbours, not overlooking himself. The countess, too, while mindful of her duties as hostess, cast significant glances from behind the pineapples at her husband, whose face and bald head struck her as looking particularly red against his grey hair. At the ladies' end there was a rhythmic murmur of talk, but at the other end of the table the men's voices grew louder and louder, especially the voice of the colonel of hussars, who, getting more and more flushed, ate and drank so much that the count held him up as a pattern to the rest. Berg with a tender smile was telling Vera that love was an emotion not of earth but of heaven. Boris was telling his new friend Pierre the names of the guests, while he exchanged glances with Natasha sitting opposite him. Pierre said little, looked about at the new faces, and ate a great deal. . . . Natasha, who sat opposite him, gazed at Boris as girls of thirteen gaze at the boy whom they have just kissed for the first time, and with whom they are in love. . . .

Nikolay was sitting a long way from Sonya, beside Julie Karagin, and again smiling the same unconscious smile, he was talking to her. Sonya wore a company smile, but she was visibly in agonies of jealousy; at one moment she turned pale, then she crimsoned, and all her energies were concentrated on listening to what Nikolay and Julie were saying. The governess looked nervously about her, as though preparing to resent any slight that might be offered to the children. The German tutor was trying to learn by heart a list of all the kinds of dishes, desserts, and wines, in order to write a detailed description of them to the folks at home in Germany, and was greatly mortified that the butler with the bottle in the napkin had passed him over (p. 53).

The authorial camera here shifts sequentially from one to another of those sitting around the table; these separate scenes combine into one composite scene. A similar device is common in film.

A scene like this one, embracing almost all the characters by moving from one to another, is particularly striking because it represents a departure from Tolstoy's usual means of description, where the narrator attaches himself in each fixed descriptive segment to one or another of the characters. The rapid sequential changes in the position of the author explain the effect of temporal acceleration which usually accompanies the survey description.

The sequential survey of guests at the banquet table seems to imitate the movement of a man's glance as he looks at the scene; this glance does not belong to any of the characters at the table, but rather to the author himself who seems to be invisibly present at the place where the action occurs.

Tolstoy uses the same device in his description of the dinner party at Count Vasily's home, on the occasion of Ellen's name day, just prior to the engagement of Ellen and Pierre (p. 189). In both of these cases the spatial position of the author is more or less concrete: the author seems to have taken up a position among the characters whom he is describing.

In other occurrences of the sequential survey, the author's spatial position is not specific, and he may be able to view a number of characters who are located in several different places—places which cannot be seen from a single viewpoint. For example, when Anatole Kuragin comes to Bleak Hills, intending to propose to Princess Marya, and when in the evening everyone has retired to his room, Tolstoy surveys all of the characters: he describes in turn what each is doing—Anatole, Princess Marya, Mlle. Bourienne, Andrey's wife, and the old Prince Bolkonsky. This sequence is similar to the banquet-table survey; the only difference is that the characters described here are not located within a space which can be realistically observed from one viewpoint. The spatial shift of the author is clearly evident here: he seems to move from room to room, glancing in turn at each character (p. 206).

The typological similarities between the technique used here and the film technique of the moving camera and montage are quite evident.

Other Instances of Shifts in the Narrator's Spatial Position

So far we have discussed those instances where the narration proceeds in terms of a shifting position—that is, when the describing observer moves through the described space. In the examples given above, the description tends to fall into separate scenes, each described from a different spatial position; only when they are joined together is the illusion of movement produced—in the same way that the movement in film is the result of the projection of a sequence of still frames.

However, the movement of the position of the narrating observer may be transmitted not only through sequences of still scenes, the summing up of which creates the illusion of movement, but through the portrayal of a single scene from a moving source, with the characteristic deformation of objects resulting from that movement.

Parallel processes may be observed in the realm of visual communication (in a drawing, in a photograph, and so on). The illusion of the movement of a human figure, for example, may be transmitted by a sequence of separate scenes in each of which the figure assumes different poses; in this instance, the viewer of the figure sums up the separate poses into a continuous movement. On the other hand, the movement of a figure may be transmitted as a single scene in which are represented certain distortions of forms resulting from the movement. For example, if we photograph an object in movement, we have two alternatives: we may take a sequence of quick shots, using a short exposure, and then arrange these pictures in an order which will allow us to reconstruct the movement; or we may use a longer exposure and let the distortion or blurring which is produced represent movement. These two types of the representation of movement may be found in the other pictorial arts as well.[4]

4. Concerning the use of these devices in pictorial art, and the possibilities of semiotic interpretation, see B. A. Uspenskij, "Per l'analisi semiotica delle antiche icone russe" (to be published). In the first case we have an analytical interpretation of move-

Analogous means for communicating movement may also be observed in literature, and our interest here is centered on the movement of the narrator's viewpoint. We have already illustrated the first technique in our discussion of the sequential survey. An illustration of the second technique is drawn from the discussion of the artistic space in Gogol by Yury Lotman. Lotman shows that in a number of cases in Gogol, we may sense a moving point of view in the description of landscape.[5]

Here is an example:

Gray haystacks and golden sheaves of corn are scattered over the fields and wander through its immense spaces.[6]

Gogol describes trees and hills as behaving in exactly the same way. The following example is particularly interesting:

The shadows of trees and bushes, like comets, were falling in sharp wedges upon the sloping flatlands.[7]

Lotman points out that the image "shadows . . . in sharp wedges" indicates that the description is carried out from the point of view of an observer who is looking down from above, and in the phrase "shadows . . . like comets" the illusion of a comet-like curve attributed to the shadows of the trees is created as a result of the swiftly moving observer himself.[8]

This particular use of the moving position of the observer is not at all frequent, and examples of it are difficult to find; we must recognize however, that such a descriptive technique is possible.

The Bird's-Eye View

When there is a need for an all-embracing description of a particular scene, we often find neither the sequential survey nor the moving narrator, but an encompassing view of the scene from some single, very general,

---

ment: the uninterrupted process of movement is analytically decomposed into a series of discrete components, which the audience (the reader) must synthesize. In the second instance, however, what takes place is a synthesis of the impressions received from spatially different points of view; this synthesis is accomplished directly within the description (the representation).

5. Iu. M. Lotman, "Problemy khudozhestvennogo prostranstva v proze Gogolia" [Problems of artistic space in the prose of Gogol], *Trudy po russkoi i slavianskoi filologii,* XI (Uch. Zap. TGU, vyp. 209), (Tartu, 1968). The following examples have been taken from this study. See also: Andrei Belyi, *Masterstvo Gogolia* [The craft of Gogol] (Moscow-Leningrad, 1934), pp. 126–127.

6. For another English translation, see "Taras Bulba," trans. Isabel F. Hapgood (New York, 1915), p. 6—Trans.

7. See "Taras Bulba," trans. Hapgood, p. 284—Trans.

8. Lotman, 1968, p. 36.

point of view. Because such a spatial position usually presupposes very broad horizons, we may call it the bird's-eye point of view.

In order to assume a point of view of such a wide scope, overseeing the whole scene, the observer must take up a position at a point far above the action. Consider, for example, the elevated position of the observer in this scene in Gogol's *Taras Bulba*:

The Cossacks leaned down upon the backs of their horses and disappeared from sight in the grass; already their black hats could not be seen, and only the lightning-swift furrowing of the grass showed their movements.[9]

It is characteristic that the observer here has assumed a specific position, not abstract, but real; that position is indicated by the fact that there are some things that the observer cannot see from his vantage point.[10]

Frequently, the bird's-eye view is used at the beginning or the end of a particular scene, or even at the beginning or the end of a whole narrative. For example, scenes which have a large number of characters are often treated in the following way: a general summary view of the entire scene is given first, from a bird's-eye viewpoint; then the author turns to descriptions of the characters, so that the view is broken down into smaller visual fields; at the end of the scene, the bird's-eye view is often used again. This elevated viewpoint, then, used at the beginning and the end of the narration, serves as a kind of "frame" for the scene, or for the work as a whole. We will return to a discussion of this particular function of point of view in connection with the problem of the "frame" of the artistic work.

This particular device is used at the end of *Taras Bulba*, where, after the death of Taras, Gogol describes the Dniester River.[11] The description is carried out from an impersonal point of view which is characterized by its broad horizons:

The River Dniester is not small, and in it are many deep pools, dense reed-beds, shallows and deep-bottomed places; its watery mirror gleams,

9. See "Taras Bulba," trans. Hapgood, p. 66—Trans.

10. When, because of the condition of the subject and because of the conventions of composition, Gogol cannot raise his observer above the field of action (this situation occurs, in particular, when the author carries out the narration from some concrete spatial position—from, let us say, the defined spatial position of a certain character), he "distorts the surface of the earth itself, bending its edges upward (not only the mountains, but seas as well)." Lotman, 1968, pp. 20, 15. As an illustration, he cites Gogol's "Terrible Vengeance" [trans. David Magarshack (New York, 1957), p. 53]. In the same article see also the discussion of the function of the view from above in "Viy," "Taras Bulba," and *Dead Souls*.

11. See also the description of the troops before the Battle of Austerlitz, *War and Peace*, p. 101.

resounding with the ringing cry of the swans, and the proud wild goose glides swiftly over it; and many are the woodcocks, tawny-throated grouse, and various other birds to be found among the reeds and along the shores. The cossacks floated swiftly along in the narrow, double-ruddered boats—rowing together, carefully shunning the reefs, disturbing the birds, which rose from the water—and talked of their ataman.[12]

The Silent Scene

A special case within this category of generalized description, carried out from a relatively remote position, is the device of the "silent scene." This device is particularly characteristic of Tolstoy[13] and employs a pantomimic description of the behavior of the characters: the gestures are described, but not the words. An example from *War and Peace,* the review of the army at Braunau, demonstrates the use of the silent scene:

Behind Kutuzov, . . . followed his suite, consisting of some twenty persons. These gentlemen were talking among themselves, and sometimes laughed. Nearest of all to the commander-in-chief walked a handsome adjutant. It was Prince Bolkonsky. Beside him was his comrade Nesvitsky, a tall staff-officer, . . . Nesvitsky could hardly suppress his mirth, which was excited by a swarthy officer of hussars walking near him. This officer, without a smile or a change in the expression of his fixed eyes, was staring with a serious face at the commanding officer's back, and mimicking every movement he made. Every time the commanding officer quivered and darted forward, the officer of hussars quivered and darted forward in precisely the same way. Nesvitsky laughed, and poked the others to make them look at the mimic (p. 101).

In the silent scene, the observer, who is located at some distance from the action, can see the characters, but because of the distance, he seems to be unable to hear them. The remote position makes it possible for the author to present a general view of the whole scene.

TIME

In the same way that the position of the narrating observer may be fixed in three-dimensional space, the observer's temporal position, in a number of cases, may also be defined.[14] The author may

---

12. See "Taras Bulba," trans. Hapgood, p. 284.—Trans.

13. On the "silent scene," see A. A. Saburov, *Voina i mir L. N. Tolstogo: Problematika i poetika* [Tolstoy's *War and Peace:* Problematics and Poetics] (Moscow, 1959), p. 430.

14. For general discussions of time in literature (from several different standpoints), see, in particular: L. S. Vygotskii, *Psikhologiia iskusstva* [The psychology of art] (Moscow, 1968); D. S. Likhachev, *Poetika drevnerusskoi literatury* [The poetics of Russian

count time and order the chronological events from the position of one of the characters (then authorial time coincides with a subjective timing of events belonging to a particular character); or he may use his own time schema.

For example, as V. V. Vinogradov has shown,[15] the account of time in Pushkin's "The Queen of Spades" is carried out in the beginning from the point of view of Lazaveta Ivanovna, who reckons time from the day she receives Hermann's letter. The narrator uses her concept of time until the death of the old countess. Then, when the story turns to Hermann, the narrator assumes his temporal point of view, reckoning time from the day when he first heard the story about the three lucky cards.

Thus, the narrator may change his positions, borrowing the time sense of first one character, then another—or he may assume his own temporal position and use his own authorial time, which may not coincide with the individual time sense of any of the characters.

Different combinations of the characters' temporal positions and authorial time determine the degree of complexity of the compositional structure of the work. Our interest here, as elsewhere, lies primarily in instances of the multiplicity of temporal points of view in the narrative.

MULTIPLE TEMPORAL POSITIONS:
COMBINATIONS OF POINTS OF VIEW

A multiplicity of temporal positions may be manifested in a work by different means and in different combinations.

On the one hand, the narrator may sequentially change position, describing the events first from one point of view, then from another. These points of view may belong to various characters, or they may belong to him. This particular technique is illustrated in the previous example from "The Queen of Spades."

In some instances, the descriptions of events from different temporal positions may overlap (that is, in the course of the narrative the same event is presented from different points of view), while in other instances, the narrator may join the events end-to-end (that is, the narrative is conducted in a strict sequential order, and the points of view of different

---

literature of the Middle Ages] (Leningrad, 1967), Chapter Four, "Poetika khudozhe-stvennogo vremeni" [The poetics of artistic time]; H. Meyerhoff, *Time in Literature*, (Berkeley and Los Angeles: University of California Press, 1960); J. Pouillon, *Temps et roman* (Paris, 1946); and the bibliographies of these works.

15. V. V. Vinogradov, "Stil' 'Pikovoi damy'" [The style of Pushkin's "Queen of Spades"], *Pushkinskii vremennik* (Moscow-Leningrad, 1936), 2:114–115.

characters are used at different stages of the account). Both of these temporal organizations are fairly elementary in their compositional design.

A more complicated form is one in which the same event is described simultaneously from several temporal positions. The narrative which results is not a juxtaposition of points of view, but a synthesis in which different temporal points of view are merged, so that the description appears, so to speak, as a kind of double exposure. Formally, this combination of temporal viewpoints may be manifested in the authorial commentary which accompanies or precedes the narration of a particular episode—and thus serves as a background against which the sequential account of the events is perceived.

In these cases, the narrative can be cast in a double perspective: it can be conducted from the temporal perspective of one or more characters who participate in the action and, simultaneously, from the point of view of the author. The author's temporal viewpoint differs substantially from that of the characters because he knows what they cannot know: he knows how this particular story will end. This double perspective derives from the double position of the narrator. In the first case, the author's temporal point of view is synchronous with that of the character, as if he had adopted his "present time." We can say, then, that the author's viewpoint and the viewpoint of the character are internal to the narrative, on the temporal plane. The author looks from within the life he describes and accepts the inherent limitations of the character's ignorance (or limited knowledge) of what is to come. When the author stands outside his characters, however, within his own time, he adopts a retrospective view, looking from the future time back into the characters' present. He knows what the characters cannot know. Then his point of view is external to the ongoing narration.

We have in mind here those cases where the author, having assumed the temporal perspective of a particular character, from whose point of view he conducts the narration, suddenly jumps ahead, revealing to us what the character—the vehicle of the authorial point of view—cannot know and will not discover until much later in time.[16] There are a number of examples of this particular technique, and our selections for discussion have been arbitrary.

Thus, throughout a substantial portion of Dostoevsky's *The Brothers Karamazov*, Dmitri Karamazov occupies the attention of both the author

16. See in this connection the many narratives which begin with the death of the character whose life story we will hear: narratives which begin with the end of the story (for example, Tolstoy's "Hadji Murad," and "Death of Ivan Ilyich").

and the reader. Dmitri serves as the vehicle of the author's point of view, a point of view which is manifested on very different planes (see for example, Book Eight). In particular, the author—or, more precisely, the narrator in whose voice the author speaks (this difference is not essential to our discussion at this point)—describes Dmitri's sensory perceptions, adopting his psychological viewpoint;[17] he borrows his speech, particularly in the form of internal monologue (that is, he adopts his viewpoint on the phraseological plane—see *The Brothers Karamazov*, p. 467); he occupies Dmitri's spatial point of view and follows him in his movements; finally, he narrates the sequence of events in terms of Dmitri's temporal perceptions. However, in some episodes, the author steps into Dmitri's future and tells the reader how the episode will end—something that Dmitri, of course, cannot know. As an example, we might take Dmitri's visit to Lyagavy, to whom he hopes to sell his father's timberland; we, as readers, have been notified at the beginning of this project that it can only end in failure. Here, our stance as readers is divided: we perceive the events, as they occur, through Dmitri's perceptions, and we live in his present time; simultaneously, we perceive the happenings differently from how Dmitri perceives them, because we also look back from Dmitri's future time—that is, we share the narrator's privileged knowledge.

Thus, the combination of two different temporal planes is achieved by means of the combined account of two different points of view: first, the point of view of the person described; second, the point of view of the describing person (the author-narrator). A similar phenomenon occurs frequently both in literature and in everyday narration.

The combination of two different temporal planes may also occur when the describing subject and the described object are the same (in first-person narration or *Icherzählung*). This occurs frequently in autobiography, where the point of view taken at the time described in the narration concurs with the point of view taken at the time of the describing.

The Life of the Archpriest Avvakum may serve as an example. On one hand, Avvakum presents the events of his narrative in a relatively straightforward chronological fashion; as D. S. Likhachev points out, his perception of time is primarily subjective, showing the "sequence of events, rather than the objective moment in time to which the particular event is attached." [18] But Avvakum's exposition of events is also con-

17. Concerning the psychological point of view see Chapter Four.
18. See D. S. Likhachev, *Poetika drevnerusskoi literatury* [The poetics of medieval Russian literature] (Leningrad, 1967), pp. 303–304, where these remarks are illustrated with concrete examples of text analysis.

nected with the time in which he is writing, and we are constantly reminded of this moment in time. Likhachev writes: "It is as if Avvakum looks upon his own past from a point in the present, and this point of view is extremely important in the narration. It defines what we may call the *temporal perspective*, and it makes his work not simply a story about his own life, but a story which gives meaning to his life at the moment he is writing." [19]

In the previous example, we moved from **Dmitri Karamazov's** present into his future; here we look, together with Avvakum, from the present into the past.[20]

For Avvakum, there is a simultaneous evaluation of both his present and his past in terms of his future (the life after death).[21] Thus, the temporal perspective may serve not only the immediate compositional goals of the description but may also function on the plane of ideological evaluation. In the same way, a phraseological device may be an autonomous compositional goal or a means for the expression of the ideological point of view. Furthermore, these points of view need not be concurrent in a work. It should be noted that there are different possibilities for the expression of ideological evaluation through the temporal perspective: the events of the present or the past may be evaluated from the point of view of the future; the events of the present and the future may be evaluated from the point of view of the past; or the past and the future may be evaluated from the point of view of the present.[22]

TENSE AND ASPECT AND THE
TEMPORAL POSITION OF THE AUTHOR

Often the temporal position from which the narrative is conducted is expressed by the grammatical form; in this way, the tense and aspect of the verb take on a direct relationship, not only to the linguistic expression, but to the poetic expression as well. As we shall see later, some grammatical forms take on a special meaning in the realm of poetics.

Leskov's short story, "A Lady Macbeth of the Mtsensk District" provides a number of examples of this phenomenon. The story is significant

19. Likhachev, 1967, p. 305.

20. For discussion of the combination of points of view in more general terms, see Chapter Five.

21. Likhachev, 1967, p. 309.

22. In connection with this aspect of the discussion, see A. M. Piatigorskii and B. A. Uspenskii, "Personologicheskaia klassifikatsiia kak semioticheskaia problema" [Personological classifications as a semiotic problem], *Trudy po znakovym sistemam*, III (Uch. Zap. TGU, vyp. 198) (Tartu, 1967), pp. 24–27.

in its use of verbal forms: the narrative past tense and the descriptive present tense are alternated throughout the story. Look, for example, at these sentences from the beginning of the sixth chapter:

Katerina Lvovna closed the window . . . she lay down. . . . She sleeps and does not sleep and she is so hot that her face is covered with perspiration and she gasps . . . Katerina Lvovna feels . . . Finally the cook came to the door and knocked: "The samovar . . ." she reminds her. . . . Katerina Lvovna . . . hardly moved . . . And the cat . . . rubs . . . Katerina Lvovna began to move . . . while it . . . crawls.[23]

What takes place here is a successive change in the tense of the verb from one sentence to another. If the past tense occurred in the preceding sentence, then we find the present tense in the next sentence and vice versa.

Further, the alternation of the present tense and the past tense is used in larger units—not from sentence to sentence but from one passage to the next.

Sergei woke up, quieted down . . . and . . . fell asleep. . . . She lies there with open eyes and suddenly she hears . . . The dogs had started to dash off and then they had quieted down.[24]

Following this section, in the next few paragraphs, the narrative is conducted in the past tense and then again we return to the present tense:

Katerina Lvovna in the meantime hears . . . but not pity but angry vicious laughter seizes Katerina Lvovna. "You can look around for yesterday," she thinks . . . This lasted for ten minutes.[25]

Following this passage, there is a long section in which the action is consistently described in the past tense: how Katerina Lvovna admitted her husband, Zinovy Borisych, to the room; how she spoke with him; how she ran to see her lover Sergei, who was hiding in the gallery. Then the description suddenly returns to the present tense:

Everything is audible to Sergei . . . He hears.[26]

Then the conversation between the husband and wife is reported as Sergei overhears it:

"What were you doing there for so long?" asks . . . Zinovy Borisych. "I was setting up the samovar," she answers.[27]

23. For another English translation, see *Nikolai Leskov: Selected Tales*, trans. David Magarshack (New York, 1961), pp. 12–13—Trans.
24. See Magarshack, p. 20—Trans.
25. See Magarshack, pp. 20–21—Trans.
26. See Magarshack, p. 21—Trans.
27. See Magarshack, p. 22—Trans.

Following this section, the use of present tense verbs continues through-out a fairly lengthy passage, and then the narration returns again to the past tense. We might easily find other examples of this technique.

In this narrative, the present tense is used to fix the point of view from which the narration is carried out. Each time the present tense is used, the author's temporal position is synchronic—that is, it coincides with the temporal position of his characters. He is at that moment located in their time. The verbs in the past tense, however, provide a transition between these synchronic sections of narrative.[28] They describe the conditions which are necessary to the perception of the narrative from the synchronic position.

All of the narration in the preceding example may be viewed as separating into a series of scenes, each being presented from a synchronic point of view and within which time seems to stop.[29] Verbs in the past tense, however, describe the shifts that take place between the scenes, forming the context against which the synchronic scenes must be perceived.

This particular kind of narrative construction may be compared to a slide show, where the individual slides are linked together sequentially to form a plot. When a slide is shown, narrative time stops; in the intervals between the slides, narrative time is accelerated and moves very rapidly.[30] In other words, the uninterrupted time flow takes here the form of discrete *quanta,* while the intervals between these *quanta* are greatly condensed.

The introduction of the present tense into narration is also common to everyday conversational storytelling. Often, in the middle of a story which is being narrated in the past tense, the teller suddenly uses a present-tense phrase ("And then he says to me . . ."); or he may use verbs in the present tense at the climactic moment of his story ("I come into the room and I see . . ."). The purpose of this device is to take the listener directly into the action of the narrative, and to put him into the same position as that occupied by the characters of the story.

28. The use of the present tense as a formal device for the fixing of time may be compared with special forms used to communicate a fixed spectator's look in ancient pictorial art. See in this connection B. A. Uspenskii, "K issledovaniiu iazyka drevnei zhivopisi" [Study of the language of ancient painting], in the introduction to L. F. Zhegin, *Iazyk zhivopisnogo proizvedeniia* [The language of art] (Moscow, 1970), p. 21.

29. If we were considering this problem in light of another approach, we might say that these scenes are characterized by their own special microtime.

30. In this connection, see Likhachev's observation about the byliny: "Those episodes in the byliny where the action occurs quickly are presented in the past tense, and those in which the action takes place slowly are given in the present tense." Likhachev, 1967, p. 241.

The alternation of grammatical tense is sometimes encountered within one sentence, demonstrating a sudden change in point of view. For instance, we find this passage in *The Life of the Archpriest Avvakum*:

On menya laet, a ya emu rekl: "blagodat' v ustnekh tvoikh, Ivan Rodionovich, da budet."	[He *is barking* at me, when I *told* him: "May there be grace in thy mouth, Ivan Rodionovich."][31]

This particular juxtaposition of verbal forms allows the author to express the relations of the actions in real time. Not only do we have a contrast in tense (present and past) but also in the durative aspects of the verbs (one indicates continuing or contemporaneous action, within the span of which a second action is completed). A similar combination of tenses in a single sentence is characteristic of Khlebnikov's poetry:

Skakala veselo kniazhna, Zveniat zhemchuzhnye strekozy.	[The Princess *was galloping* merrily, And the pearly dragonflies *jingle* in the grass.]

I piot zadumchiv russkii kvas On zamolchal i tikh kuril.	[Pensive, he *drinks* Russian kvass He *fell silent,* and being quiet, he *was smoking.*][32]

The present tense, however, is not the only grammatical form which may be used to fix a particular moment in the narrative and to convey the synchronization of the points of view of author and character.[33]

---

31. "Zhitie protopopa Avvakuma," cited according to A. N. Robinson, *Zhizneopisaniia Avvakuma i Epifaniia* [The life of Avvakum and Epiphanius] (Moscow, 1963), p. 144.

32. For other examples see V. Markov, *The Longer Poems of Velemir Khlebnikov* (Berkeley and Los Angeles: University of California Press, 1962), p. 100.

33. This may be seen especially in the use of the future tense, which may be similar to that of the present tense. Here are some lines from Andrey Bely's poem, "First Meeting":

> Mikhal Sergeich povernetsia
> Ko mne iz kresla tsveta "biskr";
> Steklo pensneinoe prosnetsia,
> Pereplesnetsia bleskom iskr.

[Literally:

> Mikhal Sergeich will turn
> Towards me, in his biskr-colored chair;
> The glass in his pince-nez will awake
> And will splash in a glitter of sparks]

Andrei Belyi, *Stikhotvoreniia i poemy* [Verses and longer poems] (Moscow and Leningrad, 1966), pp. 416–417.

Under some conditions, the imperfective aspect of the past tense of the verb may be used in Russian to perform the same functions. This phenomenon can be seen most clearly in Russian folklore:

> Vladimer kniaz' stal p'ianeshinek i veseleshinek
> Vykhodil na seredka kirpishchat pol
> S nogi na nogu perestupyval
> Iz rechei sam vygovarival.
>
> Vstaval Potyk na rezvy nogi,
> Vykhodil na seredka kirpishchat pol
> I vsem chelom bil, nizko klanialsia
> Pribegali zhareb'tsy da k koniu dobromu.

[Literally:

> Prince Vladimir got tipsy and jolly;
> He would come out to the middle of the brick floor
> And would shuffle from one foot to the other
> And would utter speeches.
>
> Potyk would get up on his swift legs;
> He would come out to the middle of the brick floor
> He would bow so low that his head would hit the floor
> And young horses would run up to the good steed.][34]

In folklore texts the present tense is characteristically used with this particular function:

> I ottul'-de Ivan skoro povorot daet,
> On vykhodit-de skoro von na iulitsu,
> On prikhodit-de skoro k koniu dobromu,
> On kak skachet-de skoro na dobra konia.
> Opet' skachet ego da non'tse dobroi kon'
> On-de s gor-de non'tse skatset non'tse na goru.
> On s ukatistoi-to skatset na uvalistu,
> Yshche gory-udoly promezh nog beret
> Po podnebes'iu letit on kak iasen sokol,
> Priezhzhat-de ko gorodu ko Kievu,
> A ezhzhaet on tut do ko bozh'ei cherkvi,
> On soskakival tut skoro so dobra konia.

[Literally:

> And from there Ivan quickly makes a turn:
> Here he comes out quickly into the street,
> Here he comes up quickly to the good steed,
> Here he jumps up quickly onto the good steed,

34. N. E. Onchukov, *Pechorskie byliny* [Byliny from Pechora] (St. Petersburg, 1904), pp. 109, 237–38.

And again the good steed now gallops;
Now he gallops down the mountains, now up the mountains.
Here he gallops from a rolling gait to a jogging gait,
And again he takes the mountains under his feet,
Upon the skies he flies like a bright falcon;
Here he comes toward the city of Kiev,
And he rides up to the Church of God,
And here he would jump swiftly from his good steed.][35]

The compositional function of the imperfective form of the past tense is to indicate in a sense, the "present in the past." Like the present-tense form of the verb in the examples we discussed earlier, the imperfective aspect enables the author to carry out his description from within the action—that is, synchronically, rather than retrospectively—and to place the reader in the very center of the scene he is describing.

More specifically, we see here a synthesis of the two viewpoints: the synchronic and the retrospective. This narrative form indicates that all of the action is going on in the past tense, where the narrator has taken up his position—a position which is synchronically related to the past events. Thus, it is possible to consider this as a combination of two narrators, each of whom speaks from a different point of view: the "general" narrator functions throughout the narrative, and all of the action he describes is, for him, in the past. For the other narrator, whose function is limited to particular scenes, the action occurs in the present. (The problems of the combination of these two points of view are discussed more specifically in Chapter Five.)

In Russian literary texts (as opposed to folklore), the use of the imperfective aspect of the past tense is encountered in only one rather narrow area—in those expressions which introduce direct speech, and particularly in *verba dicendi*.[36] For example, in Leskov's "Lady Macbeth of the Mtsensk District" we find the following dialogue:

"What are you so happy about?" Katerina Lvovna asked her father-in-law's stewards.
"Well, ma'am, dear Katerina Lvovna, we were weighing a live pig," the old steward *was answering*.
"What kind of pig?"

35. Onchukov, 1904, pp. 105–106. In this narrative fragment it is interesting to notice the narrator's care in designating time: for example, the multiple repetitions of the words *skoro* (soon), and *non'tse* (now). See further, A. F. Gilferding's observations about inserted words of the type *nyne* (now), *bylo* (was), *est'* (is) in Russian byliny, A. F. Gil'ferding "Olonetskaia guberniia i ee narodnye rapsody" [The Olonets province and its folk rhapsodes], *Sbornik Otdeleniia russkogo iazyka i slovesnosti imp. Akademii Nauk*, LIX, p. 37.
36. *Verba dicendi:* literally, verbs of speaking.

"The pig Aksinya . . ." the young man *was saying* gaily and boldly . . .

"Imps, sleek devils . . ." the cook *was scolding*.

"Before dinner it weighs eight hundred points . . ." the handsome young man *was explaining* . . .[37]

This use of the imperfective aspect of *verba dicendi* should not be considered an archaism; it is practiced in contemporary literature.

However, in spoken Russian, this use of the imperfective aspect (rather than the perfective) is considered ungrammatical, and in the examples above a form of the perfective would in every case be substituted for the imperfective aspect. In speech one would say "the steward answered" rather than "the steward was answering," and "the young man said" rather than "the young man was saying."

This particular use of the imperfective form is encountered only in continuing narration and only under special conditions in written language—in other contexts it is felt to be awkward and perhaps even unintelligible. Why should the old steward be answering, when he had already completed his answer? In ordinary speech this form might be understood to represent a repeated action or an action of some duration. But we have neither of these meanings in mind in written discourse; what controls our use of this particular verbal form is, rather, a system of narrative conventions.

Thus, the form of the imperfective past tense in Russian, in this particular application, is peculiar to the written language; it may be compared to special verbal forms, confined to narrative in other languages (the French *passé simple*, for example).

What special poetic significance does this particular grammatical form possess? The form of the imperfective aspect is opposed to the form of the perfective aspect mainly in terms of the observer's position in relation to the action (the act of speaking). The imperfective form gives the effect of extended time; it invites us to place ourselves, as it were, in a synchronic relationship to the action, and to become witnesses to it.[38] (The same function may be carried out by the use of the present tense.) In other words, the opposition of these two aspectual forms, on the plane of poetics, emerges as the opposition of the synchronic and the retrospective positions of the author.

37. See Magarshack, pp. 4–5—Trans.

38. This verb form has the same meaning as the English continuous verb form. It expresses a continuous action in respect to the observer. The observer is thus placed in the center of the action, perceiving it from within.

THE DEGREE OF DEFINITENESS
(CONCRETENESS) ON THE SPATIAL AND
TEMPORAL PLANES IN DIFFERENT ARTS

Point of view in terms of space and time is closely connected with the characteristics of artistic space in the particular work. Indeed, it might be thought that the spatial and temporal characteristics of the represented world do not necessarily concur in different works. At the moment, however, we are less concerned with the relativity of represented space and time[39] than we are with the degree of concreteness of the spatial and temporal representation of the world.

The concreteness of the modeling of spatial and temporal characteristics of the literary work is determined first of all by the specific characteristics of literature as an art form. The spatial and temporal planes are most likely to provide the analogies between the structural organization of the text in literature and other forms of representational art. The other planes on which point of view is manifested are inherent (to a greater or lesser degree) in verbal art; the spatial and temporal planes are common to literature and to the pictorial arts.

The specific organizational conventions of the artistic text determine, in different art forms, the importance of spatial and temporal characteristics—and how well defined a work of art will be in spatial and temporal terms.

If pictorial art, by nature, presupposes some spatial concreteness in its transmission of the represented world [40] but allows temporal indefiniteness, then literature (which is essentially related not to space, but to time) insists as a rule on some temporal concreteness, and permits spatial representation to remain completely undefined. In fact, a greater reliance on temporal definition is inherent in natural language, the material from which literature is made, for the difference between language as a system

39. About this question see Lotman, 1968. See also V. G. Bogoraz (Tan), *Einshtein i religiia: Primenenie printsipa otnositel'nosti k issledovaniiu religioznykh vliianii* [Einstein and religion: application of the first principle of relativity to the investigation of religious influences], No. 1 (Moscow-Petrograd, 1923); V. G. Bogoraz, "Ideas of Space and Time in the Conception of Primitive Religion," *American Anthropologist* 27, New Series (1925). The last two works examine the specifics of the spatial model of the world in mythological representations.

40. The degree of this concreteness may vary even here in some respects. See further, Uspensky, 1970, pp. 32–33; or Uspenskij, "Per l'analisi semiotica delle antiche icone russe" (to be published).

and other semiotic systems is that linguistic expression, generally speaking, translates space into time. As M. Foucault has noted, a verbal description of any spatial relationship (or of any reality) is necessarily translated into a temporal sequence.[41]

This difference has its source in the special conditions of perception of literature and the pictorial arts; in the pictorial art, perception occurs basically in space, and not necessarily in time: in literature, perception takes place first of all in a temporal sequence. Theatre and film, however, seem to assume a more or less equal degree of concreteness on both the temporal and spatial planes.[42]

The perception of the literary work is closely connected with the processes of memory. In general, the characteristics of human memory impose a series of circumscriptions on the literary work which condition its perception; the perception of a work of pictorial art, on the contrary, is not necessarily determined by memory processes. Thus, the direct connection between memory and temporal perception should not be disregarded.[43]

On the other hand, when temporal expression is a part of a pictorial work of art[44]—for example, in a series of pictures where the same figures

41. See M. Foucault, *Les mots et les choses; une archéologie du savoir* (Paris, 1966).

42. Literature and drama are different in this aspect, and their differences will appear first in the treatment of time. In older theater we often see precisely the same breaking up of simultaneous actions into sequential scenes as is necessary in literature. In this regard, in certain scenes the actors are characteristically cut off from time. For example, Chatsky, in Griboyedov's *Woe from Wit*, delivers a monologue, but Molchalin, standing next to him, is for this length of time excluded from the action. (This is especially clear in those cases where the first actor delivers a soliloquy, and the second actor cannot even pantomime his participation in the action by reacting to the words being said.) An analogous manifestation of the reordering of simultaneous actions into sequential actions may be observed in film, in connection with the use of montage: for example, the face of a man telling a joke is shown in a close-up shot, and then the face of the listener, who begins to smile, is shown; the smile does not appear simultaneously with the telling of the joke but after the joke is told, even though the reaction is meant to be a simultaneous one. In connection with the use of time in the theater as opposed to its use in literature, it is interesting to note Goethe's remarks on the temporal discrepancies in Shakespeare. Goethe explains these discrepancies by saying that Shakespeare wrote his plays to be staged, not to be read, with the condensation of time that is characteristic of the theater, a situation where "one has no time to stop and examine details critically" (and, we may add, with the impossibility of returning to a past scene, as a reader may turn back and reread earlier lines). See *Razgovory Gete sobrannye Ekkermanom* [Conversations with Goethe, collected by Eckermann] (St. Petersburg, 1905), Part I, pp. 338–341.

43. See, in particular, Dzh. Uitrou, *Estestvennaia filosofiia vremeni* [The natural philosophy of time] (Moscow, 1964), pp. 109–149.

44. See, for example, the seals on icons, the temporal sequence of fresco groupings, or the iconographic representation of the beheading of John the Baptist, where the body

participate in a left-to-right sequence—there is much greater freedom (more than in other forms of art) in our temporal ordering of it. We may choose to read the sequence from left to right in the normal order; or we may reverse the sequence, reading backward from right to left (in the same way that a film might be run backward);[45] or we may choose any scene as our starting point and move at will in any direction, completely altering the temporal arrangement. This reordering of sequence is not possible in other arts (literature and film, for instance) where the time orientation is determined. We can conclude, then, that time is not an essential factor in the structure of pictorial art forms, and that the freedom we have observed is a consequence of its relative lack of importance.

Because visual art has only a limited means of expressing time, there is little or no generation of new signs in the process of the viewer's observation of a picture. The reader of a literary work, on the other hand, is often involved during the process of reading (of perceiving), in the creation of new signs. In other words, the interplay between the author (the artist) and the audience is much less important in pictorial art than in literature.

Thus, the specifics of the translation of space in a particular literary work are determined by the degree of concreteness of the spatial characteristics. If this degree of concreteness is great enough (that is, if the work is sufficiently characterized by spatial definiteness) there arises the possibility of the concrete spatial presentation of the content, and the work may be translated into such visual media as painting and drama. But such a translation is not always possible, for clear and precise representation of space is not always a part of the author's compositional intentions. As Yury Lotman remarks, in his analysis of Gogol's "The Nose,"

---

of John is represented against the same landscape (background) and within the same frame at several different moments in time. For an analysis of similar examples, see Uspenskij, "Per l' analisi semiotica delle antiche icone russe." See also Plates 3, 4.
45. The modeling of inverted time is expressed in a poem by O. E. Mandelshtam:

> Byt' mozhet, prezhde gub uzhe rodilsia shepot
> bezdrevesnosti kruzhilisia listy.

> [Literally:

> Perhaps the whisper was born before the lips, and
> the leaves were whirling in treeless times.]

This example was quoted by V. V. Ivanov in a lecture "Vremia v nauke i iskusstve" [Time in science and in art], in the Second Summer School on Secondary Modeling Systems at Kääriku in 1966.

"the fact that the Nose has a face, that it walks, stooping, that it runs up the stairs, that it wears a full dress coat with gold embroidery and a standup collar, that it prays 'with an expression of devout piety' completely destroys the possibility of imagining it in three-dimensional space." [49]

Obviously, it would be difficult to stage or to film a work like this, in the same way that it is often difficult to film a fairy tale. Theatre (or film) demands the actualization of features that may be irrelevant in a literary text.

Gogol's "The Nose" provides a good demonstration of this difficulty, for the Nose undergoes a striking series of transformations. Not only is there a lack of spatial definiteness, but there is also marked diffuseness on other levels.

In other cases, the absence of spatial definiteness is not immediately evident, and only a careful reading may reveal that at one point a figure has changed its dimensions in relation to other figures or to objects around it—or that surroundings have changed in relation to the figure.

Note, for example, the spatial indefiniteness of the figure of the cat in Bulgakov's *The Master and Margarita*. The correspondence between the size of the cat and the size of the other characters and objects changes markedly in the course of the novel (although we can judge this change only indirectly). Sometimes we think the cat is the usual size and shape; sometimes it seems to grow imperceptibly. It performs actions that no cat could perform: it goes to the table, it pours water from a decanter, it takes a ticket from the conductor, and so forth.

In the same way, we often see a change in the dimensions of folklore figures, although these transformations are not necessarily emphasized; in fact, they are often ignored.[47] We are not talking here so much about fairy-tale transformations as about the lack of any kind of spatial definiteness: the correlation of size may appear altogether irrelevant to the storyteller.

The noncoordination that we find in the descriptions of Gogol may be treated as spatial-temporal incongruities: Chichikov, in *Dead Souls*, rides around wearing a fur coat in the summer; Manilov wears a fur coat and

46. Lotman, 1968, p. 39. In this connection, see also the remarks of Iu. N. Tynianov, *Problema stikhotvornogo iazyka* [Problems of poetic language] (Moscow, 1965), p. 173, note 3; and also Iu. N. Tynianov, *Arkhaisty i novatory* [Traditionalists and innovators] (Leningrad, 1928), Chapter 13.

47. See S. Iu. Nekliudov, "K voprosu o sviazi prostranstvenno-vremennykh otnoshenii s siuzhetnoi strukturoi v russkoi byline" [The question of the connection of spatial and temporal relations with plot structure in the Russian bylina], *Tezisy dokladov vo vtoroi letnei shkole po vtorichnym modeliruiushchim sisetemam* (Tartu, 1966).

a cap with earflaps; Kovalev, in "The Nose," sees a girl in a white dress on the streets of St. Petersburg in March; and the Nose rides around in winter in a uniform without an overcoat.[48] These incongruities are not deliberate: they occur because the careful definition of space and time is not important to the author.

All the examples we have outlined above may be interpreted as cases which lack spatial definiteness in the position of the narrator (the observer). We may interpret such instances by imagining that different characters are viewed by different observers, observers who do not communicate with one another; these observations are then brought together by the author.[49] This kind of composition is typologically analogous to the pictorial composition built on inverted perspective.

Thus, temporal indefiniteness is much less characteristic in literature than spatial indefiniteness.[50] In the pictorial arts, however, the opposite is true.

48. See G. Voloshin, "Prostranstvo i vremia u Dostoevskogo" [Space and time in Dostoevsky], *Slavia* 12 (1933): 1–2. See also, V. Buzeskul, "K kakomu vremeni goda otnosiatsia pokhozhdeniia Chichikova?" [At what time of the year did the adventures of Chichikov take place?] in his book *Istoricheskie etiudy* (St. Petersburg, 1911).

49. From a different approach it might seem that these figures are located in different spaces, only partially connected to one another. Both approaches lead to the same conclusions, however.

50. By "temporal definiteness" we understand here only the relative chronological definition of an event. Some indeterminacy, however, may be noted in other respects. For example, the absolute (not relative) temporal indeterminacy in Shakespeare's *Hamlet* has been repeatedly noted by critics. We do not know exactly how much time elapses during the action of the play: we know that in the beginning of the action Hamlet is a young student and at the end he is thirty years old—even though the action is presented to us as continuous.

4 POINT OF VIEW ON THE PLANE OF PSYCHOLOGY

When an author constructs his narration, he usually has two options open to him: he may structure the events and characters of the narrative through the deliberately subjective viewpoint of some particular individual's (or individuals') consciousness, or he may describe the events as objectively as possible. In other words, he may use the *données* of the perceptions of one consciousness or several, or he may use the facts as they are known to him. Different combinations of these two techniques are possible; the author may alternate between them or may combine them in various ways.

These two compositional processes take place in both literary and everyday narration of events or stories, for whenever we tell about an event that we have witnessed, we are confronted by the same dilemma. We can relate only our own first-hand observations, that is, the facts, or we can reconstruct the state of mind of the people who were involved and the motives that governed their actions, even though those motives are inaccessible to an observer—that is, we can adopt a point of view internal to the characters themselves. Ordinarily, we use both of these techniques in constructing our narration. Literary works manifest the same techniques: the characters are described from either the first or the second of these positions.

In those cases where the authorial point of view relies on an individual consciousness (or perception) we will speak about the psychological point of view; we will conditionally designate the plane on which this point of view may be distinguished as the psychological plane.

We have already had occasion to observe, in connection with our examination of the plane of phraseology, the reference to some particular

81

subjective consciousness during the narration. Such a phenomenon, for example, as quasi-direct discourse is in many instances simply the use of some subjective position—that is, reference to the consciousness of a particular character—manifested through speech. In some cases the psychological plane is articulated by means of phraseological characteristics, just as the ideological plane may be expressed through phraseology or through the narrator's temporal position.

At the moment, however, we are interested in the psychological plane itself, and in the specific means of expression of points of view in terms of this plane.

Let us look now at a concrete example which demonstrates both options: the "subjective" description (that is, the use of some individual perception, some psychological point of view); and the "objective" description of some event. Here Dostoevsky describes Rogozhin's attempt to murder Myshkin, in *The Idiot*:

Rogozhin's eyes glittered and a frenzied smile contorted his face. He raised his right hand and something gleamed in it. The prince did not think of checking it (p. 227).

Two paragraphs further on, the same event is described from an essentially different point of view:

It must be supposed that some such feeling of sudden horror, together with the other terrible sensations of the moment, had suddenly paralysed Rogozhin and so saved the prince from the inevitable blow of the knife which already was coming at him (p. 227).

Thus we learn that the object that flashed in Rogozhin's hand was a knife.

The description of the single event is carried out here in two essentially different ways. In the first passage, the description is "subjective," narrated through the perceptions of the prince (from his psychological point of view); accordingly, the knife is described as "something," as the prince himself perceived it at that moment. The object seems to be unknown to the author, whose point of view has completely merged at this moment with the prince's (hence the characteristic synchronic point of view from which the narrative proceeds: the knife is called "something" because the prince—and also the author—does not yet know what it is; in a moment, of course, this will become absolutely clear).

In the second passage, however, the situation is described from an "objective" position, and facts are presented rather than impressions. The author relies here on his own point of view and not on the point of view of the prince; consequently, the description is carried out from a retrospective, rather than synchronic, position.

PLATES

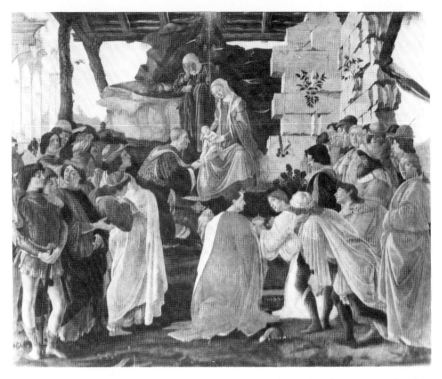

1. Sandro Botticelli. "Adoration of the Magi." The figure on the far right represents the artist himself.

2. A. Dürer. "The Feast of the Rosary." The figure by the tree (right) represents the artist himself.

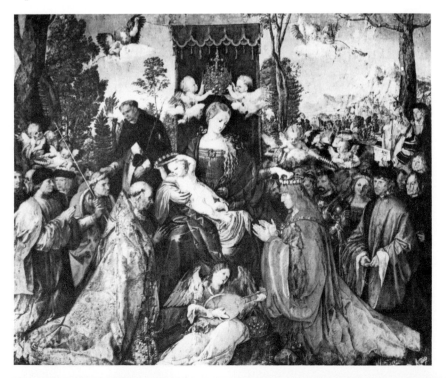

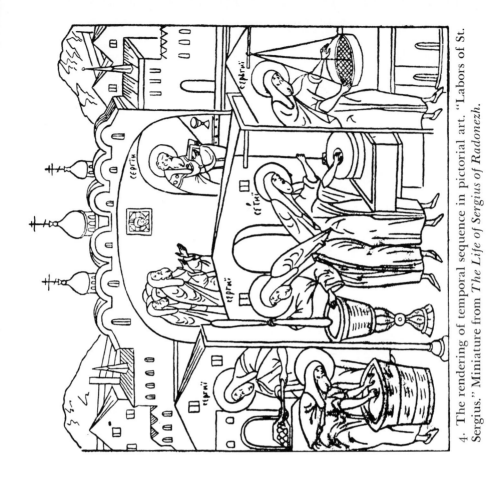

4. The rendering of temporal sequence in pictorial art. "Labors of St. Sergius." Miniature from *The Life of Sergius of Radonezh.*

3. The rendering of temporal sequence in pictorial art. "Beheading of St. John the Baptist." Icon of the fifteenth century.

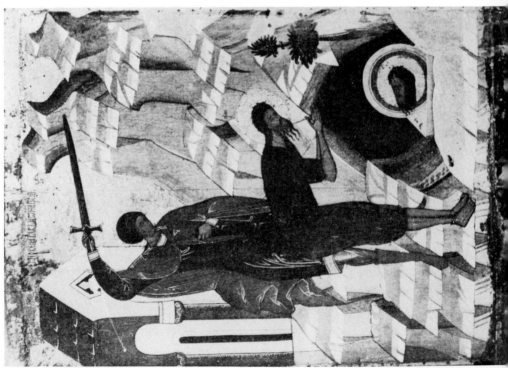

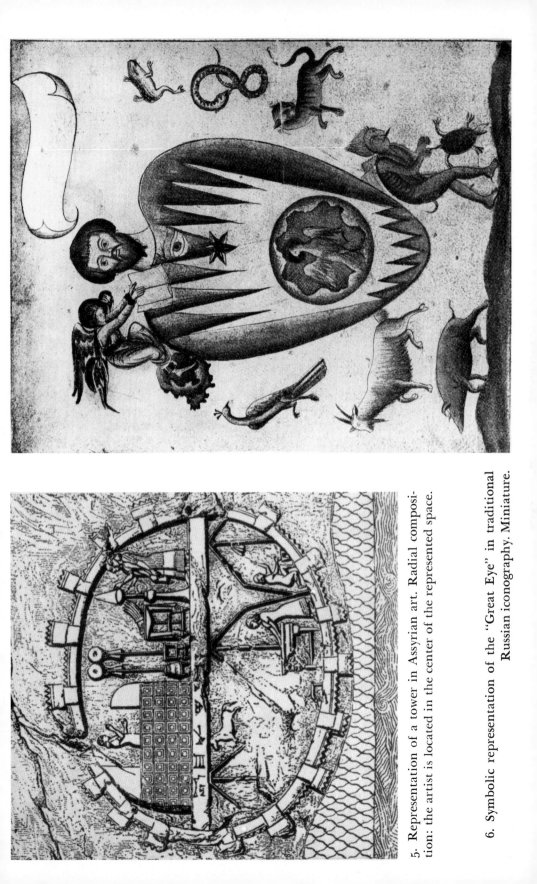

5. Representation of a tower in Assyrian art. Radial composition: the artist is located in the center of the represented space.

6. Symbolic representation of the "Great Eye" in traditional Russian iconography. Miniature.

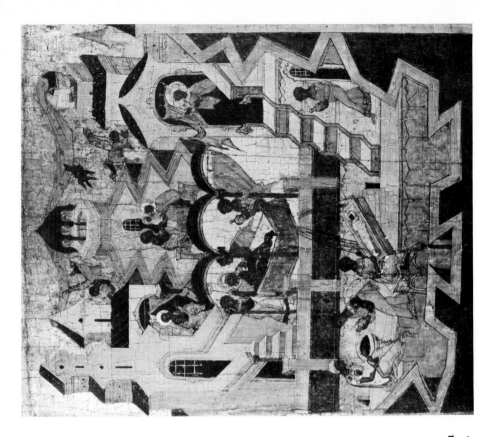

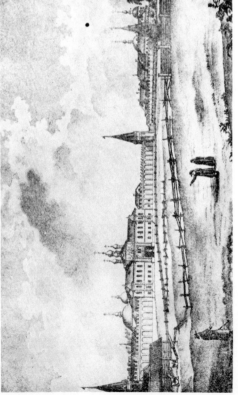

7. Foreground figures. "View toward the Preobrazhensky home for the aged and its cemetery in Moscow." Engraving of the late eighteenth or early nineteenth century.

8. Composite character of the organization of space in the Russian icon. The total space is a sum of micro-spaces.

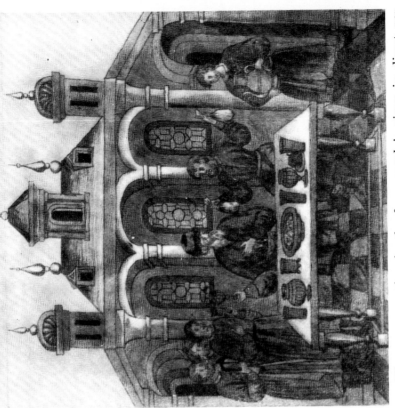

10. The representation in the foreground is given in direct perspective (see the form of the table), while the background representation is in inverted perspective (see the representation of the buildings in the background). Feast of the boyars. Miniature of the seventeenth or eighteenth century.

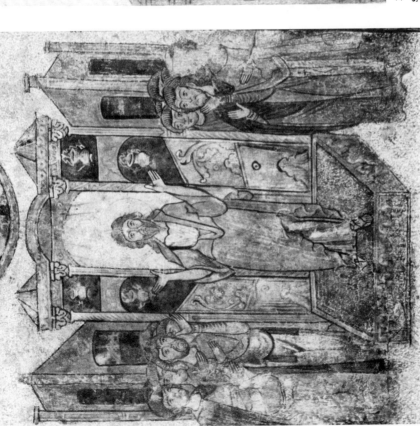

9. The representation in the foreground is in inverted perspective (see the form of the podium), while in the background it is in direct perspective (see the architectural forms in the background). Detail of a triptych "Life of the Evangelist John." Italian painting of the twelfth century.

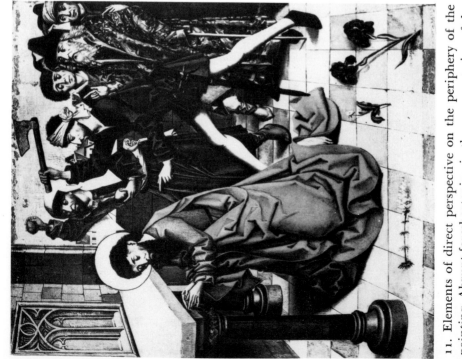

12. The laconic gestures and stressed three-dimensionality in the foreground of the painting contrast with the principles of representation in the background. Antonello da Messina's "St. Sebastian."

11. Elements of direct perspective on the periphery of the painting. Abrupt foreshortening in the representation of the floor. "Execution of St. Matthew." Fifteenth century German painting.

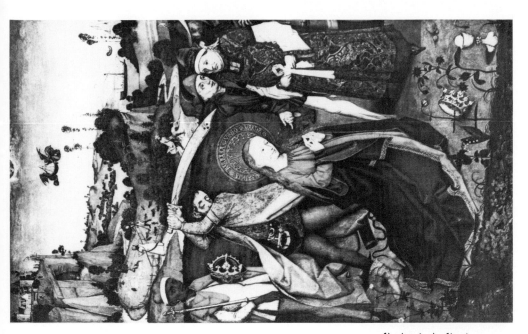

13. The Master of the Grossgmein Altar. "Madonna with Child and the Apostle Thomas." Fifteenth century.
Several consecutively represented spatial layers each have their own framing in the form of an embrasure and their own perspective position.

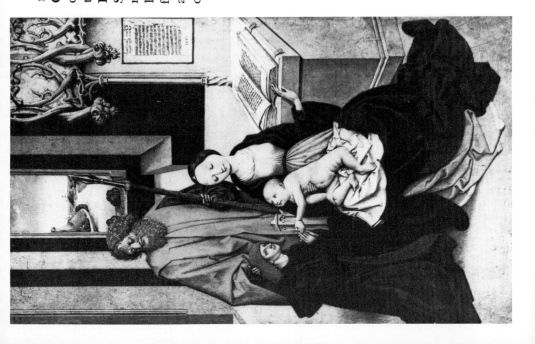

14. Hans Schuchlin. "The Execution of St. Barbara." Fifteenth century.
The background is represented as a picture within a picture.

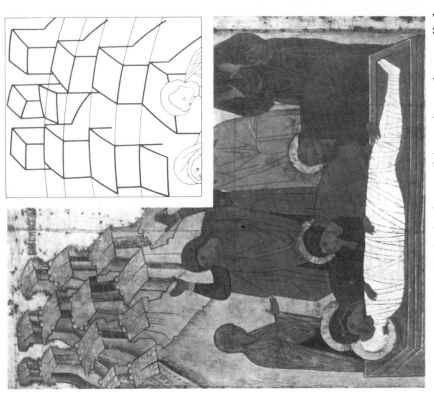

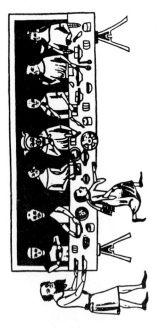

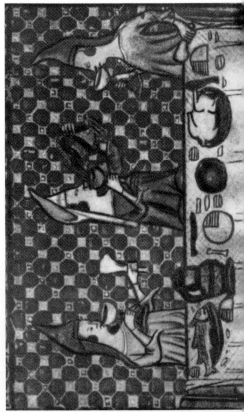

15. Collation. Illustration from an English psalmbook of the fourteenth century. The representation in the background is given as a picture within a picture.

16. The representation in the foreground (which in this instance is peripheral) is given as a picture within a picture. Displacement of the objects on the table is "toward the viewer." Illustration to a romance of the fourteenth century, *Three Ladies from Paris*.

17. Ornamentation of the background in an icon: the so-called icon hillocks "The Entombment of Christ." Icon of the late fifteenth century.

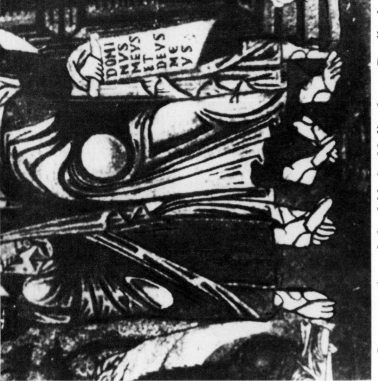

19. Ornamentation of the folds in Medieval art. Detail of a mosaic of the Cathedral of Saint Mark in Venice.

18. Ornamentation of the background in the icon: the so-called icon hillocks. "Miracle of Archangel Mikhail in Chonae." Icon of the sixteenth century.

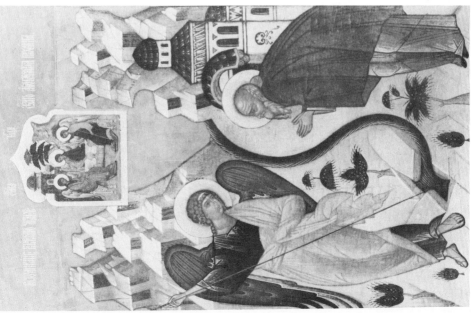

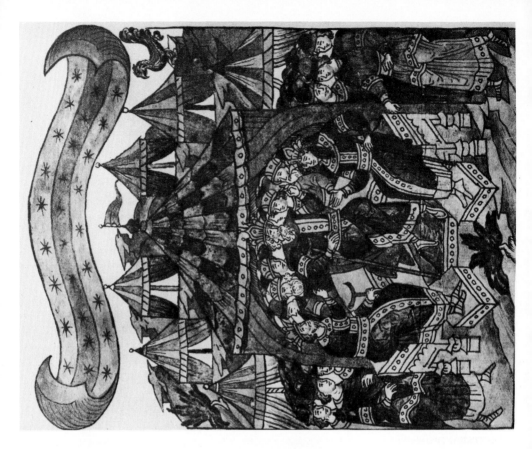

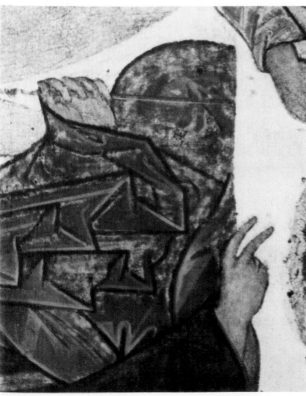

20. Ornamentation of folds in Medieval painting. Detail of Andrey Rublev: "Trinity." Fifteenth century.

21. Heightening of conventionality (or of the symbolic nature) of the background of the representation. "Night Council in the Enemy Camp." Miniature from a chronicle of the sixteenth century. The details of the background receive a highly conventional treatment: night is represented as a scroll; dawn is represented as a rooster.

We may consider that the psychological point of view in the first passage is transmitted through phraseological elements which come from some imaginary interior monologue of the count, a monologue from which, for example, the word "something" is borrowed.

We will turn now, however, to a discussion of those instances in which the psychological point of view is not connected to phraseology, but emerges in its own right, manifested by those means of expression which are specific to it.

MEANS OF DESCRIBING BEHAVIOR ON
THE PSYCHOLOGICAL PLANE

Generally speaking, human behavior may be described in two basically distinct ways. First, it may be described from the point of view of an outside observer whose position in the work may be either clearly defined or unspecified, and who describes only the behavior which is visible to an onlooker. Second, behavior may be described from the point of view of the person himself or from the point of view of an omniscient observer who is permitted to penetrate the consciousness of that person. In this kind of description we find revealed the internal processes (thoughts, feelings, sensory perceptions, emotions) which are not normally accessible to an external observer (who can only speculate about such processes, projecting his own experience onto the external manifestations of someone else's behavior). This point of view is internal to the person who is being described.

Accordingly, it is possible to speak about external and internal points of view (in relation to the object of description).[1] The opposition of external and internal points of view is of a general nature, and is not restricted to the single level of psychological perception.[2] We have already had an opportunity to observe this opposition during our examination of the phraseological level; we will attempt to make some generalizations on the nature of this opposition in Chapter Seven. For the moment, however, we shall confine our use of the terms "external" and "internal" to the narrow meaning they acquire on the plane of psychology.

1. The narrator in Dostoevsky's *The Possessed* makes the characteristic assertion: "Of course, I don't know what was inside the man; I saw only his exterior" (p. 186); his acknowledgement, however, does not prohibit this same narrator, in other moments, from adopting a point of view internal, and not external, to the character.

2. Later we will see that the opposition between internal and external points of view exists not only for literature, but also for visual art.

First Type of Description: The External View
of the Person Who Is Described

Let us turn to the first of the possibilities of description that we have outlined above. A person's behavior may be described externally in two ways. First, it may be described with reference to definite facts, without dependence on the describing subject. In this instance, the observer's location is spatially and temporally indeterminate, and his description is impersonal or, we might say, "transpersonal"; for example, it may take the form of a court recording in which the objectivity of the account and the lack of involvement of the author are deliberately emphasized, and in which only phrases like "he did," "he said," "he announced"—rather than such phrases as "he thought," "he felt," "he was ashamed"—are used.[3]

The second kind of external description refers to the opinion of some observer, through the use of such phrases as "it appeared that he thought," "he apparently knew," "he seemed to be ashamed," and so forth. In this case the point of view of the observer may be stable (for example, the viewpoint of a narrator who takes part in the action or who takes no part in it); or it may be shifting (for example, the use of the point of view first of one character, then of another: we may read "it seemed to the prince that . . . ," and a few minutes later find a description of the prince, through the perceptions of some man to whom he has been speaking).

If the behavior of one of the characters is described from the point of view of another character in the same narrative, then this second character (who presents his point of view) is described by means which are fundamentally different: his description is an internal one (a description including his internal state). Thus, if the behavior of A is described through the perceptions of B (A and B being characters in the same narrative), then A is described from an external point of view, while B is described from an internal point of view.

Second Type of Description: The Internal View
of the Person Who Is Described

In the case outlined above, the behavior of B is described with reference to his internal state—a state which is generally not accessible to an onlooker; this may occur when the particular person is described either

---

3. Judicial language characteristically attempts to eliminate all subjectivity, to approximate an objective description. A court recorder would be expected to say not "X saw an unfamiliar serviceman," but "X saw an unfamiliar man in military uniform," for the former contains, at least to a minimal degree, traces of subjectivity (the assumption that the man in question is indeed a serviceman).

from his own point of view or through a special point of view which comes from outside when the writer places himself in the position of an omniscient observer.

In this case, we may find special expressions which describe the internal consciousness—in particular, *verba sentiendi*:[4] "he thought," "he felt," "it seemed to him," "he knew," "he recognized," and so on.

The verbs which express an internal condition function in the text as formal signs of description from an internal point of view. Such verbs are marked in language and make up a relatively short list. In an analysis of a narrative, we may formally determine the particular aspect of its structure according to the presence or absence of these particular verbs.

On the other hand, special modal expressions ("apparently," "evidently," "as if," "it seemed," and so forth) enable us to recognize in the text the opposite type of description—that is, description from the external observer's point of view. Expressions of this type occur in the text when the narrator takes an external point of view in describing some internal state (thoughts, feelings, unconscious motives for action) that he cannot be sure about.

In other words, we are talking here about situations in which the author's compositional aims do not permit him the use of an internal point of view to describe a particular character. Perhaps he has already represented a character from the outside (through another character's perceptions, for instance), and then must find some means to describe his inner emotional experience. In this case, *verba sentiendi* which are used in the description of a character may be accompanied by modal expressions: "he seemed to think," "it was as if Nikolay wanted," and so on. These modal expressions function as special "operators" to translate the description of an internal state into an objective description. In other words, they make possible the transposition of the description from "within" to one from "without."

The use of operators is a device which justifies the application of *verba sentiendi* to a character who has been consistently described from an external ("estranged") point of view. We may call these operators "words of estrangement." [5]

---

4. That is, verbs of feeling.
5. A deliberate transition to the retrospective position (which allows one to know facts which may not be known to a synchronic observer) may carry a similar function. This device is particularly characteristic of Dostoevsky, for example. See in *The Brothers Karamazov* the meeting of Alyosha and Katya with Dmitri in his cell. The exposition in general is done from Alyosha's point of view. Suddenly Grushenka enters, and Dostoevsky reports: "She came in, as it turned out later, completely unexpectedly" (p. 929). The author wants to relate that Grushenka's intrusion was not foreseen by her,

As an example of the use of this device, let us turn to a passage from *War and Peace*, the scene at the Rostovs' on the countess' name day. The children have all come into the living room.

Meanwhile, all the younger generation, . . . had all placed themselves about the drawing-room, and were obviously trying to restrain within the bounds of decorum the excitement and mirth which was brimming in their faces (p. 33).

The stout boy ran wrathfully after them, as though resenting the interruption of his pursuits (p. 33).

This narrative technique is characteristic of Tolstoy, and even if we limited our search to *War and Peace*, we could find numerous examples of it. What is essential in these two instances is that Tolstoy could have omitted the words of estrangement ("obviously," "as though") without in any way altering his description of the characters; they are used here not because the author was not sure of the feelings of the characters, but precisely because he wanted to emphasize the point of view from which the characters have been described. The position from which these particular observations were made may have been that of the countess' guests, or it may have been the more remote position of an observer, who is invisibly present in the room.

Such indicators of an "alien" point of view on the plane of psychology are no less characteristic than, for example, words of a character which are used to establish someone else's point of view within the authorial context. These devices belong to different planes, but they have, in general, a single function.

The use of words of estrangement points to the presence of a synchronic narrator at the place of action.[6] We can say, then, that these words serve to fix not only the psychological viewpoint of the observer, but also his temporal and spatial viewpoint.

Thus, the presence in the description of the character's behavior of ex-

---

but he cannot say it without a special explanation because he has adopted a manner of exposition which requires him to explain how he comes to know things (and Alyosha, who is the carrier of the authorial point of view, may not know the facts at this moment). The transition to a retrospective position serves to justify the authorial knowledge and correspondingly, to justify a description from an internal and not an external point of view. We shall discuss further the restrospective position as a position justifying omniscience. This device (in this particular function) is quite often used by Dostoevsky as exemplified in the description of Ivan Karamazov (p. 337).

6. We may assume this narrator to be one of the participants (namely, the one whose inner state is described). But there are instances when all the characters are presented externally, through "estrangement." When this occurs, the author is conducting the narration from the position of a nonparticipating bystander who is invisibly present at the scene of the action—that is, from a special narrating position (see Chapter Five).

pressions which describe an internal state without these special operators indicates the use of the internal point of view. Correspondingly, the absence of expressions of the internal state or the presence of special word-operators (the words of estrangement) serve as signs of the use of the external point of view.

In conducting a formal analysis of a text and distinguishing between the two types of description (internal and external) through the use of words of estrangement, we must take into account the possibility of an elliptical construction. Occasionally these words may be omitted in a text, particularly where they may be inferred with some degree of certainty from the context. See, for example, the following passage from *The Brothers Karamazov*:

Fyodor Pavlovich . . . watched his neighbor Piotr Aleksandrovich with an ironical little smile, obviously enjoying his irritability. He had been waiting for some time to pay off old scores, and now he could not let the opportunity slip (p. 67).

It can be assumed that the modal expressions such as "evidently" or "as if" are absent from the second sentence because they occur in the preceding sentence; they are absent here for stylistic and not compositional reasons.

A TYPOLOGY OF THE COMPOSITIONAL USE
OF DIFFERENT POINTS OF VIEW

We have singled out two narrative principles, two descriptive techniques—the "internal" and "external"—by which the structures of literary works are distinguished. Remembering that we are discussing this opposition now only in terms of psychological perception, we will look more closely at different cases and attempt to provide a classification of them.

Unchanging Authorial Position in Narration

CASE ONE: CONSISTENTLY EXTERNAL   In terms of compositional complexity, the simplest case is that in which the external view is used consistently. All events are described objectively, without any reference to the internal state of the characters, and all verbs which express the internal consciousness (*verba sentiendi* and similar expressions) are absent.

Such a construction of narration is characteristic of works of epic, where actions are unmotivated. This, to a large degree, is explained by the fact that the character's internal world is hidden from us.

CASE TWO: CONSISTENTLY INTERNAL   In this case, all of the action is consistently represented from one particular point of view, through the perception of one person. Accordingly, the description of an internal state is justified only with respect to this character, while all other states are described from the outside.

The story may be presented from the point of view of a narrator in the first person (*Icherzählung*), or from the point of view of a particular character (then the story is told in the third person). The latter may be considered one of the transformations of *Icherzählung*—the first-person pronoun is replaced by a personal name or by a descriptive designation.

This construction is common in literature, and is often encountered in relatively short works.[7] A good example is Dostoevsky's *The Eternal Husband,* where all of the action is described through the perceptions of Velchaninov. While Velchaninov's behavior is analyzed and revealed from an internal point of view with respect to him, the behavior of all the other characters is presented from an external point of view.

In many cases, the narration is carried out from the point of view of one particular person, the main character (it does not matter whether he is the "I" of the story or some character X); the author—and together with him, the reader—seems to consolidate with him, and to identify with his image. Sometimes, however, the author's real compositional aim may be to show this person (this "I" or "X") as someone else observes him from the outside. In other words, this person is described from within, but the narrative as a whole is so designed that the reader must reconstruct an implicit, external view with respect to the character.[8] (Some of Hemingway's stories are constructed in this way.)[9]

The opposite situation may also be true: the main character may not be the one whose impressions are described in the work (for example, Natalie in Bunin's story of the same name, Pavel Pavlovich in Dostoevsky's *The Eternal Husband,* and so forth). The main character may be presented by means of an external description, and the author's compositional aim may be to have the reader reconstruct an internal view of this character, while the character through whom the narration is con-

7. Such a construction is particularly characteristic of Bunin and a number of other short-story writers.

8. In this case the compositional structure on the psychological and ideological levels is deliberately noncongruent, and the points of view on the psychological and the ideological levels do not concur.

9. This type of description is generally typical of people holding the romantic worldview ("romantic" is understood here not as derived from "Romanticism"). See the definition of the psychological type, "romantic," in A. M. Piatigorskii, B. A. Uspenskii, "Personologicheskaia klassifikatsiia kak semioticheskaia problema" [Personological classification as a semiotic problem], *Trudy po znakovym sistemam,* III (Uch. Zap. TGU, vyp. 198), p. 22.

ducted, and whose internal state is described, may function purely as an accessory figure, one which never acquires a concrete image. For example, it is hardly possible to imagine the narrator in *The Possessed*, in spite of the fact that he takes part in the action and we know him as Anton Lavrentevitch G.

The two cases of unchanging authorial position can be called "consistent narration." Here, the position of the narrating observer is essentially real: the author describes the behavior of the characters in literature just as an ordinary person, in an ordinary situation, would describe the behavior of another person. In consistent narration, the author belongs to the same world as his characters and is not distinguished in any way from them. Moreover, he may describe the events from his point of view or he may merge his point of view with that of one of the characters; it is essential, however, that his characteristics be such that he could participate in the events as easily as any of the characters.

In the case to which we next turn, the position of the author is less consistent and less "real," and is essentially different from the position of an ordinary observer. Here, the author uses for his description not one but several points of view which supercede each other in the course of the narrative (as in the third case), or participate simultaneously (as in case four).

The Plurality of Authorial Positions

CASE THREE: CHANGE OF THE AUTHORIAL POSITION IN SEQUENCE   In the sequential use of different points of view, each scene is described from one particular position, or point of view, but the different scenes in the work are narrated from the positions of different characters.

In this kind of description, character A may be described from the point of view of character B, and then B may be described from the point of view of A;[10] it is essential, however, that the internal states of A and B not be described at the same time, in the same situation or microscene (this condition occurs in the fourth case).

Thus, the author seems to link his point of view with that of one of the characters, as if he were taking part in the action. His position changes, in sequence, from one point of view to another during his narration—from the point of view of one character to another, or from the point of view of a character to his own point of view.[11] Each time

10. A similar method of compositional organization is often found in film. In commercial Hollywood films this device often seems to be a norm.
11. The latter device, as well as a general shift of authorial position, is often given the compositional function of framing.

this change occurs, *verba sentiendi* are used to refer to the particular character who is serving as the vehicle of the author's vision, while the other characters are described as they are seen, from the outside, by the viewpoint character.

For example, the narration of *War and Peace* is structured upon the successive alternation of the points of view of Pierre, Natasha, Nikolay, and a number of other characters. Usually, the change in point of view is determined by the scene boundaries: one scene is given from one character's point of view, the next from that of another and so on. Sometimes, however, the sequential alternation of points of view takes place within a scene. For instance, the point of view in the description of an event in the home of the Rostovs, after Nikolay has lost forty-three thousand rubles in a card game, alternates between Natasha, who is singing, and Nikolay, who is listening:

Nikolay began walking to and fro in the room.
"What can induce her to want to sing? What can she sing? and there's nothing to be so happy about in it," thought Nikolay. . . .
Natasha, too, with her quick instinct, instantly detected her brother's state of mind. She noticed him, but she was herself in such high spirits at that moment, she was so far from sorrow, from sadness, from reproaches, that purposely she deceived herself (as young people so often do). "No, I'm too happy just now to spoil my enjoyment by sympathy with anyone's sorrow," she felt, and she said to herself: "No, I'm most likely mistaken, he must be happy, just as I am." . . .
"How is it?" thought Nikolay, hearing her voice and opening his eyes wide; "what has happened to her? How she is singing today!" (pp. 312–313).

The rhythm of the transitions from one point of view to another is accelerated here, and the changes of point of view, which generally correspond to rather large sections of narration in the novel, are in this scene used to mark off short periods of time. (This speeded-up rhythm corresponds to Nikolay's state of mind.)[12]

As a result of this approach to the analysis of the structure, the narrative breaks into a series of apparently separate descriptions, each of which is narrated from the point of view of a different person. The whole constitutes a conjunction, but not a synthesis, of these separate texts.

This kind of organization of the text may be conceived as a result of a sequence of several different first-person narratives being transformed

---

12. See also the similar alternation of point of view in the dialogue between Boris and Pierre in *War and Peace* (pp. 45–47). Here, however, the condensation of rhythm is not dependent upon the characters' internal state.

into third-person narrative. This principle of organization appears in its most simple compositional form in a narrative where different parts of the story are presented through different characters, each of whom conducts the narration in the first person (for example, in Collins' *The Moonstone* and V. Kaverin's *Two Captains*). This kind of composition is probably genetically connected with the epistolary novel. The situation in *War and Peace,* where in different scenes different characters in sequence become the narrators, may be considered the next step in the progressive complication of a compositional form which has its origin in *Icherzählung,* the most elementary instance of this form.

Different actors, functioning as vehicles for the authorial point of view, may alternate in the work with the authorial "I." That is, in the work there may participate both the author himself (narrating in his own voice, and accordingly, from his own point of view or one that he has specially assumed), as well as various occasional vehicles of the authorial point of view among the characters of the work. This combination is found frequently in the work of Dostoevsky (for example, in *The Brothers Karamazov*).

The position of the narrator in this case is relatively "real," for the author seems to take part, invisibly, in the action. It is as if he were reporting directly from the field of action; his position in time and in space, therefore, can in each case be determined more or less precisely. However, the position of the narrator here may be less "real" and consistent than that of the narrator in Case One and Case Two, but it is more real than the position of the narrator in the fourth case.

When we examine the typological possibilities in compositional constructions which use different points of view in turn, we must notice that the number of persons from whose point of view the narrative is constructed is functionally limited. The author assumes the form of some of the characters, embodying himself in them for a period of time. We might compare the author to an actor who plays different roles, transfiguring himself alternatively into several characters. In this way, the internal descriptions of the state of mind of these characters are logically justified. However, if the author embodies himself in some characters of a narrative, the others remain external to him, and he perceives them only from the outside; he portrays them, but he never identifies with their image. In other words, if some characters in the work serve as the subject of the author's perceptions, others function solely as the object.

It would seem that the characters whose role the author assumes are usually the main characters, while the less important or incidental characters compose the background (they are "extras," so to speak), and do not justify internal description. This is not always true, however. In some cases the author may feel that it is important not to reveal the central character's internal being, but to show him through the eyes of someone else. When the author adopts such a compositional design, the reader may be forced to guess about the feelings and thoughts of the character, who is presented to him as a kind of enigma. Thus (and we should not consider this a paradox), the same device of external description serves in both cases: when the character is of special interest, and when he is peripheral, of little interest.

The descriptions of such characters as Tolstoy's Platon Karataev in *War and Peace* and Dostoevsky's Father Zossima in *The Brothers Karamazov* are examples of the use of external description of characters who are of special interest to the novelist. Both characters are described exclusively from an external point of view—in particular, through the eyes of one of the other characters (Pierre in *War and Peace* and Alyosha in *The Brothers Karamazov*). Each time their motivations are discussed or *verba sentiendi* are applied to them, special devices of estrangement are introduced into the description ("apparently," "as if," and so forth). For example, in the description of Father Zossima, we find: "he evidently did not want" (p. 68) and "he was apparently tired" (p. 80).

Sometimes he broke off altogether, as though to take breath and recover his strength, yet he was as if in ecstasy (p. 195).

In the description of Karataev, we find: "he seemed to be upset," "Pierre's negative answer seemed to disappoint him again," and "he evidently never thought. . . ."[13] This kind of description is in definite contrast to the description of Pierre, whose thoughts and feelings the author always reports to us. We can conclude that Karataev represents a special interest for Tolstoy primarily as the object of description, and symbolizes an important problem that Pierre must solve. The same thing is true of Zossima in *The Brothers Karamazov*.

Smerdiakov, in *The Brothers Karamazov*, is also described in this fashion. He is presented as an enigmatic character (although, of course, he is a mystery of a completely different kind than either Father Zossima or Platon Karataev) who must be understood, not by the author (who may penetrate the consciousness of the character he is describing), but by the characters of the particular work.

Throughout the major portion of *The Brothers Karamazov*, the same technique is used to describe Ivan. Indeed, for some time Ivan is de-

13. There is one exception in an earlier passage in *War and Peace* where this law is violated (p. 902), but we may assume an ellipsis of the corresponding word.

scribed only from the outside, presented through his actions and through the opinions of the people who surround him. For the reader, he is enigmatic, just as he is enigmatic (a "big-city trick") for the people of the imaginary provincial town of Skotoprigonevsk.[14] When the author first introduces us to the Karamazov family, he does not (as he might) give us Ivan's character, even though we are given definite information about the characters of the other brothers; the facts of his life are given to us drily, in a very formal way:

Why Ivan Fyodorovich had come amongst us I remember asking myself at the time with a certain uneasiness. . . . It seemed strange on the face of it that a young man so learned, so proud, and apparently so cautious, should suddenly visit such an infamous house. . . . This last fact was a special cause of wonder to many others as well as to me. . . .
It was only later that we learned that Ivan had come partly at the request of, and in the interests of, his elder brother (pp. 14–15).

Later, Ivan's behavior (which is sometimes almost incomprehensible to us) is described by the narrator from an external viewpoint and through the opinions of other characters.[15] This contrasts with the description of the other brothers, whose thoughts and feelings are open to us.

Only after Ivan has read to Alyosha his "Legend of the Grand Inquisitor" is the reader allowed to enter Ivan's consciousness—and even then only from time to time (and at first only rarely). Thus, the "Legend" represents, in a sense, the moment of transition from one descriptive technique to another and of change in the reader's relationship to Ivan, as well. The confession in the "Legend" brings Ivan close to the reader, and after this moment it is possible to see him not only through the opinions of other people but directly.

There is a sentence in an earlier passage (after the first conversation with Smerdiakov), however, which allows us a brief glimpse into the thoughts and feelings of Ivan; this appears almost as a slip on Dostoevsky's part. Immediately following this sentence, the author says:

But we will not give an account of his thoughts, and this is not the place to look into that soul—its turn will come (p. 326).

The author recognizes that description here of the internal state of the character departs from the compositional aims of the narrative as a whole. Having just mentioned Ivan's state of mind, the narrator (about

14. A coined name derived from "driving home" and "cattle" (by implication "brutes"); it implies "the place to which brutes are driven"—Trans.
15. The narrator is explicitly presented as a real person in the novel, although he does not take part in the action.

whom we had already forgotten) appears on the scene and openly emphasizes his retrospective position, in contrast to the previous description, which seemed to be synchronic. This emphasizes that in Ivan's "present" the narrator cannot yet know what Ivan feels—but he may report this to us by looking into Ivan's soul from his "future." The same emphasis on a retrospective position may be found later in the work (p. 340).

In the case of Ivan Karamazov, then, there is a gradual change in the authorial position in relation to the character. This change corresponds to the reader's growing acquaintance with Ivan and is reflected in the shift from the external view to the internal view. In other cases, the change of the author's position may take the opposite direction, and the result is the paradoxical situation in which a detailed initiation into the thoughts and feelings of a certain character is suddenly superseded by an exterior description. The reader who only a moment ago was a close acquaintance, a confidant, of the character, knowing the motives of all of his actions, suddenly finds himself completely alienated, a stranger, and occupying a position fundamentally opposed to his earlier one.[16] Occasionally this may lead to what seems like a logical inconsistency, when we suddenly learn (from someone else) something very important about the character we have known quite well—something which should not have escaped us, because we were so entirely immersed in the world of the character's feelings.

One elementary (and intentionally exaggerated) example of this particular device might be a detective story in which we discover, at the end, that the killer was the vehicle for the authorial point of view, the character with whose actions we have been closely acquainted all through the novel, and into whose thoughts and feelings we have been initiated. It is clear that such a composition is largely unsuccessful; however, we frequently encounter it in a less obvious form.

Therefore, it is characteristic that we should suddenly discover about Dmitri Karamazov—whose private consciousness is so often and in such detail described for us, and whose feelings are apparently disclosed to us—an unexpected and important detail: he has used up only half of his fiancée's money, and the other half he has hidden in an amulet which hangs about his neck. Dmitri's intention to return the money to her constantly preoccupies him, for he sees in this act the only means to regain his honor. Thus a question naturally occurs to us: if this concern has preoccupied Dmitri's thoughts so much and so often, why is it that

16. Such a device may be used in a special function, for example, as a frame.

we, who have been thoroughly initiated into his state of mind, know nothing about it?

The apparent contradiction here may be explained as the result of the superposition of two different compositional aims in the narrative: the use of Dmitri's point of view (on the psychological plane), and the reorganization of information in order to withhold some details from the reader—so that a special effect may be produced when these details are revealed (an effect which is characteristic of the detective story).[17]

Both tendencies can be noted in everyday narration. The narrator, telling a story about events which he experienced, perhaps structures his narrative by simply recounting what he perceived and felt in the process of the events—or he may reorganize his narrative material and present it to his listener in a way which he feels may more effectively transmit the information.

CASE FOUR: CHANGING OF AUTHORIAL POSITIONS; THE SIMULTANEOUS USE OF DIFFERENT POSITIONS   Finally, the author can assume several points of view not sequentially but simultaneously, so that, for example, one scene is presented in several essentially different perspectives.[18] On the psychological level this multiplicity of points of view may be manifested in the copresence of several internal views, related to different participants in the action. In this case, we have the simultaneous description of the inner consciousness of several different people—a privilege which would not be available to any one external observer, or even to a sequential alternation of observers. In this narrative type, just as in the previous one, some or all of the characters who take part in the scene may be described from the inside, while the "extras" are described from the outside. In this case, the text of the narration may not be organically segmented, as it is in the sequential alternation of points of view, into separate units which are narrated from the different points of view. The narration as a whole here represents a synthesis, and not an aggregate. If the alternation of points of view (case three) may be compared to the use of different sources

17. Concerning the effective redistributions of information in story-telling, see L. S. Vygotskii, *Psikhologiia iskusstva* [The psychology of art] (Moscow, 1968), Chapter 7, where he applies this approach to Bunin's short story, "Legkoe dykhanie" [Gentle breath]. Vygotsky is interested primarily in the relationship between the sequence of events as they are narrated (in Russian Formalist criticism: the *siuzhet*) to the sequence of events as they actually occurred (in Russian Formalist criticism: the *fabula*); he studies the events in their real temporal sequence (in the reality created by the author) and then shows in what order the author has set them forth in his story.

18. Such a case could also be considered an instance of complex (combinatory) composition, arising as a result of the superposition of different compositional structures (see Chapter Five).

of light, each of which illuminates its own assigned space (in painting, for example), the simultaneous use of viewpoints (case four) may be compared to diffused illumination, a result of the use of several light sources at once.[19]

In this case, the describer does not directly take part in the action, but stands above it, in a position that enables him to see not only all of the action, but all of the feelings and experiences of the characters. We may say that the position of the author here is unreal, for he takes the point of view of an all-seeing and all-knowing observer. On the other hand, his position in many cases may be interpreted as retrospective: it is as if he narrates experiences which took place some time ago, and has since had time to puzzle things out *post factum,* and can reconstruct the internal state of the people, imagining what they must have experienced.[20]

This particular form of narration takes place in *The Brothers Karamazov.* In the chapter entitled "An Onion," the narration is carried out from several points of view, Alyosha's, Grushenka's, Rakitin's, and in the chapter "A Sudden Resolution," the viewpoint shifts among Dmitri, Fenya, the servant, and Piotr Ilich Perkhotin. The author's point of view here seems to be dispersed among a number of characters; it is as if he held a camera which moved confusedly from character to character.

This instance might be considered an occurrence of the sequential transference of point of view from one character to another discussed above. However, the alternations in sequence are here condensed and the tempo quickened to such an extent that the boundaries of the micro-descriptions, constructed from discrete, fixed points of view, are blurred, and the separate descriptions merge indistinguishably. The compositional rhythm of the work, with frequent transitions from one point of view to another, is accelerated, and, at least in Dostoevsky, there may be a correspondence between this rhythm and the inner state of the characters who are participating in the particular scene. Indeed, this type of narrative occurs often in the work of Dostoevsky at moments of great stress or crisis in the inner lives of the characters. For instance, the chapter entitled "An Onion" reflects an internal crisis in Alyosha after the death of Father Zossima as well as an internal crisis for Grushenka:

19. Both devices may correspond with devices used in representational art.

20. We already know, from our examination in the preceding chapter, that the retrospective narrative position is typical of both literature and everyday story-telling. Linguistically, this retrospection appears first of all in the use of the past tense, traditionally accepted in narrative (in a variety of languages); some languages even have a special narrative verb form related to the past: in French, the *passé simple,* in Hausa, the *suka,* and so forth. In Russian the form used is the imperfective aspect of the past tense.

the Pole, her former lover, arrives while her love for Dmitri is growing. The chapter "A Sudden Resolution" describes the crisis in Dmitri's consciousness: he has found out about Grushenka's departure, and, believing that he has killed the old servant Gregory, he decides to commit suicide.

Thus, this general synthetic point of view plays a definite functional role in the work of Dostoevsky.

The Possibilities of the Transformational Concept

Of the four different cases of narrative organization described above, the last three (in particular, those which are connected with internal point of view) may be obtained by combining more and more complex transformations of *Icherzählung*.

The second case, the consistently internal description of one particular person (while all the others are given through his perception), may be a straightforward case of *Icherzählung,* or it may be easily transformed into *Icherzählung* narration by the substitution of a first-person pronoun, of a personal name, or of a descriptive designation.

In the third case, the author's point of view may shift, and several different points of view may be used, but each fragment of the narration is consistently given from a single point of view, and the narrative thus divides into separate pieces, each of which is structured according to the patterns we found in the second case. Thus, in the final analysis this case again may be transformed into *Icherzählung*.

Finally, the last case is constructed, as we have said, of descriptions joined together, not sequentially, but synthetically, in the same way that the second case is constructed: however, separate descriptions (of the same scene), produced from different positions, seem to be indistinguishably merged together here.

Character Types: Internal and External Views

We shall exemplify three types of characters in terms of the concept of internal and external description.

First are those characters who never function as vehicles for the psychological point of view. They are never described from within, but always from the point of view of an external observer.

Second are the characters who are never described from the point of view of an external observer. In a description of these characters' inner life, the author never uses the modal expressions "as if," "apparently," and so forth. When we are attempting to define formally the type of a character in a narrative, it is important that we not consider the beginning and the end of the narrative, that is, the text which serves as the frame. This frame is often based on an external description of the character, whose internal description will be developed in the central part of the narrative.

Third are the characters who may be described in the work either from their own point of view or from the point of view of an observer. By virtue of this fact, such a character may act as a vehicle of authorial perception and as the object of it.

In different works, we may encounter different variations of these particular types. The author's choice of character type is generally determined by his compositional aims; for this reason, the definitions of character types may serve as distinctive features in the description of the composition of a particular literary work.

THE PROBLEM OF THE PSYCHOLOGICAL POINT OF VIEW
AS A PROBLEM OF AUTHORIAL KNOWLEDGE

The approach to the psychological point of view based on the presence or absence of *verba sentiendi* shows that formal analysis may be applied in this sphere, but by no means does it exhaust the possible manifestations of point of view on the psychological level. It is possible to make reference to a subjective consciousness without the use of *verba sentiendi*.

We have already cited an example in Dostoevsky's *The Idiot*: in the case of Rogozhin's attack on Myshkin, the internal point of view of Myshkin is established by the reference to a knife as a "flashing object" in Rogozhin's hand. A similar example occurs in *War and Peace*:

A week after his arrival, the young Polish count, Villarsky, whom Pierre knew very slightly in Petersburg society, came one evening into his room with the same official and ceremonious air with which Dolohov's second had called on him (p. 324).

Here, the clear reference to Pierre's consciousness is in no way connected with the use of verbs which refer to the internal state. For the reader, the association between Villarsky and Dolohov's second is meaningless, for he knows nothing about the appearance of Dolohov's second (Tolstoy does not describe him). The similarity is important only to Pierre himself: it is a personal association. What we have in this particular passage, then, is not so much a description of how Villarsky enters the room, but rather a description of associations in Pierre's consciousness. Consequently, this case must be attributed to the psychological plane.

If we want to generalize about all of the possible manifestations of point of view on the plane of psychology, we should perhaps give central place to the question of the author's knowledge and the sources of this knowledge. Does the author put himself into the position of a person who knows practically everything about the events he describes, or does he impose limitations on his knowledge? If his knowledge is limited, we must attempt to discover the conditions which impose those limitations. They may be brought about by the fact that the author has adopted the point of view of a particular character. But limitations of authorial knowledge may not be connected with the adoption of a certain character's point of view; then we must speak about a special narrator (stylized monologue such as *skaz* provides a typical instance of this situation).

On this question, G. A. Gukovsky writes: "The abstract all-embracing author takes for himself the privilege of knowing everything—what has happened to all of his characters, what they think, and how they feel; this privilege, or this claim to privilege, is one of the most serious and difficult problems in the study of literature, and raises the most difficult questions: what makes the omniscience of the author convincing for the reader and what is the objective ideational meaning of omniscience in the conception of reality itself." [21]

The problem of authorial knowledge is a central one in terms of psychological point of view, and in some cases may be relevant for the spatial and temporal point of view as well. It does not seem to be important, however, for the other levels that we have discussed.[22]

Specifica IN THE DISTINCTION OF POINTS OF VIEW ON THE PLANE OF PSYCHOLOGY

The distinction of points of view on the psychological level is important for different literary genres, except for drama. The text of a play is composed of direct speech, together with some authorial comments. On the stage we have only the character's actions and his words— his "objective" behavior. We may conjecture about the character's internal state only to the extent to which it is expressed in his objective behavior. (If we read the play, however, the psychological characteristics which are included in the author's comments become accessible to us.) Correspondingly, those actions in drama which belong by their nature to the subjective (internal) plane of behavior (and which may be established

---

21. G. A. Gukovskii, *Realizm Gogolia* [Realism in Gogol] (Moscow-Leningrad, 1959), p. 47.
22. Concerning the problem of conscious limitations imposed by the author upon his own knowledge of the narrative events, see Chapter Five, where the problem is treated on a larger scale—in connection with the author's general artistic conception.

only by means of a description from within) are necessarily translated, in the staging of the play, to the objective (external) plane; in other words, both planes merge in drama.

This is one of the determining factors in dramatic conventions. On the stage, the internal monologue cannot be distinguished from an ordinary monologue; when one character on-stage says something to himself, he must speak loudly enough for the audience to hear—while another character, even though he stands beside him, is conventionally supposed not to have heard it. Sometimes, however, we encounter in drama situations where a character speaks aloud to himself while another eavesdrops[23] (misusing the obligatory conventions of dramatic action). Both situations are clearly conventional and are caused by the concurrence (in ways specific to drama) of subjective and objective behavior.

23. For example, in Russian drama of the eighteenth century, see *Iudif'* in N. S. Tikhonravov, *Russkie dramaticheskie proizvedeniia, 1672–1725* [Russian dramatic works, 1672–1725] I (St. Petersburg, 1874), p. 159. Also see *Svad'ba Krechinskogo*, by A. V. Sukhovo-Kobylin (Act 1, sc. 12), where one character, Krechinsky, "thinks" (the word "thinks" appears in the author's stage directions), while another character, Nelkin, accidentally overhears him.

5 | THE INTERRELATIONS OF POINTS OF VIEW ON DIFFERENT LEVELS IN THE WORK

We devoted our preceding discussions to the different manifestations of points of view considered in terms of planes: in terms of ideological evaluation and phraseological characteristics, in terms of spatial-temporal perspective, and in terms of subjective-objective description—each on the corresponding plane. These different types of point of view, we have argued, constitute various positions from which the narration may be conducted.

In the simplest case, someone's point of view may manifest itself simultaneously on all planes, or at least on several planes. For example, in *Icherzählung*, the author may carry out the narration from his own position, without ever adopting someone else's point of view in any of the aspects we have mentioned (although this is not a necessary condition of *Icherzählung*).

Or, the author may assume the point of view of one of his characters in all the possible aspects. In this case the author would consistently describe the internal state of the viewpoint character, while all of the other characters would be described from the outside, as they are perceived by the viewpoint character. Thus the authorial position would fully concur with the position of the viewpoint character on the psychological plane. Also, the author would move through time and space together with this character, adopting his horizons—accordingly, the position of the author would concur with that of the character on the spatial-temporal plane. In describing what the character has seen and observed, the author would use the character's language—in the form of quasi-direct discourse, internal monologue, or in some other form; thus the author's position would also concur with the position of that particular character on the phraseological plane. Finally, the position of the author and that of the character can concur on the plane of ideology.

When, in our analysis of a work, points of view concur on different levels, the compositional structures of the different levels of this work also concur. This case would be considered trivial in terms of the possibilities of compositional options.

The concurrence of all points of view on different levels of analysis in one person, however common it may be, is not by any means obligatory, for the manifestation of someone's point of view on one level of analysis does not entail that it be manifested as belonging to the same person on any other level. Accordingly, in a single work complex compositional designs are formed when structures articulated on each level of analysis are different. Theoretically, it should be possible to discover laws which govern the interrelationships of various structures of the artistic work, articulated on different levels—that is, to discover in what ways one structure may determine another, and to what extent the structures may differ. At this point in our investigation of the subject, however, it is hardly possible to be specific about these laws, and we shall limit ourselves to a description and exemplification of possible types of nonconcurrences in viewpoint among different levels of analysis.

THE NONCONCURRENCE OF POINTS OF VIEW ARTICULATED IN THE WORK ON DIFFERENT LEVELS OF ANALYSIS

THE NONCONCURRENCE OF THE IDEOLOGICAL POINT OF VIEW AND OTHER POINTS OF VIEW

First of all, the point of view manifested on the level of ideology may be nonconcurrent with points of view manifested on other levels.

The Nonconcurrence of the Ideological
and the Phraseological Planes
The nonconcurrence of points of view on the phraseological and ideological levels takes place when the narration in a work is conducted from the phraseological point of view of a particular character, while the compositional aim of this work is to evaluate the character from some other point of view. Thus, on the level of phraseology a particular character emerges as the vehicle of the authorial point of view, while on the level of ideology he serves as its object.

The nonconcurrence of the phraseological and the ideological positions is characteristic of such stylized narration as *skaz* and is a typical device in the creation of irony.

For an example of this particular kind of nonconcurrence, let us turn to the following lines of authorial speech in *The Brothers Karamazov*, where Dostoevsky borrows the speech of one of his characters, a schoolboy named Kolya Krasotkin:

A report once spread at school that Krasotkin played horses with the little lodgers at home, prancing with his head on one side like a tracehorse. But Krasotkin haughtily parried this thrust, pointing out that, really, to play horses with boys of one's own age, boys of thirteen, would certainly be disgraceful "at this date," but that he did it for "the kids" because he loved them, and no one had a right to call him to account for his feelings (p. 654).

Here we have seen the most obvious case of the authorial use of someone else's speech; the author indicates definitely that Kolya Krasotkin's point of view has been used, a point of view manifested on the plane of phraseology; but at the same time, we find imprinted upon it the irony of the authorial attitude; thus Kolya Krasotkin's point of view emerges as a constituent element in a more general authorial point of view. The author associates himself with Kolya's phraseology, but not with his ideology: he speaks in Kolya's voice (using his phraseology in authorial speech) but from his own authorial position. In terms of the plane of ideology, Krasotkin functions not as the vehicle of the author's point of view, but, on the contrary, as the object of the author's evaluation. Thus, in terms of phraseology, the author incorporates himself with his character, while in terms of evaluation he "estranges" himself from the character.

A similar nonconcurrence of points of view—authorial estrangement on the evaluative plane brought together with an association in point of view on some other plane (phraseology, psychology, and so forth)— is most important in the creation of irony. Irony occurs when we speak from one point of view, but make an evaluation from another point of view; thus, for irony the nonconcurrence of point of view on the different levels is a necessary requirement.[1]

In his investigation of the use of reported speech in Dostoevsky's narration of "Nasty Story," Voloshinov comes to the conclusion that "almost every word in the narrative (what concerns its expressivity, its emotional coloring, its accentual position in the phrase) figures simul-

1. For another discussion of irony, see Chapter Six.

taneously in two intersecting contexts, two speech acts: in the speech of the author-narrator (ironic and mocking) and the speech of the hero (who is far removed from irony)." [2] We may observe in this case the nonconcurrence of the ideological and phraseological points of view, with the phraseological point of view subordinated to the ideological.

The dual function of any reported speech in general and of quasi-direct discourse in particular, on the phraseological plane and the ideological plane, may be explained by the dual nature of quasi-direct discourse—it is, as Voloshinov notes, speech within speech and at the same time speech about speech: "A message may be received as a certain particular ideational position of the speaker, and, in that case, by the agency of the indirect discourse construction, its exact referential makeup (what the speaker said) is transmitted analytically. . . . On the other hand, a message may be received and analytically transmitted as an expression characterizing not only the referent but also, or even more so, the speaker himself." [3]

The Nonconcurrence of the Ideological and the Psychological Planes

In our analysis of the psychological plane, we noted that the number of actors or characters described from within, rather than from without (that is, the number of characters from whose psychological point of view the narration in a particular work may be structured) is often limited. The author assumes the roles of some characters for a time, "existing" in them, describing the world through their perceptions; other characters interest him primarily in terms of an external perception.

In order to characterize a work, it is essential to determine whether there is a relation between the fact that a character's state of mind is open (accessible) or closed to our observation, and the author's ideological attitudes to that character—or, in other words, to determine the relationship between the "inner" and "outer" descriptions of characters and the distinction of characters as "sympathetic" or "unsympathetic."

Indeed, one may suppose that the description of the character from the outside or from the inside is conditioned by the author's attitude toward him: the author may take the point of view of a character whose

2. See V. Voloshinov, *Marksizm i filosofia iazyka* [Marxism and the philosophy of language] (Moscow, 1930), p. 161. [For an English translation see "Reported Speech," in Matejka and Pomorska, eds., *Readings in Russian Poetics: Formalist and Structuralist Views* (Cambridge: MIT Press, 1971), pp. 149–175.]

3. Voloshinov, 1971, pp. 162–163.

outlook he feels he can accept; the psychological state of another may be alien, even incomprehensible to him; perhaps he cannot identify with him even for a time. Consequently, the author presents the character exclusively from an external view without ever describing his state of mind. The author in this case may be compared to actors who cannot assume all roles, but only those with which they can associate their "I."

The position of the author in this case merges with that of the reader: the author assumes only the point of view of those characters with whom, according to the author's intention, the reader will identify.[4]

Thus, in this case, the differentiation between characters described on the psychological plane internally, and not externally, corresponds to their division into sympathetic or unsympathetic characters, and as a result, the psychological and the ideological points of view concur. (This concurrence is typical of Tolstoy.)

The concurrence of the ideological point of view and the psychological point of view is by no means obligatory, however, for in many cases the differentiation of the characters as sympathetic or unsympathetic, and their description from within or from an external point of view, do not correspond, but intersect, and the author may describe the inner states of both the sympathetic and the unsympathetic characters. (For example, in *The Brothers Karamazov,* Dostoevsky often presents a description of the inner state of Fyodor Pavlovich Karamazov.)

In this case the author's and the reader's positions diverge; the author deliberately assumes a particular point of view, knowing that the reader will not associate himself with that particular view.

THE NONCONCURRENCE OF THE SPATIAL AND TEMPORAL POINTS OF VIEW WITH OTHER POINTS OF VIEW

The Nonconcurrence of the Spatial and Temporal Points of View and the Psychological Point of View

The nonconcurrence of the spatial and temporal points of view with the psychological point of view (one of the more common forms of nonconcurrence) may appear, for example, when the vehicle for the temporal and spatial point of view, i.e. the character whose field of vision the author has borrowed, is not shown from within but from an external point of view, through the perception of some other observer. The vehicle of the psychological point of view, that is, the character

4. On the possibility of a difference between the author's and the reader's position, see Chapter Six.

whose perceptions the author has used in his description, may in turn
find himself within the field of vision of some other character.

We may use as our example a scene from *War and Peace*, the name-
day celebration of Countess Rostov and of Natasha. At one point,
Countess Rostov wants to speak alone with her friend, Anna Mihalovna
Drubetskoy, and she asks Vera, the eldest daughter, to leave. Vera rises
and goes to her room, and for a short period the author, and the reader
with him, become her companions. When Vera walks through the sitting room, the group of young people comes within her field of vision
and is described as she sees them (see *War and Peace*, p. 38). Thus for a
period of time we see the world from her perspective. Vera's perspective
is only spatial, however; the author does not adopt her perspective on
the psychological level or on any other level. The author accompanies
Vera, but he does not embody himself in her, as he often does in other
instances with other characters: each time he records Vera's perceptions,
he finds it necessary to distance himself from her by prefixing his observations with such words of estrangement as "evidently" and "apparently." Thus, Vera herself is presented through an external observer,
as are those whom she sees: the author assumes a place next to her but
he never adopts her system of perceptions. We may recall a similar
example from *War and Peace* when, throughout an entire scene, the
author follows Anatole Kuragin's spatial movements but never assumes
his psychological point of view (in the passage where Anatole attempts
to abduct Natasha, pp. 543 ff.).

A passage from Dostoevsky's *The Possessed* (Part II, Chapters 1 and
2, pp. 211 ff.) provides another example of nonconcurrence between the
spatial-temporal point of view and the psychological point of view. For
the most part, Dostoevsky presents Stavrogin from an alienated viewpoint as an enigma that we can resolve only toward the end of the
narrative; consequently, descriptions of Stavrogin's psychological state
are infrequent.

For example, in the narration of Stavrogin's journey at night through
the city, Stavrogin is almost exclusively described from the outside
through the eyes of an observer. The author constantly stresses the distancing: external signs of Stavrogin's behavior are described—the expressions on his face—but we almost never are told about his feelings
or his thoughts.[5]

The invisible observer (or the author's camera) from whose point of
view Stavrogin is described, and who is present, so to speak, even when

5. Some exceptions here may be disregarded.

Stavrogin is completely alone, seems to move along with him without ever becoming a part of him. We follow Stavrogin during his long night journey, seeing what he must have seen. The room he enters, the street along which he walks, are described as they must have presented themselves to Stavrogin. Actually, however, these surroundings are described not as Stavrogin sees them, but as an observer who has borrowed Stavrogin's spatial and temporal perspectives would have seen them. Here, for example, is the description of Captain Lebyadkin's room, as Stavrogin steps into it:

Nikolay Vsyevolodovitch looked around. The room was tiny and low-pitched. The furniture consisted only of the most essential articles, plain wooden chairs and a sofa, also newly made without covering or cushions. There were two tables of limewood; one by the sofa, and the other in the corner was covered with a tablecloth, laid with things over which a clean table-napkin had been thrown. And, indeed, the whole room was obviously kept extremely clean.
Captain Lebyadkin had not been drunk for eight days. His face looked bloated and yellow. His eyes looked uneasy, inquisitive, and obviously bewildered. It was only too evident that he did not know what tone he could adopt, and what line it would be most advantageous for him to take (pp. 265–266).

This detailed picture is not really transmitted through the eyes of Stavrogin; it is prompted by his observation of the room, but is hardly a result of his impressions of it.[6] In considering this scene, we should speak about Stavrogin's field of vision rather than his point of view. Stavrogin does not function here as a camera which views the scene, but rather as an object of our examination.

During the course of the events which surround this particular scene, Stavrogin moves into the field of perception of two characters—he is described by his mother (p. 206) and by Captain Lebyadkin (pp. 239–246). Although the spatial-temporal point of view belongs only to Stavrogin, on the psychological level Stavrogin may become the object of the points of view belonging to various characters.

The Nonconcurrence of the Spatial and Temporal Points of View
and the Phraseological Point of View
This case may be illustrated by another scene from *War and Peace*—

6. See also a similar example in V. Shklovskii, *Mater'ial i stil' v romane L'va Tolstogo 'Voina i Mir'* [Material and style in Tolstoy's *War and Peace*] (Moscow, n.d.), p. 197. Shklovsky suggests that although the description of the military council at Fili is given from the point of view of the peasant girl Malasha, there are details in the description that a child could not have captured.

the description of the relationship between Nikolay Rostov and Dolo-hov. During this scene, the spatial-temporal perspective belongs only to Nikolay (and in part the psychological point of view as well). On the phraseological plane, however, at one particular moment Nikolay's point of view is combined with that of Dolohov's mother:

Marya Ivanovna, who had taken a fancy to Rostov, seeing his attach-ment to her Fedya, often talked to him about her son (p. 300).

The use of the name "Fedya" (the mother's affectionate name for her son) indicates that the phraseological point of view belongs to the mother, to Marya Ivanovna—and she in fact uses this particular name in direct speech in a later passage. Thus Nikolay's point of view and the point of view of Dolohov's mother coexist in this passage.

THE COMBINATION OF POINTS OF VIEW
ON THE SAME LEVEL

As we have remarked earlier, different points of view, articulated on different levels of analysis, do not necessarily concur in a work; accordingly, the composition of such a work is characterized by the combination of several distinct compositional structures. When the narration as a whole is conducted with a simultaneous use of several points of view, related to one another in different ways, the result is a complex (combined) compositional structure, which, if we were to repre-sent it graphically, would be multidimensional. The points of view used during narration may enter into both syntagmatic or paradigmatic re-lations.

In other instances, the combination of different points of view takes place not on different levels of the work, but on the same level. In other words, the narration is produced directly from two or more differ-ent positions on the same plane; this phenomenon may be compared to the use of two sources of light—double-lighting—in painting, for ex-ample, in the works of the medieval masters, Rubens, and others.[7]

We are not talking now about changes in the authorial position (that is, about the author's shift from one point of view to another during the process of narration), but about the combination of points of view —that is, about the simultaneous use of several different positions. This

7. See L. F. Zhegin *Iazyk zhivopisnogo proizvedenia* [The language of a pictorial work] (Moscow, 1970).

instance occurs when there are several superimposed discrete compositional structures, articulated on the same level of analysis.[8]

Most common, perhaps, is the instance in which one of the points of view in the combination is that of a special narrator, either openly present in the narrative or concealed. This point of view may merge during the narration with the point of view of one character, and sometimes even with the point of view of another narrator. Thus, in the structuring of the work we have an instance of the combination (which may be persistent or intermittent) of the narrator's position with some other positions. There are many examples of this particular phenomenon in *War and Peace* and in Tolstoy in general.

The Combination of the Narrator's Position with Various Other Positions in the Narration of War and Peace

The narration in *War and Peace* is usually carried out simultaneously from at least two positions (later we shall see that in some instances, there may be more than two positions): from the point of view of one of the characters (Natasha, Prince Andrey, Pierre, and so forth); and also from the point of view of an observer or narrator who is inconspicuously present at the scene of the action. This observer (who seems to be relatively close to the author himself, but does not necessarily identify with him) assumes the role of a person who is well acquainted with the people about whom he speaks, who knows their former history, and often knows the motives behind their action. He may know things which are hidden from the consciousness of the characters themselves, since he may penetrate not only their consciousness but their subconscious as well. This narrator, however, is not an all-seeing observer with a gift of absolute insight, but simply a penetrating and intelligent human being,[9] with his own likes and dislikes, with his own human experiences,

8. Andrey Bely has made conscious use of this descriptive device. In analyzing (*post-factum*) the description of the child's illness in his autobiographical short story "Kotik Letaev," Bely writes: "The author pictures the interesting state of flashes of consciousness, generated during a high fever during a case of the measles; then there is a distinct moment of consciousness between the measles and the scarlet fever; then there is the feverish stage of the second illness; and after it the first glimpse of the bedroom by the child who has recovered from his illness." But having adopted the point of view of a small child who does not realize that he is ill and that what he feels is fever, the author tries to transmit the details of the child's feverish state through an adult consciousness, as it is echoed in his memory. See Andrei Belyi, *Na rubezhe dvukh stoletii* [On the borders of two centuries] (Moscow, 1931), p. 169.

9. The latter, however, is by no means a necessary quality of the narrator. In Tolstoy the narrator is usually more intelligent (or at least not less smart) than his characters; in Dostoevskii the narrator often maintains a lower (or equal) position, and as a result Dostoevskii's characters can be more shrewd and intelligent than their narrator.

and with the limited knowledge that is inherent to all human beings (although such limitations are not necessarily those of an author). The following description of Anatole Kuragin relates fairly clearly the psychological position of this narrator:

But Anatole was dumb and swung his leg, as he watched the princess' hair with a radiant face. It was clear that he could be silent with the same serenity for a very long while. "If anybody feels silence awkward, let him talk, but I don't care about it," his demeanor seemed to say. Moreover, in his manner to women, Anatole had that air, which does more than anything else to excite curiosity, awe, and even love in women, the air of supercilious consciousness of his own superiority. His manner seemed to say to them: "I know you, I know, but why trouble my head about you? You'd be pleased enough, of course!" Possibly he did not think this on meeting women (it is probable, indeed, that he did not, for he thought very little at any time), but that was the effect of his air and his manner (pp. 200–201).

On the one hand, the narrator assumes the position of an external observer who does not know for certain what Anatole thought and felt, but who can make assumptions to that effect (in this respect, the expressions of estrangement in the text are significant). On the other hand, although this narrator may not know for certain about Anatole's feelings at any particular moment, in general he knows Anatole fairly well —he knows him as a close acquaintance or a friend might know him; his reference to Anatole's behavior with women and his remark that Anatole does not think a great deal, bear witness to this familiarity. Finally, this particular narrator possesses his own personal experience; he tells us, for example, from his own point of view and not from the point of view of Anatole, about the kind of manner that fills women with "curiosity, awe, and even love." He conducts the narration not from some abstract or impersonal position, but from a fairly concrete human position.

Sometimes, however, this narrator steps aside and the narration then is carried on exclusively from the point of view of one of the characters—as if the narrator were not there at all. The episode of the breakup between Pierre and Ellen may serve as an example. The greater part of the description, which begins with the dinner given at the English club in honor of Bagration, is narrated from the point of view of Pierre, and occasionally the narration turns into Pierre's narrated monologue (see p. 283). The description from Pierre's point of view is interrupted only a few times by descriptions from other points of view: for example, by an external observer's "objective" viewpoint on Pierre or by a viewpoint belonging to Nikolay Rostov, whose attitude toward Pierre is one of ill-will and mockery. But the penetrating and knowing narrator is absent here; we know only as much about Ellen's affair with Dolohov as Pierre himself knows. Together with Pierre, we can only speculate about her faithlessness, and until the end, we know only the outer signs of this affair—for example, the existence of an anonymous letter, or the fact of Dolohov's provocative behavior, and so forth. Here, the narrator who knew so much in other situations has retreated behind the scene, leaving to the reader only Pierre's perceptions.[10]

In other instances, usually at the beginning of a new section of narrative,[11] the point of view in *War and Peace* definitely does not belong to any of the characters. But even though the characters themselves do not provide the viewpoint for the narration, the description is not simply an impersonal account, registering a series of objective facts about the behavior of the characters: from the description we learn about the subjective experiences and feelings of the characters, even about motivations which may have been hidden from the characters themselves; we may also learn how their behavior appears to someone; this "someone" may not be associated, however, with any of the participants in the action.

The narrator in *War and Peace*, then, plays the same part as a character; both may become the vehicles for the author's point of view: both possess a subjective perception.

Curiously enough, the narrator's perception may be at variance with the perception of a character, just as the impressions of two different witnesses to a single event may disagree. In this connection the scene in *War and Peace* which describes the execution of Vereshchagin is of particular interest. Tolstoy describes this scene from a distance, for the author has recourse here neither to the point of view of Count Rastopchin (whose viewpoint he had used previously—p. 828) nor to that

10. In literature, generally speaking, we may note two types of narrators, A and B. This typology does not depend on whether the narrator is a concealed one (where special analysis is needed to demonstrate who he is, as in the case of *War and Peace*) or an openly manifested narrator, who may speak from his own point of view and in the first person, as in *The Brothers Karamazov*. Type A is present fairly consistently during the whole action; if another point of view is used in the same narrative we have a combination of points of view, and a complex compositional structure is formed as a result. Type B is a narrator who frequently disappears, and in such narration the viewpoint may go from one character to another; also the narrator may reappear and speak from his point of view. The function of narrator B is the same as that of other characters in the given work.

11. This, of course, is connected with the function of the frame. See the discussion of this problem in Chapter Seven.

of any of the characters;[12] here Tolstoy uses an authorial point of view which clearly possesses a subjective perception.[13]

In this scene the narrator describes how Count Rastopchin, after the execution, rides in his carriage through the streets of the abandoned Moscow. The psychological point of view of Rastopchin himself is used, and his feelings of guilt for his part in the execution of Vereshchagin are presented to us in detail:

He seemed to be hearing now the sound of his own words: "Tear him to pieces, you shall answer for it to me!" (p. 834).

But in fact we may question whether Rastopchin did utter the words which now sound in his head.

Previously, the narrator has described in detail the execution scene for us, and reported everything that Rastopchin said—and these particular words were not spoken, although he did utter something similar. In any case, these words did not register in the perception of the narrator.

Thus, the perceptions of the narrator and of the character do not agree here, and this variation may serve as a testimony to the subjectivity of the perceptions of both the narrator and the character.

It is thus possible to talk about the presence of a special narrator in *War and Peace*, a narrator who is not clearly manifest, in the sense that he does not as a rule conduct the narration in his own voice. Compare this with Dostoevsky's *The Brothers Karamazov* or Gogol's *Evenings on a Farm near Dikanka*, where the narrator is clearly present, even if he does not take part in the action: sometimes he conducts the narration in his own voice, in the first person; and sometimes he retreats, and completely adopts the perception of one of the characters.

But more importantly, a careful investigation of *War and Peace* indicates that the narrator speaks from not just one, but at least two dis-

12. Indeed, each time in this scene the feelings of a character are spoken of, the author feels obliged to use "words of estrangement," operators which translate the action onto the plane of external description. For example, concerning Rastopchin: "Rastopchin looked about him . . . as though seeking someone" (p. 829). Also, " 'Ah,' called out Rastopchin, as if struck by some unexpected reminiscence" (p. 829). Concerning Vereshchagin: "He gazed at the crowd and, as though made hopeful by the expression he read on the faces there . . ." (p. 830).

13. The subjectivity of the authorial description may be seen, for example, in the following phrases: " 'Count!' . . . the timid and yet theatrical voice of *Vereshchagin* broke in" (p. 830); "Vereshchagin uttered a brief 'Ah!' of surprise, looking about him in alarm, as though he did not know what this was done to him for" (p. 830). The author describes this scene in the same way as a character would have described it.

tinct positions—or we could say that there are two different narrators.[14]

One narrator is the astute and intelligent observer about whom we spoke earlier: he is closely acquainted with the characters he describes; he knows their past (but not their future[15]); he is able to analyze their actions in the light of their conscious and subconscious motives; he has his own conceptualizations about life and history. There is no real reason to differentiate this narrator from the author of the digressions in *War and Peace*.

To question the source of this particular narrator's knowledge about a character would be essentially incorrect; that is, we are not justified in asking where and how he learned what he knows about the characters' conscious and subconscious states. When the question (which clearly lies outside the province of the issue under discussion) is raised at all, it might be answered by suggesting that those intimate facts are within his range of knowledge because he has "created" the characters. But while this answer may seem incorrect in the framework of our discussion, we want to emphasize here that the question itself should not even be asked. In other words, the position of this narrator is by no means the position of a direct, first-hand observer, but is rather that of a narrator who is one step removed from his characters, occupying an intrinsically different position, more general than that of the other characters.

There is yet another narrating position which is clearly defined in *War and Peace*, however: the position of the immediate observer who is present (although he remains unseen) in the scene which he describes, and who reports the action, synchronically, as it progresses. The narrator here must function under the same restrictions which control the characters in the work, and the limits of his knowledge are accordingly fixed by the same constraints that govern their knowledge.

Thus, on the temporal level, this second narrating position is defined as a synchronic position; the narrating position which we discussed before, on the other hand, is "panchronic." In general, the temporal and spatial position of the synchronic narrator has an immediate connection with the time and space of the events which he describes, while the "panchronic" narrator is removed to a broader and more abstract plane.

In more general terms, the synchronic narrator conducts his narration

---

14. Compare the several narrators singled out in the works of Gogol. See G. A. Gukovskii, *Realizm Gogolia* [Realism in Gogol] (Moscow-Leningrad, 1959), pp. 46–48, 51–52, 206, 222.

15. A narrator may occupy a temporal position from which he may hint not only at his knowledge of the past, but also at his knowledge of the future.

from inside the action he describes, while the "panchronic" narrator adopts a position external to the action. (For a typological analogy with painting, see the concluding chapter of this study.)

Both aforementioned narrating positions appear in the first scene in *War and Peace*, Anna Pavlovna Scherer's soirée. The description of the gathering is not presented from the point of view of any of the characters themselves.[16] The presence of a synchronic observer (whose position may or may not concur with the position of one of the participants in the action) becomes manifest a number of times in this scene by the use of words of estrangement ("evidently," "as if," etc.). For example:

"No, do you know that that boy is costing me forty thousand roubles a year?" he [Prince Vasily] said, evidently unable to restrain the gloomy current of his thoughts (p. 4).

But in the midst of these cares a special anxiety on Pierre's account could still be discerned in her [Anna Pavlovna] (p. 7).

The author could, of course, have simply remarked that Prince Vasily was incapable of restraining the current of his gloomy thoughts when speaking about Anatole, his son; he could easily have noted that Anna Pavlovna feared that Pierre might disgrace himself. However, the author finds it necessary (this is very significant) to assign these remarks to some other perception, as if he felt that he did not have the right to assert that these thoughts actually did take place (even if references to actuality seem out of place in view of our approach).

It is typical that the author has recourse to the same descriptive method even when there is no reason to question the feelings of the characters he is describing:

Evidently all the people in the drawing room were familiar figures to him, and more than that he [Prince Andrey] was obviously so sick of them that even to look at them and to listen to them was a weariness to him (p. 10).

The subsequent account of Andrey's behavior confirms us in our initial belief that it not only seems to be as the narrator has reported it, but it is so; the acquaintance with Prince Andrey which the author claims at other moments would seem to give him sufficient reason not to speculate about Andrey's feelings, but to describe them in quite definite terms. However, the author feels it necessary here, as he often does

16. With exceptions. Thus, at one moment traces of the point of view of Anna Pavlovna may be felt (pp. 9–10), at another moment those of the point of view of Pierre (p. 7); even these passages, however, could be attributed to an omniscient narrator.

elsewhere, to speak about those things which are evident by making reference to someone else's estranged impressions.

We are then, of course, prompted to ask whose impressions these are. Do they belong to one of the characters who participate in the action of the scene? This answer seems plausible, but here is another passage, from the conversation between Anna Pavlovna and Prince Vasily:

> *"Avant tout, dites-moi, comment vous allez, chère amie?* Relieve a friend's anxiety," he said, with no change of his voice and tone, in which indifference, and even irony, was perceptible through the veil of courtesy and sympathy (p. 1).

Whose subjective impressions are these? It is clear, of course, that they belong neither to the prince himself nor to Anna Pavlovna. Yet we know that the two are alone in the drawing room, and so we must conclude that these are the impressions of a first-hand observer who is invisibly present on the field of action.

Sometimes the author puts himself into the position of a narrator who not only describes his characters at the particular moment of the action, but who knows them well in general—that is, he places himself in the position of an all-knowing narrator. See, for example, in the same chapter of *War and Peace,* this description of Anna Pavlovna Scherer:

> Anna Pavlovna Scherer, in spite of her forty years, was on the contrary brimming over with excitement and impulsiveness. To be enthusiastic had become her pose in society, and at times even when she had, indeed, no inclination to be so, she was enthusiastic so as not to disappoint the expectations of those who knew her (p. 2).

This description does not come from Anna Pavlovna herself (she would scarcely think these things about herself), but neither does it come from any of those around her. This point of view belongs, rather, to a narrator whose position is essentially different from that of the direct observer. Here is another example:

> "Tell me," he [Prince Vasily] added, as though he had just recollected something, speaking with special nonchalance, though the question which he was about to ask was the chief motive of his visit: "is it true that *l'imperatrice mère* desires the appointment of Baron Funke as first secretary to the Vienna legation? He is a poor creature, it appears, that baron." Prince Vasily would have liked to see his son appointed to the post (p. 3).

The author here knows what only Prince Vasily may know; however, he speaks not from the point of view of Prince Vasily himself, but from the point of view of some observer external to Prince Vasily. Here again we have an instance of the narrator who knows his characters thoroughly; he not only portrays them at a given moment, but he knows everything about them in general.

The distinction of two narrators in *War and Peace* might appear artificial, and we might want to say that there is only one narrator who is fairly well acquainted with his characters, but who may want to limit himself sometimes and to adopt the position of a reporter, recording synchronically from the field of action. Indeed, in most cases we may interpret the narrator's remarks in this way. However, passages attributed to the narrator which cannot be consolidated into one authorial position are of particular interest; see, for example, this sentence from the same passage:

"Yes, do promise, promise, *Basile,*" Anna Mihalovna said, pursuing him with the smile of a coquettish girl, which must have been once characteristic of her but was now utterly incongruous with her careworn face (p. 13).

The phrase "must have been once" definitely shows that the narrator's knowledge about this particular character is limited, and indicates that the description in this particular case belongs to a direct, first-hand observer, an unseen participant in the action. This position is inconsistent with the unlimited knowledge about his character which the narrator has displayed previously.

Here is another example:

Anna Pavlovna's countenance showed signs on seeing Pierre of uneasiness and alarm, such as is shown at the sight of something too big and out of place (p. 6).

The author does not tell us here what Anna Pavlovna really felt. He wants to transmit the expression on Anna Pavlovna's face and resolves his problem by using expressions usual in situations like this one. He emerges at this moment not as an all-seeing observer, but as an ordinary person with a background of actual experience.

Tolstoy often emphasizes those restrictions and limitations of the narrator's knowledge which are typical of a first-hand synchronic observer (narrator). The following example is characteristic in this respect:

"Listen, dear Annette," said the prince, suddenly taking his companion's hand, and for some reason bending it downwards (p. 4).

Special emphasis upon the limitations of authorial knowledge may be seen in the following examples from *War and Peace*:

The little princess did not hear or did not want to hear his words (p. 88).

The face of Prince Andrey was very dreamy and tender. . . . Whether he felt dread at going to the war, or grief at forsaking his wife—or possibly something of both—he evidently did not care to be seen in that mood, for, catching the sound of footsteps in the outer room, he hastily unclasped his hands, stood at the table, as though engaged in fastening the cover of the case, and assumed his habitual calm and impenetrable expression (p. 90).

Either from awkwardness or intentionally—no one could have said which—he [Ippolit] did not remove his arms for a long while after the shawl had been put on, as it were, holding the young woman in his embrace (p. 18).

The two positions which the narrator takes in *War and Peace* are two distinct positions, yet they may coalesce during the narration, and either of the two positions may combine with the position of one of the characters. This results in a combined viewpoint formed on one level.

"Substituted" Point of View: An Instance of a Combination of the Points of View of the Narrator and of the Character

If we return to the example we discussed earlier, Anna Pavlovna's apparent reaction to Pierre's entrance into her salon, we can see that the narrator has substituted his psychological viewpoint for hers. He speaks not so much about what she actually felt, but rather about what he assumes that she must have been feeling. In other words, the narrator interprets the expression on Anna Pavlovna's face as if he were seeing through her (he puts into her those feelings and perceptions which he would have had in her place). At the same time this interpretation appears to be rather close to the fictional reality; it seems probable that these feelings correspond to what Anna Pavlovna felt.

This device is typical of Tolstoy. Here is another example:

The presence of Natasha—a woman, a lady, on horseback—excited the curiosity of the uncle's house-serfs to such a pitch that many of them went up to her, stared her in the face, and, unrestrained by her presence, made remarks about her, as though she were some prodigy on show, not a human being, and not capable of hearing and understanding what was said about her (p. 473).

Here the psychological position of the characters (the servants) merges with the narrator's psychological explanation and interpretation of their position.

We can consider this instance and those like it as the combination of two separate psychological points of view—here one belongs to the characters (the house-serfs) and the other to the narrator who interprets the feelings of the characters by substituting his own feelings for theirs.

This substitution process often takes place in those descriptions of a character's inner state where the author makes use of such expressions of estrangement as "evidently," "as if," and so forth. We have already noted that such words in general testify to the narrator's estranged or alienated position, which can also be identified with the position of an external observer. This estranged point of view may primarily be attributed to the narrator; however, it may also be intermittently combined with the viewpoint of one of the characters.

The following description of the hunting scene at Otradnoe is typical of the device of "substituted" viewpoint. The old uncle, Nikolay, and Natasha, ride to hunt; the uncle's dog is first to the kill:

The uncle himself twisted up the hare, flung him neatly and smartly across his horse's back, seeming to reproach them all by this gesture, and with an air of not caring to speak to anyone, he mounted his bay and rode away. All but he, dispirited and disappointed, rode on, and it was some time before they could recover their previous affectation of indifference (p. 472).

An authorial estrangement is clearly manifested here—that is, the narrator interprets the situation from his own openly estranged viewpoint, replacing to some degree the feelings of the characters with his own interpretations of their feelings. Actually, there seems to be no reason to think that the uncle is "reproaching" or "abusing" the others by his actions; the narrator simply interprets the characters' actions and manner in this way, attempting to communicate not so much their actual feelings as the way their behavior could have been perceived by a spectator who observed this scene.

Interestingly enough, however, we learn in the next paragraph that the viewpoint that we have been tracing here, the viewpoint of the distanced narrator, may be identified with the viewpoint of Nikolay, one of the participants in the action:

When the uncle rode up to Nikolay a good deal later, and addressed a remark to him, he felt flattered at the uncle's deigning to speak to him after what had happened (p. 473).

Here we can speak about an influence that the narrator's point of view exercises over the character's point of view (the narrator seems to attract the character's viewpoint to himself), and in the final account, about a special case of the combination of the narrator's point of view and the character's point of view.

The examples above indicate some combinatorial possibilities in the linking of different points of view on the psychological plane. A similar situation on the phraseological plane takes place in what we have called "substituted direct discourse"—that is, when the author speaks for his character, putting into his mouth the words which the character must have said in a particular situation. One example of this substitution is provided by a poem we mentioned earlier, Pushkin's *Prisoner of the Caucasus,* in which the author pronounces for one of his characters, a Cossack, a parting speech to his motherland. Here the author assumes the character's voice, and yet retains his own authorial voice; the two points of view concur on the phraseological plane. (For a discussion of this particular problem, see Chaper Two.)

Generally, the device under discussion, the combining of points of view by means of substituting the narrator's viewpoint for the character's viewpoint (on any level) should perhaps be designated as an instance of the "substituted" point of view. The substituted viewpoint may also appear on the ideological plane, when the evaluation from the point of view of the character is replaced by the evaluation from the position of the narrator.

And finally, in regard to the spatial and temporal planes, we can refer to a situation we commonly encounter: the description is attached to the spatial position of a particular character, and yet the narrator borrows horizons which are wider than those of the character. Thus, the narrator substitutes for the spatial point of view of a character, a point of view that the narrator would have had in his place.[17]

17. We might interpret in a similar way the example we offered earlier from *The Possessed*; however, we may note in this passage a nonconcurrence of the spatial and the psychological viewpoints.

6

SOME SPECIFIC COMPOSITIONAL PROBLEMS OF THE ARTISTIC TEXT

Until now, our aim has been to illustrate points of view on different levels and in different kinds of interrelationships; we have, however, deliberately avoided the discussion of some specific compositional possibilities which would have represented additional complexities. We shall now consider two of these problems.

THE DEPENDENCE OF POINT OF VIEW ON THE OBJECT OF DESCRIPTION

Previously, we examined the simpler and more general compositional organization of a text, in which the choice of the narrative position is dependent only upon the author of the narration.

There is, however, another possibility: the descriptive mode (and in particular the choice of point of view) may depend not only upon who is describing, but also upon what is being described. In other words, the point of view is determined not only by the describing subject (the author) but by the described object (which may be a particular character or a particular situation). Moreover, these typologically distinct descriptive modes, each characteristic of different works and of different authors, may coexist in one work, in applications to various objects of description.

In general, the behavior of a particular character in a literary work may be motivated either by his personal characteristics (that is, by what kind of person he is—by what he is) or by the context, by those situations in which he is found (that is, where he is).[1] Each type of motivation is

1. A. M. Piatigorskii and B. A. Uspenskii, "Personologicheskaia klassifikatsiia kak semioticheskaia problema" [Personological classification as a semiotic problem], *Trudy*

characteristic of different literary schools; there may be, however, a consolidation of these two types in one work. In the works of some writers (for example, Stendhal, Dickens, and Tolstoy), specific situations usually grow out of the personalities of the characters. The opposite tendency is illustrated in folklore, where the behavior of the character may be determined by the specific "place" in which he finds himself; here we may also include the works of those writers who have followed the traditions of folklore, such as Melnikov-Pechersky.[2]

The dependence of the author's point of view upon the object of description is best demonstrated by examples from the phraseological level. In our earlier discussion, we suggested that particular phraseological points of view are most readily apparent when personal names and appellations are used, for the naming of a character in authorial speech indicates which point of view the author (narrator) has adopted toward the character at that particular moment. But different modes of description may be applied to different characters in the same work. Some characters in a work may be described from several different points of view, while others are seen consistently from a single viewpoint. Here the descriptive mode is thus wholly dependent upon the object of the description.

Several illustrations of this principle may be found in *War and Peace*. If we exclude from our consideration the clear cases of quasi-direct discourse (that is, those instances when it is apparent from the immediate context which is the particular character whose point of view the author adopts in the authorial text), then it is not difficult to see that certain characters are named in a more or less uniform way throughout the novel (the character has the same name, or there are a limited number of variations on that name), while other characters are named in different ways.

Thus, Natasha Rostov is always "Natasha" (or "Natasha Rostov"). Nikolay, however, is called by several names in the authorial text: he may be referred to as "Nicolas," "Nikolenka," or "Nikolushka" (here,

---

po znakovym sistemam, III (Uch. zap. TGU, vyp. 198) (Tartu, 1967), pp. 17–18. The study provides a psychological interpretation of this particular problem.

2. See S. Iu. Nekliudov, "K voprosu o sviazi prostranstvenno-vremennykh otnoshenii s siuzhetnoi strukturoi v russkoi byline" [Spatial and temporal relations in the plot structure of the Russian bylina], *Tezisy dokladov vo Vtoroi letnei shkole po vtorichnym modeliruiushchim sistemam* (Tartu, 1966). Compare this with the approach of Iurii M. Lotman, "O poniatii geograficheskogo prostranstva v russkikh srednevekovykh tekstakh" [The concept of geographic space in Russian medieval texts], *Trudy po znakovym sistemam*, II (Uch. zap. TGU, vyp. 181) (Tartu, 1965), where Lotman discusses the connection between the change in moral status and the shift in space which is characteristic of the consciousness of medieval Russia.

the author apparently adopts the point of view of Nikolay's family); as "Rostov" (the point of view is that of Nikolay's comrades in the army and of his friends in society); as "the young count" (the point of view of his servants); and so forth. Sometimes the author describes Nikolay from an estranged viewpoint, as though the reader did not know him—for example, in the hunting scene at Otradnoe, Tolstoy calls him "a young hunter, Rostov," as if Nikolay had just been introduced to us for the first time. This estrangement of the character follows immediately after he has been called by a familiar name "Nikolushka" (p. 458).

We could say, then, that while Tolstoy describes Natasha from a fixed position (it is as if he refuses to adopt the point of view of any of the others, and sees and represents her from his own point of view), he describes Nikolay from many different points of view, showing him in different perspectives.

The dispersion of points of view (or the absence of that dispersion) is an important factor in the compositional organization of a text.

We can trace this same principle in the different possible manifestations of the phraseological point of view. In our earlier discussion of *War and Peace,* we noted that French speech (when it is spoken either by the French or by the Russian aristocracy) may be quoted in Russian and in French, and that this is connected to the authorial position in relation to the person who is being described (the character to whom the direct speech belongs). But the speech of some characters (Captain Rambal and Colonel Michault, for example) is consistently given in French; the position of the author in relation to these particular characters never changes. (We might conclude, therefore, that Rambal and Michault are interesting to the author only in terms of an external description [pp. 874–876].)

In the same way, quasi-direct discourse may be used by the author with more or less dependence upon the object of description. Thus, the linguistic characteristics which appear in the text may depend not only upon the particular person in whose voice the author speaks, but also upon the situation in which he speaks or about whom he speaks.

The dependence of descriptive devices upon their referent is generally characteristic of linguistic behavior and is not limited to the artistic text. In ordinary conversation, we can often observe the connections between different linguistic features (lexical, phonetic, and so on) and the object about which we speak. For example, when we speak about a child or about a matter related to children, we sometimes adopt an intonation with special phonetic features—this phenomenon is called literally "lisping" (*siusiukan'e*). We may even use a special grammar (characterized by special diminutive suffixes, which are optional in normal speech).

Another example occurs in Russian literary language: the pronunciation of the letter g in the words *Bog* (God) and *Gospodi* (Lord) is not plosive but fricative, a sound generally alien to the Russian language in its literary form; this relic of the traditional church pronunciation is now lost from Russian literary pronunciation and survives only in these two words, because of their special meaning. Thus, the object of the speech may define the specifics of language (the use of particular phonetic, grammatical, or lexical systems).

In literary texts, a similar dependence upon the object of the description may also be found on the ideological level. The fixed epithets of folklore, for example, often express the author's ideological point of view. But their use may be conditioned not so much by the author's attitude as by the object of description: a particular epithet may be required to appear each time some object is described or even mentioned. The fixed epithet here enters into the general pattern of the situation and of its etiquette which in epic and oral poetry is connected with the corresponding object of narration. As D. S. Likhachev has observed: "If a writer describes the behavior of a prince, he subordinates it to the standards of princely behavior; if he writes about a saint, he follows church etiquette; if he describes a campaign undertaken by the enemy of Russia, he subordinates it to the concepts of his time about an enemy of Russia. The military episodes he subordinates to military concepts, the everyday episodes to concepts about ordinary life, and the peacetime episodes in the life of a prince to the etiquette of the court, and so on." [3] The described situation originates, therefore, in the object of the description and defines and determines the ideological point of view of the author.

The same phenomenon occurs in a literary work of the nineteenth century: the different images of Alyosha Lokhmaty in Melnikov-Pechersky's epic novels *In the Forest* and *In the Mountains*. Alyosha's behavior and the author's evaluation of it are primarily determined not by his personal qualities, but by the situational context in which his actions take place. During the course of the narrative the author's attitude to Alyosha changes markedly, not so much because of changes in Alyosha himself (i.e. his personality) as because of the change in his place in life: he moves from country to city, from the position of a worker to that of a merchant, and so on.

3. D. S. Likhachev, *Poetika drevnerusskoi literatury* [Poetics of Old Russian literature] (Leningrad, 1967), p. 95. Concerning "the etiquette of the situation," see further, D. S. Likhachev, "Literaturnyi etiket russkogo srednevekov'ia" [Literary etiquette of the Russian Middle Ages], *Poetics* (Warsaw, 1961). Concerning fixed epithets, see A. N. Veselovskii, "Iz istorii epiteta" [From the history of the epithet], in *Istoricheskaia poetika* (Leningrad: 1940).

Tolstoy's treatment of Sonya in *War and Peace* is similar, for his attitude toward her changes as her situation changes. His relationship to Ellen, on the other hand, remains the same throughout the narrative and does not change even in the account of her death. Ellen's dying is described casually and with irony, as though Tolstoy were describing another of her tricks.

Thus in these examples the relationship toward the character is a function of the *"topos"* (in the broad sense of the term) in which he is shown; it does not depend immediately upon the describing subject but upon what is described.

In the same way, the spatial-temporal position of the author in relation to a character in the narrative may depend not only upon the general characteristics of a particular author, but upon the qualities of a particular character: some characters may be described from one definite position, and others from several different positions. The same is true on the psychological level.

A parallel in pictorial art is the system of representation in old icons, where the figures who are semantically more important are represented primarily as stationary, forming a stable center in relation to which the whole representation is organized; less important figures are represented in dynamic poses, and they are fixed in their relationship to the center. In other words, the more important figures are described from a well-defined and stable point of view, while the others are described from various more or less incidental points of view.[4]

Thus, different descriptive modes which, generally speaking, may be considered characteristic of a specific author, may sometimes be found in the same work when conditioned by the specifics of the represented material. Works of this kind are structured as if different objects of the narration were described by different authors—and consequently, according to different principles of narrative organization. Such cases may be treated as further complications of the elementary compositional possibilities which were discussed earlier.

POINTS OF VIEW: THE PRAGMATIC ASPECT

*The Nonconcurrence of the Positions of
the Author and Reader*

Earlier, speaking about the different points of view in a literary work and about the shifts in point of view which occur during a narration

4. See B. A. Uspenskij, "Per l'analisi semiotica delle antiche icon russe" (to be published).

(or a representation), we referred to the point of view of the author—that is, to the point of view of the one who carries out the description (or conducts the narration or constructs the representation). Usually, this point of view belongs simultaneously to the receiver of the description (the reader or the viewer), who joins with the author and assumes different points of view along with him. In most cases, then, to differentiate between the position of the describer (the author) and the position of the perceiver (the reader) is not necessary.

There are, however, cases in which these two positions do not concur, but where that nonconcurrence is deliberately planned by the author.

We are not talking now about the author's unsuccessful execution of the work—that is, when the positions of the author and reader do not coincide in spite of the author's intention, either because he fails to achieve his purpose or because the reader assumes a position which the author did not foresee. (These cases of nonconcurrence are more likely to occur when the reader and the author are culturally distant from one another.)

In our present discussion, we are concerned with the concurrence and nonconcurrence of the author's and reader's positions as intended by the author. This kind of nonconcurrence is found in various comic effects, and is particularly important in the creation of irony.

An example of irony based on the deliberate opposition of the points of view of author and reader is the following passage from Avvakum, accusing the icon painters who have begun to paint in a more modern style, following the reforms of Patriarch Nikon:

Spasi Bog su vam—vypravili vy u nikh morshchiny ikh u bednykh. Sami oni v zhivote svoem ne dogadalis' tak sdelat', kak vy ikh uchinili.

God will certainly bless you for having smoothed out the wrinkles in the faces of the poor saints. You made them look better than they actually looked in this life.[5]

Avvakum has deliberately adopted a point of view opposed to the one he intends his reader to adopt. The author has in effect assumed the role of a fool, putting himself in a position that he would never have assumed in reality. We could say that the author's position here is double; it might also be correct to say that in this instance the positions of the author and the reader diverge, because the author has deliberately taken on a role which is by no means his own.

5. From the conversation "Concerning outward wisdom," in *Zhitie protopopa Avvakuma, im samim napisannoe, i drugie ego sochineniia* [The life of the Archpriest Avvakum and other of his works, written by himself] (Moscow, 1959), p. 138.

Another example can be found in *War and Peace*, in the passage which describes the opinions in society about the divorce of Ellen and Pierre, and about her new marriage. Tolstoy writes:

There were, indeed, certain strait-laced people who could not rise to the high level of the subject, and saw in the project a desecration of the sanctity of marriage, but such persons were few in number, and they held their tongues (p. 781).

Clearly, Tolstoy does not speak in his own voice here. Adopting in this instance a new point of view, he departs from his usual position (which is not apparent here, but which can be easily deduced from the context) and from the position he intends the reader to adopt.

There are, of course, many similar examples. The intentional nonconcurrence of the reader's and the author's position is the basic technique of irony. Indeed, it is characteristic of irony that the author speaks or acts through an assumed character, yet that character appears as the object (not the subject) of evaluation. We have discussed earlier the effect of irony as an instance of nonconcurrence of the ideological point of view and some other point of view. Irony is thus a special case of authorial pretense, in opposition to the reader's "natural" position as defined by the author.[6]

The examples above are instances where the author changes his position for a time, after he and the reader have held identical positions; the reader, then, automatically retains the same position, while the author unexpectedly shifts from it. In other cases, the nonconcurrence of the positions of the author and the reader may be more extensive—it may be maintained throughout the narration. This technique is true of the *skaz*, for instance, and we can point to it in the short stories of Zoshchenko, where the person from whose point of view the story is told emerges simultaneously as the object of the reader's evaluation.[7]

In the examples we have discussed, the author's position shifts in respect to that of the reader. It is not difficult, however, to offer examples in which the reader's position changes in respect to that of the author. The shifting of the author's position is characteristic of irony; the shifting of the reader's position, on the other hand, is typical of the grotesque.

In Gogol's *The Inspector General*, for example, Khlestakov begins to tell lies, lies that soon reach almost cosmic proportions. We, as the

6. This is in accordance with the Greek etymology of the word: *eironeia*, literally, "dissimulation."

7. See also in this connection a somewhat different interpretation of Leskov's short story "Levsha" [The Lefthanded] by V. V. Vinogradov in his work, *O iazyke hhudozhestvennoi literatury* [The language of literature] (Moscow, 1959), pp. 123–130.

audience, have just become adapted to the conventional reality presented to us, when suddenly we are confronted by something which clearly exceeds the limits of the convention; as a consequence, the norm of our perceptions, our notions of probability and possibility, suddenly undergoes a change.[8] The shift which occurs in the point of view (in the evaluative system) of the reader testifies to a dynamic reader's position which conforms to the author's intentions.[9]

A similar shifting in the reader's position, an empirical adaptation to a norm which is alien to him, is common in various types of fantastic literature. It may also become apparent in the anecdote. Here, the reader at first perceives the events from one point of view, and then unexpectedly discovers that he should have been perceiving those events from an entirely different point of view—he discovers, that is, that the narrator had spoken from a different point of view than he had suspected. In these and other compositional designs, the shifting position of the perceiver with respect to the author's position seems to be characteristic of comedy.

The Semantics, Syntactics, and Pragmatics of Compositional Structure

If we apply to the study of the artistic work the division into syntactic, semantic, and pragmatic aspects of the semiotic phenomena, we can then discuss a work on three levels: the *semantic* level, on which we consider the relationship of the description (narration) to the described reality (the relationship of the representation to the represented); the *syntactic* level, on which we investigate the internal structural laws and regularities which govern the construction of the text; and the *pragmatic* level, on which we deal with the relations between the text and the audience for whom it is intended. We may speak, then, about the semantic, the syntactic, and the pragmatic aspects of *composition* of the artistic work (that is, in terms of point of view).

The semantics of the compositional structure examines the relation of point of view to the described reality, and, in particular, that distor-

8. V. V. Gippius has remarked that what is distorted in the grotesque is not the "reality," but some "norm." "Liudi i kukly v satire Saltykova" [People and puppets in Saltykov's satire], *Ot Pushkina do Bloka* (Moscow-Leningrad, 1966), p. 296. At the same time, the distortion of the norm is connected specifically with the shifting of point of view.

9. In similar situations the viewpoints of both author and reader undergo a change; here, however, the reader's view departs from that of the author, and we are still justified in considering the reader's point of view (in relation to the author's position) as a dynamic one.

tion of reality which is produced in its transmission through a particular point of view. Often the same reality (the same event) may be described from different points of view, each of which distorts reality in its own way. These different points of view may be mutually complementary, and when they are brought together they offer the reader a more nearly adequate image of the described reality. The organization of multiple points of view in a literary work with respect to the problem of adequate representation of the referent thus belongs to the semantic aspect of composition.

The pragmatics of compositional construction examines the composition of the work in connection with the audience, that is, with the person to whom the text is addressed. The compositional structure of a literary work may specifically foresee some responses on the part of the reader, in such a way that the reader's reactions enter into the author's calculations, as if the author were programming those responses into the work.[10] Particularly, as we have seen, the author may rely on a definite shift in the reader's position.[11] Various compositional relations between the author's and the reader's points of view occur first of all in terms of their relative horizons—that is, how informed they are about the events. The author may be presented as omniscient (he may have absolute knowledge about the events of the narration) while some circumstances may be hidden for a time from the reader, and the horizons of the characters may be even more strictly limited. In other cases, the author (the narrator) may intentionally impose constraints upon his own knowledge, so that he appears to be ignorant of facts which a character knows. The knowledge of the author (the narrator) may be deliberately restricted in comparison to that of the reader, and so forth.

The syntactics of the compositional structure examines the relationships

10. Here we are speaking about the pragmatic relations of a literary work only in terms of its compositional aspect. If we had to speak about the pragmatics of the artistic work in general, we would face the much larger problem of the classification of a work of art in terms of the reader's pragmatic relations to it (here, however, we might want to distinguish those relations which have or have not been foreseen). For example, we read some novels in order to find out "what happens" (sometimes this motivation is so strong that we may even read ahead to discover the ending); other works are read so that we may view an old problem in a new way; and so forth. Related to the question of pragmatics is the fact that while some works may be easily reread, others are read again with difficulty, or with less enjoyment. These are complex and specialized problems, however, and a discussion of them is not within the scope of this study.

11. For a discussion of pragmatic compositional relations in painting (the consideration of the positions and the movements of the spectator during the structuring of the representation), see my introduction to L. F. Zhegin, *Iazyk zhivopisnogo proizvedeniia* [The language of a pictorial work] (Moscow, 1970), p. 31.

of different points of view in the work, outside of any relation to the represented reality. Here we are concerned with such questions as the function of one or another point of view in the work—that is, the syntactic meaning (without reference to the depicted reality—the *denotatum* of the text) established within the boundaries of the work. It is primarily the syntactic aspect of composition which we examine in this study.

In terms of communication theory, we may treat the literary work as a message, the author as the sender and the reader as the receiver. Correspondingly, we can distinguish the point of view of the author (the sender) and the point of view of the reader (the receiver); we can also distinguish the point of view of a person whom the message describes (a character in the narrative).

Furthermore, some of these types of point of view may be combined in the narrative; for example, the position of the author and the reader, or the position of the author and one of the characters, may be consolidated in such a way that they cannot be distinguished.

If the position of the reader is external to the narrative (the reader necessarily sees the work from the outside), then the character holds primarily an internal view, while the position of the author may change. Thus, if the author adopts the point of view of the reader, the events will be described from the outside (from an alienated position); if the author adopts the point of view of a character, the events will be described from "within." (The problem of internal and external points of view are examined in Chapter Seven of our study.)

7

THE STRUCTURAL ISOMORPHISM OF VERBAL AND VISUAL ART

INTERNAL AND EXTERNAL POINTS OF VIEW

The Manifestation of Internal and External Points of View on Different Levels of Analysis in Literature

We have singled out several planes on which differentiations in point of view may be manifested. Our emphasis was on the particular ways (for the corresponding level of analysis) in which types of point of view reveal themselves on each individual plane. We have observed, meanwhile, that at least one set of oppositions in points of view is of a pervasive character, manifesting itself on all of the planes. This opposition has conditionally been designated as the opposition of the "external" and "internal" points of view: in the one case the author, during his narration, assumes a position which is deliberately external to the represented events (he seems to describe them from an outsider's point of view); in the other case, he may place himself in a position which is internal to the narration: specifically, he may adopt the point of view of a particular character taking part in the narrated events, or he may assume the position of an observer who does not participate in the events but who is present at the scene of action.

When the author's position is internal in respect to the action he is describing, his position may be either internal or external in respect to different characters. When the author has adopted the point of view of one of the characters, we may say that the character is described from within. However, if the author reports from the scene of action without placing himself in the position of a participant in the action, he is a non-involved observer whose point of view is necessarily external to the characters, although his viewpoint is still internal to the action he is describing. This instance may be illustrated by a passage from Bulgakov's *The Master and Margarita*. Ivan and the Master are holding a conversation in Ivan's cell of the insane asylum where he is an inmate. No one else is present during the conversation. The author tells us: "The visitor began to whisper into Ivan's ear so softly that only the poet [Ivan] could hear what he was saying, except for the first sentence." After this first sentence is reported, the description becomes noticeably estranged: the author describes the speaker's facial expressions and other external signs in his behavior. The speaker's words, however, do not reach us; the author (and together with him, the reader), it seems, is not able to hear them. It is then reported: "When all the noise outside had stopped, the visitor [the Master] pushed himself a little distance from Ivan and began to speak louder." [1] We, as readers, then hear the end of the Master's story.

The point of view which the author adopts here is that of an invisible observer who is present in the scene, but does not take part in it. This is a particularly clear manifestation of this type of point of view, which in other instances may be less evident.

The external point of view, as a compositional device, draws its significance from its affiliation with the phenomenon of *ostranenie*, or estrangement. The essence of this phenomenon resides primarily in the use of a new or estranged viewpoint on a familiar thing, when the artist "does not refer to a thing by its name, but describes it as if it had been seen for the first time—and in the case of an event, as if it were happening for the first time." [2] In the context of our approach, the device of estrangement may be understood as the adoption of a point of view of an outside observer, a position basically external to the things described.

In a narrative, external and internal points of view may appear, theoretically, on each of the given planes—and various complex compositional constructions may be realized by matching an internal description on one level with an external description of the same object on another level.

On the ideological plane, the person from whose point of view the described events are judged may be a direct participant in the action

---

1. M. Bulgakov, *Master i Margarita* [The Master and Margarita], (Moscow, 1966), p. 92. [See Michael Glenny's translation (New American Library, 1966), p. 148—Trans.]
2. See V. Shklovskii, "Iskusstvo kak priem" [Art as device], *Poetika. Sborniki po teorii poeticheskogo iazyka* (Petrograd, 1919), p. 106. The phenomenon of estrangement, includes in addition to the alienated point of view, another, closely connected device: the impeded form [*priem zatrudneniia formy*]. This device consists in heightening the difficulty of perception, and it is used in order to awake an active response in the perceiver, to compel him, in the process of the perception of the thing, to experience it in its essence.

(whether he is a major character or a secondary figure), or he may be a potential participant who, although he does not take part in the narrated events, seems to belong among the characters. In this case, the world (on the ideological plane) is described as if from within, rather than from without.

In other instances, the evaluation in a narrative may proceed from a position deliberately external to the narrated events—from the position of an author and not of a narrator. Here, the author is basically opposed to his characters; he is above them, not among them. This position of estrangement on the ideological level is typical of satire.[3]

On the plane of phraseology, the author's use of speech borrowed from a character (quasi-direct discourse or narrated monologue) indicates that the author has adopted a point of view internal to the character he is describing. The use of stylized narration such as *skaz* (in its pure form) indicates, on the other hand, that an internal view in respect to the described action has been adopted, although it is external to the characters who take part in that action.

The opposition of external and internal points of view on the phraseological plane is relevant not only in respect to the authorial speech, but also in the transmission of the direct speech of the characters. As we have shown previously, the naturalistic reproduction of foreign or ungrammatical speech can be an indication of the author's estrangement from the character (as in the reproduction of Denisov's speech in *War and Peace*); in other instances it can be indicative of an external position in relation to described action as a whole (the reproduction of French speech in *War and Peace* may be interpreted as an example of this instance).

The same opposition of the internal versus the external clearly emerges on the spatial-temporal plane. Specifically, in spatial characteristics, the concurrence of the position of the describer and the position of a particular character indicates the use of the internal point of view (in relation to the character); nonconcurring positions (for example, instances of the sequential survey, the silent scene, and the bird's-eye view) indicate

3. See the opposition of the medieval carnival humor and modern satire in M. Bakhtin's book *Tvorchestvo Fransua Rable i narodnaia kul'tura srednevekov'ia i Renessansa* [The work of François Rabelais and the popular culture of the Middle Ages and the Renaissance] (Moscow, 1965), p. 15. Bakhtin characterizes the folk humor of the Middle Ages as laughter directed at oneself (the one who laughs does not exclude himself from the world at which he laughs). Bakhtin sees in this a mark which distinguishes popular festive laughter of the Middle Ages from the "purely satirical laughter of the modern period" (negating laughter), where the one who laughs "stands outside of the phenomenon he ridicules, in opposition to it."

In general, concerning the internal point of view as characteristic of the medieval world view, and the external position as characteristic of the modern period, see below. [See also M. Bakhtin, *Rabelais and His Work* (Cambridge, 1968).—Trans.]

the use of an external point of view. In the same way, on the temporal plane the internal point of view is presented through the synchronization of the narrator's time and the time he is describing (he narrates as if he were in the participants' present time); the external point of view is represented by the retrospective position of the author (he reports what the characters do not yet know, as if he were conducting the narrative not from a viewpoint in their present, but from a viewpoint in their future).

On the psychological plane, as our earlier examination suggests, the opposition between the description from within and from without is particularly important. On this level, the author's position may only be external or internal in relation to a particular character, not in relation to the described action.

The Combination of Internal and External
Points of View on One Level of Analysis

In Chapter Five, we discussed the possibility of the combination of various points of view within a narrative, both on different levels of the work and on a single level. In the same way, we can now discuss the possibility of combining (on one or another level) descriptions from an external point of view with descriptions from an internal point of view. We will present this possibility in terms of the various planes.

THE IDEOLOGICAL PLANE   In analyzing the structure of Dostoevsky's work, Bakhtin, primarily concerned with the level of ideological evaluation, writes: "The consciousness of the character is presented as a different, *alien* consciousness, but at the same time it is not 'objectified' nor closed up; it does not become simply the object of the author's consciousness." [4] Bakhtin notes in Dostoevsky a combination of points of view, both internal and external to the particular character; these points of view are distinguishable solely on the ideological plane.

THE PSYCHOLOGICAL PLANE   A combination of the internal and external points of view may also be noted on the psychological plane. As we noted earlier in an example from *The Brothers Karamazov*, Dmitri's state of mind is described in detail for us, but we are not told about the subject of his greatest anxiety, about that to which his thoughts must constantly return. Indeed, we might say that two different points of view are combined in the description of Dmitri—the point of view from within (which

---

4. M. M. Bakhtin, *Problemy poetiki Dostoevskogo* [Problems of poetics in Dostoevsky] (Moscow, 1963), p. 7. [M. Bakhtin, *Problems of Dostoevsky's Poetics*, Ann Arbor, in press).—Trans.]

assumes a description of the character's inner state); and the point of view from without (which is that of an outside observer estranged from the character), the latter presupposing the absence of any description of the character's consciousness. This combination of points of view takes place throughout the novel, whenever Dmitri is described, but it is clearest at those moments when the two viewpoints conflict, when they start to contradict one another.

THE SPATIAL AND TEMPORAL PLANE   The combination of points of view which relate to time brings together a character's temporal position (his "present") with the temporal position of the narrator (who knows the further development of the events and who, in relation to the character, looks back at the events from the future). The description in this case is conducted simultaneously from both points of view, and may be considered an instance of the combination of the external and internal positions of the narrator (in relation to the events he describes), manifested on the level of spatial-temporal characteristics.

THE PHRASEOLOGICAL PLANE   The combination of the author's external and internal positions in respect to a particular character is exemplified on the phraseological plane by parallel descriptions; in such cases both the authorial speech and the speech marked by phraseological characteristics of an individual speaker are used. In *War and Peace* this is exemplified by a combination of the authorial speech with a speech referring to Napoleon's perceptions: "When he saw . . . the expanse of the steppes (*les steppes*). . . ." (p. 567). The combination of the external and the internal positions of the author in relation to the action rather than to a particular character is also exemplified in *War and Peace* by the description of the hunt at Otradnoe, which is carried out simultaneously on two planes: in the terminology of the hunt, and in neutral terminology.

External and Internal Viewing Positions in Pictorial Art

We have noted various possibilities for the manifestation of external and internal points of view in a literary text. A similar opposition is of no less significance in the structuring of the representation in pictorial art.

In Europe since the Renaissance, the artist has usually assumed a position external to the representation; in ancient and in medieval painting, however, the artist seemingly placed himself within the represented world which he then portrayed as being around him—not from an estranged or external viewpoint, but from a point of view internal to the representation.

Some ancient representations are clearly indicative of the artist's internal position in respect to the represented space. As an example, we might refer here to the landscape on one of the reliefs in the palace of Sennacherib in Nineveh (Assyria, eighth century B.C.). There the hills and trees on both sides of the river are represented as lying flat: on one side of the river the tops of the hills and the trees point upward, while on the other side they point downward.[5] No less characteristic are the representations of fortresses encountered in various cultural areas (for example, in Assyrian art), the towers of which are spread out flat and point from the center of the representation to its periphery: upwards, downwards, and to the sides (see Plate 5). This kind of representation must originate from the fact that the artist mentally placed himself in the center of the represented space.

In later art, particularly in medieval art, the use of an internal source of illumination is particularly characteristic in opposition to a shadowed foreground in the peripheral parts of the picture. The internal source of illumination corresponds to the internal positioning of the observer or artist with respect to a representation.[6]

The use of the internal or external point of view is manifested most importantly in the system of perspective chosen by the artist. Linear perspective portrays an object as it is perceived from the outside (from a fixed point of view external to the represented reality).[7] The picture is drawn as a view from a window might be drawn—with a necessary spatial barrier between the artist and the world he represents. Indeed, in Renaissance art theory, the painting is a "window into the open" (compare Alberti's *fenestra aperta* and Leonardo da Vinci's *pariete di vetro*). In the system of linear perspective, the point of view of the artist may be considered as corresponding to that of the spectator.

However, inverse perspective, a perspective system which is characteristic of both medieval and ancient art, supposes an internal position of

5. See further, N. D. Flittner, *Kul'tura i iskusstvo Dvurech'ia i sosednikh stran* [The culture and art of Mesopotamia and the neighboring lands] (Leningrad-Moscow, 1958), p. 260.

6. See L. F. Zhebin, *Iazyk zhivopisnogo proizvedeniia* [The language of a pictorial work] (Moscow, 1970), p. 60. [L. Žegin. *The Language of a Pictorial Work,* tr. by S. Rudy (The Hague and Paris: (Mouton, in press).—Trans.]

7. The principle of direct or linear (geometric) perspective in general presupposes some sort of imaginary transparent wall onto which is projected the viewed pattern (compare Dürer's well-known experiments in the construction of a mechanism for drawing in perspective). This imaginary wall signifies the inevitable barrier between the artist and the reality represented according to laws of direct perspective.

the artist, rather than an external one.[8] One of the typical features of inverse perspective is the diminution in size of the represented objects—not in proportion to their distance from the spectator (as in direct perspective), but in proportion to their proximity to him—so that the figures in the background of the painting are represented as being larger than those in the foreground. We may interpret this phenomenon by suggesting that in the system of inverse perspective the diminution in size of objects in the representation occurs not in relation to our point of view (the point of view of the spectator outside the painting) but with respect to the point of view of an abstract internal observer whom we may visualize as being located in the depth of the painting.[9]

In ancient painting we sometimes find the symbolic representation of an eye (see Plate 6), apparently unrelated to the general structure of the painting. This phenomenon is encountered in Egyptian art, Eastern art, and sometimes in medieval art; it has also been long preserved in the iconographic tradition.[10] The eye may symbolize the point of view of some abstract viewer within the painting, who might be identified, in some cases, as the Divine observer from whose position the image is presented.[11] In Japanese engravings we may note the representation of the eyelashes of a person looking at the world pictured within the engraving (a representation which symbolizes the point of view of an abstract spectator outside the painting).[12]

In some cases the internal and external viewing positions may conflict with one another. The medieval dispute about the representation of Peter and Paul in relation to Christ in Roman mosaics[13] could serve

8. See O. Wulff, "Die umgekehrte Perspecktive und die Niedersicht," *Kunstwissenschaftliche Beiträge A. Schmarsow gewidmet* (Leipzig, 1907). See also A. Crabar, "Plotin et les origines de l'esthétique médiévale," *Cahiers archéologiques* (1945) fasc. 1.

9. Miriam S. Bunim, *Space in Medieval Painting and the Forerunners of Perspective* (N.Y.: Columbia University Press, 1940).—Trans.

10. The phenomenon we have indicated was noted especially by P. A. Florensky, who treated it in one of his unpublished works; it was also noted by G. K. Chesterton in *St. Thomas Aquinas* (New York, 1933). Concerning the representation of eyes in Buddhist art, see E. S. Semeka, *Istoriia buddizma na Tseilone* [The history of Buddhism in Ceylon] (Moscow, 1969), p. 121, note 40.

11. In Russian iconographic art, even in the nineteenth century, it was habitual to draw on the icon the so-called great eye and on it to write the word "God." See I. F. Nil'skii, *Vzgliad raskol'nikov na nekotorye nashi obychai i na poriadki zhizni tserkovnoi, gosudarstvennoi, obshchestvennoi i domashnei* [The opinion of the schismatics about some of our customs and about the traditions of the life of the church, the nation, the society, and the home] (St. Petersburg, 1863), p. 9. Cited in *Khristianskoe chtenie*, Part II, 1863.

12. S. M. Eizenshtein, *Izbrannye proizvedeniia* [Collected works], vol. 3:516. I am grateful to V. V. Ivanov for calling my attention to this passage.

13. See M. Schapiro, "On Some Problems in the Semiotics of Visual Art: Field and Vehicle in Image Signs," *Semiotica* 1, no. 3 (1969): 233.

as an example of this conflict. It could not be determined whether Peter should be represented at the right side of Christ from the spectator's point of view or at the right of Christ in relation to Christ himself. This conflict apparently stems from the confrontation of two opposing artistic systems (one using an internal point of view and one using an external point of view), either of which may be employed in representation.

THE FRAME OF AN ARTISTIC TEXT

The Problem of the Frame in
Different Semiotic Spheres

The importance of the problem of the frame, that is, of the borders of the artistic work, is evident. In a work of art, whether it be a work of literature, a painting, or a work of some other art form, there is presented to us a special world, with its own space and time, its own ideological system, and its own standards of behavior. In relation to that world, we assume (at least in our first perceptions of it) the position of an alien spectator, which is necessarily external. Gradually, we enter into it, becoming more familiar with its standards, accustoming ourselves to it, until we begin to perceive this world as if from within, rather than from without. We, as readers or observers, now assume a point of view internal to the particular work. Then we are faced with the necessity of leaving that world and returning to our own point of view, the point of view from which we had to a large extent disengaged ourselves while we were experiencing (reading, seeing, and so forth) the artistic work.

The transition from the real world to the world of the representation is particularly significant as one of the phenomena in the creation of the "frame" of the artistic representation. Compositionally it is expressed in a definite alternation between description structured from within and description structured from without and in the transitions between them.

Before we turn to a discussion of the specifically compositional aspects of the problem of the frame, and to a description of the formal means of its expression in the artistic text in terms of point of view, we must first emphasize the general semiotic importance of framing. In this connection, the concepts of the "beginning" and the "ending" have a particular significance. Their importance becomes manifest in the formulation of systems of culture which we understand to be systems of the semiotic representation of the world view (or more precisely, systems relating social and personal experience). In some cultures the notion of "beginning" is marked, in others the "ending" (as in eschatological cultures); other cultures represent cyclical systems, and so forth.[14]

The relevance of the concepts of the "beginning" and the "ending" is apparent in such cultural texts as the worship service, for example. Here they are expressed by special ceremonies: the obligatory act of crossing oneself upon entering a Russian Orthodox church; or, for the Russian Old Believers—with their particular emphasis upon the beginning ritual —a complex series of bows upon entering the church. The significance attached by the Old Believers to the marking off of borders in the act of worship is expressed again in the reproach they addressed to the followers of Patriarch Nikon's reform of the Orthodox service for not emphasizing the beginning and the ending enough: "in church they have neither beginning nor end." [15]

In many instances, it seems to be psychologically necessary to mark out the boundaries between the world of everyday experience and a world which has special semantic significance. Thus in the theater the frame is expressed through such stage devices as footlights, curtain, and so forth. In some situations (often prompted by the desire to break down the frame of the artistic space), the actors may enter the auditorium, address the audience directly, or attempt in other ways to establish contact with the audience; nevertheless, the borders between the conventional (imaginary) world of the performance and the ordinary world remain inviolate. Sometimes the borders of the conventional artistic space may fluctuate, without, however, being entirely destroyed, as in the case of carnival or mystery plays where theatrical conventions expand into life.

Intrusion of art into life changes the borders of the artistic space without destroying them. These borders may be destroyed, however, in a fundamentally different situation: not in the intrusion of art into life, but in the intrusion of life into art—that is, in those cases where the audience, rather than the actor, attempts to break down the barriers of the artistic space and "enter" into the text of the artistic work, forcibly violating it. Some examples of this phenomenon are: the well-known attack upon Repin's painting, "Ivan the Terrible Killing his Son"; the murder by a medieval audience of an actor who played Judas (similar incidents occurred during the performances of Moslem religious plays); and the famous attempt of a New Orleans audience upon the life of an

14. See Iu. M. Lotman, "O modeliruiushchem znachenii poniatii 'kontsa' i 'nachala' v khudozhestvennykh tekstakh" [Concerning the modeling signification of the "end" and the "beginning" in artistic texts], *Tezisy dokladov vo Vtoroi letnei shkole po vtorichnym modeliruiushchim sistemam* (Tartu, 1966).

15. See the journal *Istina* [Truth] 59 (Pskov, 1878), p. 343.

actor who played Othello. We might also include among these examples attempts, well known in ethnology, to inflict harm by damaging a representation—and other corresponding acts.[16]

Efforts to violate the borders of the artistic space, generally speaking, seem to be motivated by an understandable desire to bring together, as closely as possible, the represented world and the real world, in order to achieve the greatest degree of verisimilitude—of realism—in the representation. Attempts to break down the frame are many:[17] the removal of the curtain in contemporary theater; the many cases in pictorial art where the representation extends beyond the frame;[18] and the overcoming of the borders of the artistic space and the joining of life and art, as expressed in the motif of the living portrait (a motif which is characteristic of the work of Wilde and Gogol).

Florensky writes in this connection: "Reality is described through symbols or images. Yet a symbol would cease to be a symbol and become, in our consciousness, a simple reality in its own right, without any relation to the thing symbolized, if the description of reality had as its object only reality: description must necessarily contain the symbolic nature of these very symbols; it must deliberately and consistently hold on to both the symbol and the thing symbolized. The description must be double. This duality is obtained through a critique of the symbols themselves. . . . It is appropriate to the artistic image that it possess the ultimate degree of incarnation, concreteness, and living truth, but the wise artist probably spends his greatest effort to keep his images, which have become symbols, from slipping from their pedestals of esthetic isolation and mixing with life, like elements which are homogeneous with it. The representations which extend beyond the frame, the naturalistic paintings so real that you are almost tempted to reach into them, the

16. See Iu. M. Lotman and B. A. Uspenskii, "Uslovnost' v iskusstve" [Conventionality in art], *Filosofskaia entsiklopediia* (Moscow, 1970), 5:287–288.

The attempts to discuss characters as real people are characteristic of the interpretations of the naive reader as well as of traditional criticism. See Iu. Tynianov, *Problema stikhotvornogo iazyka* [Problems in the language of poetry] (Moscow, 1965), p. 25. These attempts may to some degree be considered a violation of the frame of art and an expansion of life into art.

17. There is a tendency in twentieth-century art to introduce into the artistic text some concrete objects from the real world (for example, newspaper clippings in Cubist paintings, in the work of Braque and others); this tendency is carried to its extreme in pop art. In literature, the introduction of documentary newspaper reports (in Dos Passos, for instance), advertisements, announcements, and so forth play the same role.

18. In medieval and ancient art, especially in the miniature, the representation often extends beyond the formally designated borders of the artistic work; for example, a hand or a foot of a figure may protrude from the artistic space and be shown on the outside of the outlined frame.

onomatopoeic imitations of sounds in music, factualness in poetry—generally speaking, every substitution of art by a copy of life is an offense both against art and life." [19]

The Frame in Pictorial Art

The frame takes on special significance in painting, where it functions either as the immediate designation of the limits of the painting (as the actual frame), or as a special compositional form which structures the representation and invests it with symbolic meaning (that is, which gives to the work of art a semiotic quality characteristic of representational art in general). Here we might refer to G. K. Chesterton's remark that a landscape without a frame means almost nothing, but that it only requires the addition of some border (a frame, a window, an arch) to be perceived as a representation.[20] In order to perceive the world of the work of art as a sign system, it is necessary (although not always sufficient) to designate its borders: it is precisely these borders which create the representation. In many languages the meaning of the word "represent" is etymologically related to the meaning of the word "limit."

Even in those cases where the borders of the representation are not explicitly designated, the artist seems to regard them as naturally and inevitably present. This observation might enable us to understand why a primitive artist draws not on a clean surface but on top of another picture, without attempting to erase it, as if it does not occur to him that the first representation will be visible to the viewer. The artist here does not seem concerned that one representation might mix with another, primarily because he knows that the two cannot fuse: each possesses its own homogeneous artistic space.[21] In the same way, in Chinese art, the owner of a painting, or the artist himself, did not hesitate to write his comments or to affix a seal directly on the representation itself. If we remember that in China calligraphy and drawing were related arts,[22] then we can consider this instance as another superposition of two representations. The same may be said about the artist's placing of his signa-

19. See P. Florenskii, "Simvolicheskoe opisanie" [Symbolic description], *Feniks*, I (Moscow, 1922), 90–91.

20. See G. K. Chesterton, *Novyi Don Kikhot* [*The Return of Don Quixote*] (Moscow-Leningrad, 1928), p. 152.

21. In connection with similar representations see M. Schapiro, 1969, p. 223. Schapiro disagrees with the interpretation offered here, however, and suggests that there is evidence that the frame did not exist for the prehistoric artist.

22. See, for example, N. Popov-Tativa, "K voprosu o metode izucheniia kalligrafii i zhivopisi Dal'nego Vostoka" [Toward the question of the study of calligraphy and painting in the Far East], *Vostochnye Sborniki*, I (Moscow, 1924).

ture directly on the representation, as the European masters did,[23] and about handwriting exercises and various inscriptions that appeared on Old Russian manuscripts (even liturgical books), which paradoxically went hand in hand with elaborate decoration and in general with a special reverence for the book.[24]

The frame is an extremely important element of the artistic representation. It is particularly significant when the artist structures the representation from an internal position (which may become apparent in different aspects of the representation, particularly from the system of perspective used).

If a painting is structured from the point of view of an outside observer, as though it were a "view from a window," then the frame functions essentially to designate the boundaries of the representation. In this instance the artist's position concurs with that of the spectator. However, if the painting is structured from the point of view of an observer located within the represented space, then the function of the frame is to designate the transition from an external point of view to an internal point of view, and vice versa.[25] In this instance the position of the artist does not correlate with that of the viewer; it is, rather, opposed to it.

23. Schapiro, 1969, p. 225.

24. In old Russian church services (which we may judge here according to the practices of the Old Believers) remarks of a purely technical nature ("metaliturgical") which are not a part of the content of the service but deal only with its procedures (the direction "turn the page," for example) may be pronounced not in a whisper, but in a loud voice—precisely because they do not fundamentally violate the liturgical act, having no essential relationship to it. For the same reason, incorrect pronunciation was corrected aloud directly during the course of the worship service. The Old Believers even now practice this kind of correcting. See A. M. Selishchev, *Zabaikal'skie staroobriadtsy* [The Trans-Baikal Old Believers] (Irkutsk, 1920), p. 16; and B. A. Uspenskii, *Arkhaicheskaia sistema tserkovno-slavianskogo proiznosheniia* [The archaic system of church Slavic pronunciation] (Moscow, 1968), p. iii. The casual observer might react to such an "interruption" of the act of the service as he would react to the intrusion of stage directions into a performance; however, this is no interruption for someone who is concentrated on the content of the worship service itself. Similarly, in Japanese puppet theater, the puppeteers are not hidden from the spectator, but they are never noticed in the performance.

Similar conjectures can be made about the ancient liturgical act: individual moments of the liturgy—the robing of the bishop, for instance—became ritualized in the course of time and were incorporated into the structure of the liturgy as part of the ceremony.

25. For the same reason an ancient icon (in contrast to a modern painting) does not require a frame; the representation does not need formally outlined borders, because the foreground figures themselves make a natural frame for the picture. See V. Lazarev, "Vstupitel'naia stat'ia k al'bomu" [Introductory article to the album], in *SSSR: Drevnie russkie ikony*, UNESCO World Art Series (New York, 1958), p. 23. In ancient painting a part is not mechanically separated from the whole but is a space which is self-enclosed and independently organized within the frame.

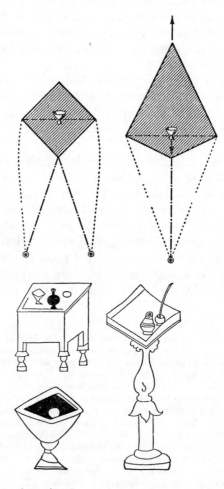

Examples of distortions in the system of inverse perspective: (a) separation of the viewing positions; (b) merging of the viewing positions: the far corner becomes an acute angle and moves "away from the viewer"; the nearest corner widens into an obtuse angle; the center is displaced "toward the viewer"; (c) objects situated in the center of the table are displaced "toward the viewer." (See Zhegin, 1970, pp. 44, 48.)—Trans.

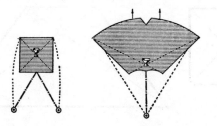

Example of distortions of rectangular objects in the system of inverse perspective: a straight line may become concave; a break in the concave line may occur in the rear part of the object (see Zhegin, 1970, pp. 44, 46)—Trans.

We may say that the frame of a painting (primarily, its real frame) belongs necessarily to the space of the external observer (that is, of the person who views the painting and who occupies a position external to the representation)—and not to that imaginary three-dimensional space represented in the painting.[26] When we mentally enter the imaginary space, we leave the frame behind, just as we no longer notice the wall on which the picture is hung; for that reason, the frame of a painting may possess its own independent decorative elements and ornamental representations. The frame is the borderline between the internal world of the representation and the world external to the representation.

When the artist structures his image from an internal point of view, the frame is created by the shift from the internal point of view, which structures the central part of the representation, to the external point of view, which structures the periphery. This shift may be realized in a picture in the alternation between forms in the central part, represented in inverse perspective, which is manifested by concave forms, and forms on the periphery, represented in "sharply converging" low-eye level perspective, which is manifested by convex forms.[27] We should remember that forms of low eye-level perspective may be understood as mirror images of forms of inverse perspective. Zhegin writes: "Forms of sharply-

26. Schapiro, 1969, p. 327.
27. See Zhegin, 1970, pp. 56–61. Also see L. F. Zhegin, "Nekotorye prostranstvennye formy v drevnerusskoi zhivopisi" [Some spatial forms in old Russian painting], *Drevnerusskoe iskusstvo: XVII Vek* (Moscow, 1964), pp. 185–186. See Wulff, 1902.

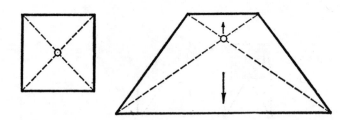

In the system of low eye-level perspective the center shifts "away from the viewer." (See Zhegin, 1970, p. 57.)—Trans.

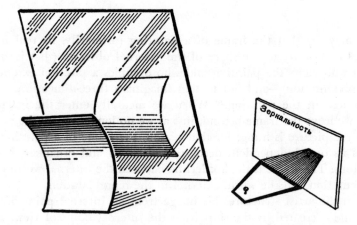

Forms of low eye-level perspective are the mirror image of forms in inverse perspective. Concavity appears in a mirror as convexity. (See Zhegin, 1970, pp. 59, 60.)—Trans.

converging perspective (the figures in the foreground frame, for example) are presented as an observer inside the painting (vis-à-vis us) sees them— 'from the reverse side,' so to speak. Because he must see the figures in the foreground as concave (in the inverse perspective), they are presented to us as being convex. . . . This 'mirror-ness' pertains only to the *system* in which the representation is interpreted, not to the representation itself. . . . As system, the foreground frame represents the mirror image

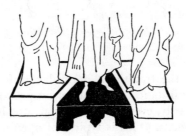

Horizontal alternations of forms in inverse perspective (on the sides) and low eye-level perspective (in the center). (See Zhegin, 1970, p. 60.)—Trans.

of the central plane." [28] In other words, the "closed" world of the image, presented from the point of view of someone within the work, appears to us, along the periphery of the represented space, from its reverse, external side.

The combination of the point of view of the internal viewer (located in the central part of the representation) and the point of view of the external viewer (on the periphery of the representation) is exemplified by the typical representation of a building in medieval painting: the interior is represented in the center of the picture, and the exterior is represented on the periphery. We can simultaneously see both the internal walls of a room, for example (in the main part of the painting), and the roof of the house to which this room belongs (in the upper part of the representation).[29]

The transition from the external to internal point of view and vice versa may be considered as a natural frame in a painting. The same phenomenon may be noted in a literary work.

---

28. Zhegin, 1970, pp. 59–60, 76.

29. On the contrary, in Japanese painting, with its characteristic use of the point of view of the external observer looking from above (which might be explained by the fact that the Japanese artist usually draws by putting the painting down on the floor, and not in the standing position characteristic of European art) the interior of a building is represented by removing the roof, rather than by taking off the front wall. See B. Vipper, *Problema i razvitie natiurmorta* [The problem and the development of still life] (Kazan', 1922), pp. 70–71; also C. Glaser, Die Raumdarstellung in der japanischen Malerei," *Monatshefte für Kunstwissenschaft* (1908).

The Shift from External to Internal Point of View as a
Formal Device for the Designation of the Frame of a Literary Work.
Traditional opening and closing formulae form natural frames in folk-lore or literature.[30]

When we turn to the traditional formulae which end the folk tale, we find that in many instances the first-person pronoun, the "I," appears here rather unexpectedly, even though no narrator has taken part in the action until this moment. (This is typical of opening formulae, as well.) The appearance of the narrator may be linked in some way to the action, but that link appears to be conventional.

See, for example, these popular formulae for a happy ending: *I ia tam byl, med-pivo pil, po usam teklo, da v rot ne popalo.* [And I was there, mead-beer I did drink, down the whiskers it ran, in the mouth it did not go.] Or: *A pri smerti ikh ostalsia ia, mudrets; a kogda umru, vsiaku rasskazu konets.* [And upon their death I remained, the wise man; and when I die, all the stories will be ended.]

It would seem that sentences like these must violate the whole preceding narrative by a paradoxical introduction of a narrator (the "I") who clearly could not have participated in an action which took place in the past, in a distant land. However, these sentences do not violate the narrative, but bring it to a conclusion; moreover, they are required to end the story—to provide a final transition from the internal point of view in the life of the tale to the external point of view belonging to the everyday world. (In connection with the shift from one system of perception to another, the shift from prose to rhyme in these concluding formulae is significant.)

The mention of a miracle, for example, is a typical beginning of a bylina. It usually appears only at the beginning of the narrative or at the beginning of a new section, and its use has a compositional function. Within the fantastic world of the bylina, or of the fairy-tale, the miracle would not be a surprising event, but an ordinary one. The unusual quality of a miracle may be conceived only from a point of view basically external to the narration, a point of view which may only be adopted at the beginning of a narrative (because from a point of view internal to the narrative any miracle belongs to the order of things). Here are two openings typical of Serbian epic poetry: *Bozhe pravyi, chudo-to kakoe!*

30. See their description (based on Slavic materials) in the study of J. Polivka, "Úvodní a závěrečné formule slovanských pohádek" [Entry and conclusion formulae of Slavic fairy tales], *Národopisný věstník československý* XX (Prague, 1927).

[Mighty God, what a miracle!] *Slushaite, pro chudo rasskazhu vam!* [Listen, I'll tell you about a miracle!][31]

We have presented examples from folklore, but the same principle is evident in literature. Thus, for example, it is typical for some narratives that a first-person narrator who did not appear earlier in the story suddenly appears at the end. In other cases, this first-person narrator appears only at the beginning of the story, and then disappears (like the narrator in Leskov's "A Lady Macbeth of the Mtsensk District"). In terms of content, the narrator here would seem completely superfluous; indeed, his function, unrelated to the plot of the narrative itself, is only to provide a frame for the story.

Exactly the same function may be attributed to the unexpected address to a second person which occurs at the end in some narrative forms—that is, an address to the reader, whose presence had been completely ignored until that moment. An example is the traditional dedications to the prince at the end of Villon's ballads.[32]

Addressing a second person at the end of the narrative is compositionally justified, in particular, in those cases when the narration itself is in the first person. Thus, both the intrusion of the first person (the narrator) and the intrusion of the second person (the reader) may have the same function: the representation of a point of view external to the narrative, which is presented for the most part from some other point of view.

The first-person narrator who appears at the end of a narrative has the same function as the self-portrait of the artist at the periphery of a painting and as the on-stage narrator in drama, who in some instances may represent the author. The function of the second person, representing the audience or a viewer, may be compared in some cases to that of the chorus in ancient drama, which represented the spectator for whom the action was performed. The author often finds it necessary to establish the position of a perceiver—to create an abstract subject from whose point of view the described events acquire a specific meaning (and become significant and, correspondingly, semiotic).[33]

31. See S. Iu. Nekliudov, "Chudo v byline" [The miracle in the bylina], *Trudy po znakovym sistemam,* IV (Uch. zap. TGU, vyp. 236) (Tartu, 1969), p. 158.

32. As an example from contemporary Russian poetry we might cite the passage at the end of Novella Matveeva's poem "Veter" [The Wind]: *a ty sidish' tikho"* [while you sit quietly].

33. In this respect the practical hints often given to beginning photographers are characteristic: the photograph of a landscape should have a foreground, allowing us to reconstruct the point of view of the subject-observer; it is also advisable to include in

The function of the frame becomes even more apparent when, at the end of the story, first-person narration shifts to third-person narration. This technique is used by Pushkin in *The Captain's Daughter,* where the main hero, Grinev, tells the story in the first person, and a "publisher," speaking about Grinev in the third person, presents the epilogue. The transition from the internal position to the external position in all preceding examples functions as the frame.

The significance of the frame in the perception of the artistic text becomes evident when we consider such characteristic devices as the pseudo-ending in narrative. What gives the feeling of cessation when the narrative is still to continue is the use of one of the formal compositional devices of framing in the middle of the narrative. In film comedies the effect of the pseudo-ending may be produced by the embrace of the lovers when they are rejoined after a separation, because the device of the happy ending has acquired the function of the frame, as it signals the cessation of action. The cessation of time is indeed part of the function of the frame. In literature this effect is produced through various ways of shifting to the external point of view, particularly when the shift in point of view is made irreversible by the plot: for example, when the dominant representative of the authorial point of view in the story dies. Death of the main hero is felt, as a rule, to be a sign of the ending of a work.

The phenomenon of framing—of alternation between a point of view internal to the narrative and a point of view external to the narrative—may be observed on different levels of an artistic work.

Thus, on the psychological plane, before the author adopts the perceptual point of view of a particular character, he first presents that character from the point of view of an external observer. The opening of Bunin's story "The Grammar of Love" may serve as an example of this technique: "A certain Ivlev rode once at the beginning of June to some remote corner of his country." Immediately after this sentence, in which Ivlev is described as a stranger, he becomes the vehicle of the authorial point of view; his thoughts and feelings are consistently described, and the whole world in general is presented through his per-

---

that foreground a human figure, usually off to one side, so that we can adopt his point of view. (The same principle is often applied in old landscape etchings. See Plate 7.) When these elements are missing, the landscape becomes impersonal, and because it cannot be attributed to any real point of view it may be uninteresting. Here we might also refer to the fundamental difference between our perception of a story which is entirely imaginary and our perception of a story about actual events: the latter makes real the position of the subject perceiving the events and therefore appears to hold more interest.

ceptions. The position of the external observer suddenly disappears; we forget about it in the same way as we forget about the frame when we look at a painting. But even more striking may be the transition from internal to external positioning at the end of the story, when the detailed description of the feelings of the character is unexpectedly replaced by a description of that character from the point of view of an outside observer—as if the reader had never been familiar with that character. (For an example see Jack London's "Love of Life.")

The same principle may be detected on the spatial-temporal plane. In terms of space, a point of view with a broad horizon (like a "bird's-eye view" or the narrator's position in a "silent scene"), which indicates an observer outside the action, is characteristically used in framing a narrative. Temporal framing may be realized by the use at the beginning of a narrative of the retrospective point of view and subsequently, as the narrative proceeds, of the synchronic point of view. In fact, the narrative often begins with hints about the denouement of the plot which has not yet begun; this indicates the use of a point of view external to the story, a point of view located in the future in respect to the time which unfolds within the narrative. Subsequently, the narrator may shift to an internal position, adopting, for example, the point of view of a particular character and assuming his limited knowledge about what is to come—so that the reader forgets about the predetermined course of events in the story, despite allusions to it made previously. Beginnings of this kind are common in narratives of different periods; as an example we may cite the Gospel of Luke, which begins from a retrospective position with a direct address to Theophilus.

The same phenomenon is also common in the epilogue, where a point of view synchronized with the time of a particular character may be replaced by an all-embracing temporal point of view. Acceleration (or condensation) of time related to the broadened temporal span of the ending of the narrative is also characteristic of the epilogue.[34]

Another closing device is the complete cessation of time. In this connection, D. S. Likhachev writes: "The tale ends with a statement that there are no more events to come: prosperity, death, marriage, feast. . . . Final prosperity is the end of fairy-tale time." [35] Similarly, the final, motionless scene of Gogol's *The Inspector General,* where all the characters are frozen in fixed poses, signifies the complete cessation of time and thus serves the function of a frame. It concurs with the Constable's

34. See D. S. Likhachev, *Poetika drevnerusskoi literatury* [Poetics of old Russian literature] (Moscow, 1967), p. 218.
35. Likhachev, 1967, pp. 232–233.

violation of the limits of the dramatic space when he addresses the audience: "Who are you laughing at?" (although the audience has never been acknowledged during the course of the play).[36] Both phenomena signal a transition from a point of view internal to the action to an external point of view.

Cessation of time brought about by the characters' freezing into poses is indicative in Gogol of the transformation from action into image, from living people to puppets.[37] It is also characteristic of the traditional Chinese theater, where at the end of an act the actors assume special poses to form a *tableau vivant*.

Fixation of time at the beginning of a narrative in Russian may also be realized by the use of the imperfective aspect of the past tense (in *verba dicendi*). In the first paragraphs of *War and Peace,* for example, the author introduces the dialogue between Anna Pavlovna Scherer and Prince Vasily by means of the imperfective: "Anna Pavlovna . . . was saying. . . . The prince, who had just appeared . . . was answering." The use of imperfective forms is succeeded in the next passage by the use of perfective forms. The same use of the imperfective can be found in the beginning of Gogol's *Taras Bulba* (in the dialogue between Taras Bulba and his wife, for example).

Framing may be realized on the plane of phraseology by the same principle. For instance, we may refer to G. A. Gukovsky's analysis of the function of the narrator in Gogol's *Evenings on a Farm near Dikanka*: "Rudyi Panko [the narrator—Trans.], a figure and a vehicle of the authorial speech, disappears from the text almost immediately after the introduction and reappears distinctly and in person very seldom—in fact, he appears again only in the introduction to 'St. John's Eve,' in the preface to the second volume of the collection, in the introduction to 'Ivan Fyodorovitch Shponka,' and finally, at the very end of the collection in a stylized list of errata." Therefore, Gukovsky concludes: "Rudyi Panko figures only in the frame of the book; he does

36. See Iu. M. Lotman, "Problema khudozhestvennogo prostranstva v proze Gogolia" [Problems of artistic space in the prose of Gogol], *Trudy po russkoi i slavianskoi filologii,* XI (Uch. zap. TGU, vyp. 209) (Tartu, 1968), p. 12, note 9.

An actor's addressing the audience, which signifies that he has stepped out from the limits of the stage space, is a formal ending device which commonly occurs in theater —for example, at the end of *The Minor,* a play by D. I. Fonvizin, Starodum points to Prostakova and says: "Here lie the fruits of bad mores!" This phrase, of course, is addressed to the audience more than to the characters of the comedy.

37. Concerning the significance of the puppet theater in Gogol, see V. V. Gippius, *Gogol* (Leningrad, 1924); concerning the significance of painting for Gogol, see Lotman, 1968.

not enter into the text of the stories." [38] Moreover, while the narrator Rudyi Panko functions as a frame for the whole of Gogol's *Evenings on a Farm near Dikanka* and only appears sporadically at the beginning of some stories, the individual stories are generally introduced from the point of view of another narrator, a vaguely romantic poet,[39] who is then replaced by a point of view internal to the narrative proper. Thus we may observe here the formation of frames within frames in a hierarchical order. Such a pattern can be found in various aspects of a work of art when the internal and the external authorial positions alternate in the formation of frames on the phraseological level.

Finally, the same principle may also be observed on the plane of ideological evaluation. Here, to give an example, it may account for the endings of Dostoevsky's novels which Bakhtin calls *"conventionally literary, conventionally monologue-style* endings," observing that in Dostoevsky there is "a peculiar conflict between the internal incompleteness of the characters and dialogue on the one hand and the external . . . completeness of each separate novel on the other." [40]

THE COMPOUND NATURE OF THE ARTISTIC TEXT

We have discussed how the frame of a work is created by a shift between the internal and external authorial positions. This principle of framing may apply not only to the whole narrative but also to parts of the work. These parts (microdescriptions) have their own organization, based on the same principles as the organization of a whole work —that is, each has its own internal composition and its own frame.

We noted, for example, that the fixation of time through the use of the imperfective aspect of the verb (*verba dicendi*) may serve as a framing device for a narrative. The same device of compositional framing may be adopted in order to isolate a part of the narrative and turn it into a relatively independent text. As an example of this use of the imperfective aspect, we might turn in *War and Peace* to the dinner-table scene at the Rostovs', when little Natasha is dared to ask, before the guests, what will be served for dessert:

"You don't dare to ask," her little brother *was saying* to Natasha, "And you won't ask!" "I will ask," Natasha *was answering* (p. 55).

Further on, Tolstoy returns to the use of the perfective:

38. G. A. Gukovskii, *Realizm Gogolia* [Realism in Gogol] (Moscow-Leningrad, 1959), p. 41.
39. Ibid., p. 40.
40. Bakhtin, 1963, pp. 55–56.

"Mama!" Her voice sounded down the whole length of the table (p. 55).

And so on throughout the passage. The imperfective form of the verb is used again, however, at the end of the scene:

"Well, what will it be: Marya Dmitryevna, what will it be?" she *was* almost *shrieking.* "I want to know!" (p. 56).

The same device for "stopping time" is used in a passage of *War and Peace* to end the description of Prince Andrey's country life:

"Mon cher," Princess Marya *would say,* coming in at such a moment, "Nikolushka cannot go out for a walk today; it is very cold."

"If it were hot," Prince Andrey *would answer* his sister with peculiar dryness on such occasions, "then he would go out with only his smock on . . ."

On such occasions Princess Marya *would think* what a chilling effect so much intellectual work had upon men (p. 390).

This use of the imperfective verb forms ("would say," "would answer"), which generally indicated repeated action, expresses the nonuniqueness of the scene, its typicality as it takes place over a period of time. As a result of this technique, temporal definiteness fades, and time, rather than being represented in sequentially developing actions, is cyclic. The use of the device of "stopping time" is typical in endings of narratives.

Parallel compositional organization of the whole work and of a relatively self-contained part of the work may be observed in other instances.

On the phraseological level, differences in naming may be used to mark transitions. Look, for example, at this sentence:

There was no formal betrothal and no announcement was made of the engagement of Bolkonsky and Natasha; Prince Andrey insisted upon that (p. 444).

After this passage, Andrey is once more referred to only as "Prince Andrey." The formal reference to "Bolkonsky" is a momentary transition to the external position for the sake of drawing a frame around a new part of the narrative.

Alternation between the internal and external positions of the author, realized in the alternation between the Russian and French speech in *War and Peace,* may now be understood and interpreted as a device similar to that of the unexpected transition to the voice of the narrator intruding in the middle of a narrative.

On the psychological plane the same purpose is achieved by transitions between external and internal point of view. This is realized through shifting from an external (objective) point of view to a description of the thoughts and feelings of a character (that is, the use of the character's own psychological point of view as opposed to some other point of view of him). We can turn to the scene where the wounded Prince Andrey lies on the battlefield after the Battle of Austerlitz; the representation of his state of mind, to which the whole chapter is devoted, is preceded by an exposition carried out from an external point of view:

Prince Andrey Bolonsky was lying on the hill of Pratzen, on the spot where he had fallen with the flagstaff in his hands. He was losing blood, and kept moaning a soft, plaintive, childish moan, of which he himself knew nothing (p. 265).

After this introductory sentence, the remainder of the scene is transmitted through the perceptions of the character. In exactly the same way, the description of Pierre's state of mind, when he is seated at the table in the English Club, is preceded by a section showing him from an external point of view:

But those who knew him well could see that some great change was taking place in him. . . . He seemed not to be seeing or hearing what was passing about him and to be thinking of some one thing (p. 283).

Sometimes the change from one character's internal point of view to that of another serves the same function. For example, the scene in *War and Peace* in the house of the old and dying Count Bezuhov is presented through Pierre's perceptions; however, before Pierre's point of view takes over, in the introductory passage to this scene, Anna Mihalovna Drubetskoy's perceptions are used:

Anna Mihalovna convinced herself that he was sleeping (p. 66).

Immediately we shift to Pierre's point of view:

Rousing himself, Pierre . . . began to think (p. 66).

In this instance the frame is created by the viewpoint of Anna Mihalovna Drubetskoy. Although this point of view is internal—a reference to someone's perception—and not external, as is usually the case in framing, it should be explained only functionally. Its function is to be different from the position of Pierre, which is central to the next section of the narrative. This instance may thus also be considered an example of framing created by the transition from an external point of view (with respect to Pierre) to an internal point of view.

Thus, the whole narrative text can be sequentially divided into an

aggregate of smaller and smaller microtexts, each framed by the alternation of the external and internal authorial positions.[41]

The same principle may be observed in the spatial organization of
pre-Renaissance painting, where the internal viewer's point of view
may be utilized.[42] Here, the space of the painting is a complex aggregate,
divided into discrete microspaces (Plate 8), each of which is organized
in the same way as the total space: each small space has its own peripheral
foreground constructed from the position of an external viewer, while
the central part of each microspace is organized from the position of an
internal observer (the viewer situated within the represented space).
This is manifested, for example, in the characteristic alternation of
forms of sharply converging low eye-level perspective and inverse perspectives. The low eye-level perspective appears, generally speaking, on
the periphery of the painting, while the representation itself is structured—from the point of view of an internal viewer—by the system of
inverse perspective. This alternation of viewpoints is also manifest in
the alternation of light and dark planes: an internal source of illumination is characteristic of the system of inverse perspective; consequently,
the shading takes place on the periphery of the picture. These alternations may take place horizontally or vertically, as well as in the depth
of the painting; they provide the "layered" appearance that is characteristic of the spatial system of ancient painting. This layered spatial
organization is exemplified in ancient painting by the system of representation of the so-called "icon hillocks" [ikonnye gorki]—the traditional
representation of landscape—and by the "overlapped" representations (of
angels, heavenly bodies, and so forth) when one part of the image is hidden behind the succeeding spatial layer.[43]

In literature the phenomenon of conjoining microdescriptions or
particular texts in a more general text is represented by a composition
employing a story within a story. The most obvious and simplest in-

41. With regard to the organization of time, in our study of this problem in Chapter
Three, we noticed a similar principle: time may be defined, in the work, in the form of
separate and discrete scenes, each of which is presented from the point of view of a
synchronic observer and is characterized by its own special microtime. When either
space or time is defined in this way, the frame is found at the seams of these separate
pieces, marking the transition between them.

42. Zhegin, 1970. This principle is represented in its most schematized form in
ancient Egyptian art. The spatial representation here is in the form of rows, arranged
one above another.

43. Zhegin, 1970, pp. 84–85. See also Zhegin, 1964; and Zhegin, "'Ikonnye gorki.'
Prostranstvenno-vremennoe edinstvo zhivopisnogo proizvedeniia" ["Icon hillocks": spa-
tial and temporal unity in a work of pictorial art], Trudy po znakovym sistemam, II
(Uch. zap. TGU, vyp. 181).

stance may be found in framed novellas and other clear-cut cases in which the change in narrator is presented explicitly, and the reader clearly perceives the borders between the separate stories. In other instances the microdescriptions may organically merge within the work. Here, the changes in the narrator's position are hidden from the reader; the borders between constituent parts of the text can be detected only by discovering the implicit framing devices (which, so to speak, constitute the internal seams of the work) as distinct from the compositional devices internal to each separate microdescription. In this case, the fused parts are inseparable, and the work does not naturally divide into its constituent parts.

A more complex composition is possible when different microdescriptions overlap one another. In this kind of composition the frames of the microtexts on one level (on the plane of phraseology, let us say) do not concur with the frames which are manifested on another level (for example, on the plane of spatial-temporal characteristics). A text which is organized in this way cannot be broken down into its constituent microdescriptions, although the separations may be defined in terms of each level. In the case of a story inserted within a story, the borders concur on all levels. In the same way, speech within speech may be inserted as a discrete unit in the form of direct discourse within a larger text, or, as in the case of quasi-direct discourse, speech within speech may merge organically with the whole text.

In the pictorial arts the same phenomenon may be described as representation within a representation. The hierarchy of the most primitive organizational form may be recognized in the placing of one picture within another. Linked series of small pictures (*kleima*) forming the frame of the icon or ancient linked fresco compositions are examples of this form.

The layered spatial organization of medieval painting is a more complex case. There, the separate representations of the microspaces organically and indivisibly merge into the general spatial representation of the painting—and the borders between the constituent microspaces can be apprehended only as internal compositional frames.

The special compositional function of the representation within a representation (and, in general, of the work within a work) will be discussed in the following section.

SOME PRINCIPLES OF BACKGROUND REPRESENTATION

Our observations concerning the composite nature of space in ancient painting indicate that the organization in each constituent microspace depends on the place and function of each microspace within the representation; thus, each microspace may have its own artistic system and its own principle of organization.

Thus the background in medieval painting is often presented in a different artistic system than the central part. The background, in contrast to the figures in the foreground or center, may be presented from a bird's-eye viewpoint, for example.

Here we might draw a direct parallel with literature. In literature the all-encompassing point of view from the seemingly elevated position of the observer contrasts compositionally with descriptions from specific points of view, which permit a more detailed description. Characteristically in both cases, the bird's-eye view appears in the periphery of the representation.[44]

We might also mention the characteristic alternation between "perspective" representations (following the rules of linear perspective) and "nonperspective" representations in order to oppose the various planes in a work of pictorial art (see Plates 9, 10, 11).[45] For example, in painting, a flat decorative background (represented in linear perspective) contrasting with three-dimensional figures in the central part gives the effect of live actors in front of painted scenery.[46] Note also the frequently used opposition of laconic gestures and frontality of representation in the foreground of a painting, and sharp foreshortening and baroque elements in the representation of the background figures, the "extras" (see Plate 12).[47]

In Renaissance art, the represented space is formed by a combination of several microspaces, each structured according to the laws of linear perspective with its own independent organization (that is, with its own

44. The background belongs to the periphery of the representation—see further about this below.

45. The characteristic representation of a building both in seventeenth-century Russian art and in Italian art of the late Middle Ages is the building shown with its front wall removed. The internal view is represented in perspective, and the result is a picture within a picture. See B. V. Mikhailovskii and B. I. Purishev, *Ocherki istorii drevnerusskoi monumental'noi zhivopisi so vtoroi poloviny XIV v. do nachala XVIII v.* [Essays on the history of old Russian monumental painting from the second half of the fourteenth century to the beginning of the eighteenth century] (Moscow-Leningrad, 1941), p. 121.

46. Here we might refer to those *quattrocento* nude figures which are in the foreground, on a background of architectural decor treated in linear perspective.

47. In this connection the main figures in an icon are presented frontally; the secondary figures may be presented in profile. See B. A. Uspenskii, "K sisteme peredachi izobrazheniia v russkoi ikonopisi" [Towards a system of transmission of the depicted object in Russian iconography], *Trudy po znakovym sistemam*, II (Uch. zap. TGU, vyp. 181) (Tartu, 1965).

horizon line).[48] The background space often has its own special frame—in the form of a doorway or a windowpane, exemplifying the concept of the painting as "a view through a window," which was current during the Renaissance. Several sequentially-arranged spatial layers may be found in a painting, each with its own special frame and perspective position.[49]

The background in a painting, therefore, can often be understood as a picture within a picture, an independent representation organized according to its own specific laws (Plates 14, 15, 16).

Moreover, background figures, more frequently than the peripheral foreground figures, are used for purely decorative purposes;[50] often what is represented in the background is not a world, but the scenery of a world. The background is not a representation, but a representation of a representation.

This phenomenon relates to the fact that in pre-Renaissance art the representation of the background is, as a part of the periphery of the picture, oriented toward an external point of view (that is, toward the

48. The line of the horizon may be defined as a line at the convergence of all parallel lines in the perspective representation.

49. As an example we might refer to Botticelli's *Annunciation* and to I. van Kleve's *The Adoration of the Magi*. See also *Madonna with Child and the Apostle Thomas*, by the master from Grossgmain (see Plate 13).

50. This fact might explain the curious phenomenon that occurs in the background and at the periphery of ancient paintings, where we find elements of an artistic system more advanced (in the evolutionary sense) than that used in the foreground. See M. Schapiro, "Style," in *Anthropology Today: An Encyclopedic Inventory* (Chicago, 1953), p. 293. In other words, when an artist represents a background or figures which have a generally auxiliary nature in a painting he may be ahead of his time: thus, for example, the background may be constructed according to the laws of linear perspective or to principles of the baroque (with the typical foreshortening and expressive facial expression) at a time when these artistic principles are not dominant in art. Forms in linear perspective and baroque forms are oriented toward the external spectator and depend directly on his spatial and temporal position (a fact which makes unavoidable the subjectivism implicit in this kind of representation); this orientation is, indeed, to be expected on the periphery of the painting.

We might add, in this connection, that the laws of direct perspective were known rather early (by the fifth century B.C.), but their application was limited to applied forms of art; first of all, they were used in the representation of theatrical scenery (the discovery of direct perspective in ancient Greece was related to the art of theater scenery (skēnographia). See P. A. Florenskii, "Obratnaia perspektiva" [Inverted perspective], *Trudy po znakovym sistemam*, III (Uch. zap. TGU, vyp. 198), pp. 385–386; and Flittner, 1958, pp. 175–176, where the representation in linear perspective on some of the Sumerian objects is explained by the fact that this representation belongs to applied art.

Conjectures have been made that in the Renaissance the application in painting of direct perspective was also originally connected with the theater (this connection is sometimes postulated with regard to Giotto's landscapes). In this connection see Uspensky, 1970, pp. 10–11.

position of an outside observer), while the central representation is oriented toward the internal point of view of a hypothetical observer placed in the center of the painting. In support of the argument that the background in ancient painting was represented from an external point of view, we may refer to a parallel phenomenon characteristic in Russian icons: here, the building in the interior of which the main action takes place serves as background, and is represented from the outside, never from the inside.[51] We will note in a later discussion that the devices of background representation and of framing are the same.

Here we might also refer to the purely decorative scenic backgrounds in Giotto's paintings, which A. Benoits spoke of as "stage-property" houses and pavilions and "flat, scenery-like rocks which look as though they were carved from cardboard,"[52] and to Tintoretto's and El Greco's backgrounds, which were painted from wax-figure models suspended from the ceiling. They all represent not reality itself, but a representation of reality.[53]

A "representation within a representation," in the majority of instances, is constructed in an artistic system which is different from the one applied in the rest of the painting. Thus, for example, the representation of the face in profile is characteristic of Mayan art (and of ancient Egyptian art); however, the representation of a mask or a sculpture (that is, the representation of a representation) may be given full-face. In Egyptian art, the treatment of the figure of a statue or a mummy is different from that of the figure of a living being. The representation of a living man's figure is a combination of profile and frontal views (that is, the figure is usually presented as being three-dimensional); a statue or mummy is presented only in profile (only in two-dimensional space).[54] In the same way, Russian art generally treats cer-

51. See Uspensky, 1965, p. 254.

52. A. Benua, *Istoriia zhivopisi* [A history of painting] (St. Petersburg, 1912), I, 1, 107–108.

53. Florenskii, 1967, 396–97; T. Kaptereva, *El Greco* (Moscow, 1965), pp. 5, 31.

54. A painting on a sarcophagus from Kerch, located in the Hermitage, represents the workshop of an Egyptian artist; see the reproduction in V. V. Pavlov, *Egipetskii portret I–IV vekov* [The Egyptian portrait from the first to the fourth centuries] (Moscow, 1967), plate 26. There we can see clearly the contrast between the profile representation of the artist and the *en face* (full-face) representation of the paintings on the wall. See also the explanation of the full-face representation of the Demon Bes in Egyptian art, where Bes' face was pictured as a mask. (See B. Vipper, 1922, p. 61, note 2, p. 64, note 3.)

We may assume that the portrait *en face* in Egyptian art was originally connected wtih the representation of the funeral mask (which is a representation of a representation) and not directly of a human being. Indeed, the portrait originally functioned in Egypt as a replacement for the funeral mask; the portrait was placed upon the mummy-like

tain figures in profile—for example, a live horse is usually represented by a stylized profile flattened against a plane. However, when the statue of a horse is represented, this rule is violated (see the full-face representation of the statue of Justinian's horse on the sixteenth-century Novgorod icon of Pokrov).[55] In all these cases, the representation of the representation of the object is indirectly opposed in its treatment to that of the representation of the object itself.

Thus the background and, generally, the periphery of a painting are treated in some special way, as a representation within a representation. This fact permits us to recognize formally the figures which belong to the background of a painting (that is, various secondary figures who play the role of "extras").[56]

In the same way, in literature "extras" who appear, so to speak, in the background of the narrative are usually represented through compositional devices which are in opposition to those used to describe the main characters. The latter may serve as vehicles for the author's point of

---

mask, and for a long time both were used interchangeably. (See Pavlov, 1967, p. 46); in this connection, we can consider also those works which investigate the genetic relationship of the portrait and the representation of the magic double. It is possible that originally the funeral mask was copied, and that in later times the *en face* representation was separated from the mummy and came to have an independent function.

The evolution of the still life may be similar to the process outlined above. The representation of whole objects may be observed first in the art of the Bronze Age, in the form of weapons represented on sarcophagi and sacral monuments—serving as substitutes for the real weapons, which had been placed on the covers of the coffins (see Vipper, 1922, p. 53, note 1).

It is interesting that in paintings on Greek vases figures are generally represented in profile, but the figures of corpses may appear noticeably foreshortened and *en face* (see Vipper, 1922, pp. 61, 94–95; see also p. 95, note 1, concerning foreshortening in relation to the representation of the dead body in Egyptian art, also concerning the studies of Uccello and Mantegna in representing dead bodies. In semantic terms, the dead body seems related in the artist's consciousness to the background—and it was therefore represented according to the rules for the representation of the background. This brings up the question of the still life (or *nature morte*) and its connection with the problem of the representation within a representation. See also V. K. Malm'berg, *Staryi predrassudok: K voprosu ob izobrazhenii chelovecheskoi figury v egipetskom rel'efe* [An old prejudice: toward the question of the representation of the human figure in Egyptian relief] (Moscow, 1915), pp. 15–16, esp. note 38.

As Vipper has remarked (1922, pp. 60–61), corpses are represented in Egyptian art by the same devices that are used to represent statues (see the preceding note).

55. See A. I. Nekrasov, "O iavleniiakh rakursa v drevnerusskoi zhivopisi" [Foreshortening in Russian medieval art] *Trudy otdeleniia iskusstvoznaniia Instituta arkheologii i iskusstvozaniia RANIION,* I (Moscow, 1926).

56. The relation between background (scenery) and "extras" in the dramatic performance may be observed in the change of stage setting in Shakespearean theater: the actors who played the minor parts carried the stage properties on and off stage. See A. Anikst, *Teatr epokhi Shekspira* [Theater in the time of Shakespeare] (Moscow, 1965), p. 146. Compare the similar function of the uniformed men who help with the scenery in the contemporary circus.

view (in one aspect or another), but the extras, generally speaking, do not have this function, and their behavior is usually presented through an accentuated external point of view. In the most characteristic of these cases, the extras are described not as people but as puppets—another example of the representation within the representation that we noticed in painting.[57]

An example of this technique is found in Kafka's description of the boarders in *The Metamorphosis*. These characters are typical extras; they always appear in the background of the action. They are puppet-like, as is immediately evident from the marked automatization of their behavior. They behave in exactly the same way; they always appear at the same time, and in the same order (one of them is called "the man in the middle" as if they never changed their relative positions); their motions are automatic. Most of the time, only their gestures are described; when they speak, only one ("the man in the middle") utters the words for all of them. We might say that Kafka's boarders are presented as a single three-part mechanism, as three puppets on the same string, controlled by one actor.

A similar kind of description of automatized behavior among the background figures in *War and Peace* is represented by two puppetlike characters who seem to be connected according to the same principle as communicating vessels in physics. This is the description of a woman whom Nikolay courts in Voronezh, and of her husband:

Towards the end of the evening, however, as the wife's face grew more flushed and animated, the husband's grew steadily more melancholy and solid, as though they had a given allowance of liveliness between them, and as the wife's increased, the husband's dwindled (p. 880).

Another illustration of the same principle may be found in the beginning of *War and Peace,* at Anna Pavlovna Scherer's soiree, where the automatic behavior of the background characters is emphasized by the author's comparing them to spindles in a spinning mill (p. 7).

Even more characteristic is the description of the crowd in Dostoevsky's "The Diary of a Writer": "Someone was making faces in front of me, hiding behind this fantastic crowd and pulling some sort of string, working a spring, which made the puppets move—while he laughed and laughed" (From "Petersburg Dreams in Verse and Prose," 1861).

57. In general, concerning the representation of the characters as puppets, irrespective of their functions in the particular work, see V. V. Gippius," Liudi i kukly v satire Saltykova" [People and puppets in the satire of Saltykov], in his book *Ot Pushkina do Bloka* (Moscow-Leningrad, 1966).

In *Crime and Punishment,* Dostoevsky describes the Kapernaumov family, who rent the room to Sonia Marmeladov, in much the same way —as puppets. The Kapernaumovs are typical extras: we do not hear them speak at all. For example, Svidrigailov's conversation with Madame Kapernaumov is presented as if it were a telephone conversation:

You see, that's the way to Sofya Semyonovna. Look, there is no one at home. Don't you believe me? Ask Kapernaumov: she leaves the key with them. Here is Madame de Kapernaumov herself. Hey, what? She is rather deaf. Has she gone out? Where? Did you hear? She is not in and won't be till late in the evening probably.[58]

Svidrigailov speaks to Madame Kapernaumov and answers for her just as one might speak to a puppet.

Finally, characters can often be divided into groups: those who can move about freely; and those who remain stationary, who cannot change their environment, but are bound to a particular place. The roles of the mobile characters are commonly played by the central figures of the narrative, while the stationary characters are usually secondary figures.[59] Thus, the extras may be bound to a particular environment; the description of the extras forms an integral part of the description of the background. A typologically similar principle may also be noted in theater.[60]

The same tendency toward stereotyping which increases in the background of a narrative may also appear in the naming of the minor characters. So, for example, in the story of Katerina Ivanovna, in Dostoevsky's *Crime and Punishment,* we find such grotesque and improbable surnames as Princess Bezzemelnaya [Landless] and Prince Schegolskoy [Dandy], even though the surnames of other characters in this novel are

58. Fyodor Dostoevsky, *Crime and Punishment,* trans. Constance Garnett (New York: Bantam Books, 1958), part 6: chapter 5, p. 418—Trans.
59. See S. Iu. Nekliudov, "K voprosu o sviazi prostranstvenno-vremennykh otnoshenii s siuzhetnoi strukturoi v russkoi byline," [The connections between the spatial-temporal relationships and the structure of the plot in the Russian byliny], *Tezisy dokladov vo Vtoroi letnei shkole po vtorichnym modeliruiushchim sistemam* (Tartu, 1966), p. 42; and Iu. M. Lotman, "O metaiazyke tipologicheskikh opisanii kul'tury" [The metalanguage of typological descriptions of culture], *Trudy po znakovym sistemam,* IV, (Uch. zap. TGU, vyp. 236) (Tartu, 1969), 464.
60. It is characteristic in older drama that elements of pantomime appear in the background and also that conventionality markedly increases in the representation of a play within a play. See F. S. Boas, "The Play within the Play," in his book *A Series of Papers on Shakespeare and the Theater,* 1927. The same phenomenon is manifest in ancient theater in the use of masks only for the actors who play character roles: the old man, the rogue, and so forth. (This may be inferred from the representation of theatrical presentation in Pompeian painting and from the illustrations in some manuscripts of Terence.)

realistic. Here we have a sharp change in descriptive principles: from realistic description to stereotypic description. What is essential is that the story told by Katerina Ivanovna is a narrative within a narrative, and the characters who appear in it do not take part in the main action of the book. They do not "really" exist in the narrative which forms the foreground. Accordingly, they are presented by means of devices belonging to the representation within a representation.

This tendency toward stereotyping in the naming of secondary figures in the background of a narrative occurs in a number of Dostoevsky's works. In "Uncle's Dream" we find Countess Zalikhvatskaya [Daredevil]; in *The Gambler*, Dur-Zazhigin [Stupid-Glow]; in *The Double*, Prince Svintchatkin [Pigkin]; the teacher Dardanellov [Dardanelle Straits] and the high school pupil Bulkin [Breadroll] in *The Brothers Karamazov*; the materialist and atheist Kislorodov [Oxygen] in *The Idiot*. The device is obvious in naming such secondary figures as the clerk Pisarenko [the clerk Clerky] in "Mister Prokharchin"; Doctor Kostopravov [Doctor Bone-twister] in *Private Thief*. The author may even call attention to this technique: in *The Adolescent*, the owner of the gambling house where the Adolescent wins by betting on zero is called Zershchikov [Zero]; in *The Eternal Husband* Dostoevsky notes that at the Zakhlebin's house, Trusotsky [Trotter] "trotted along after the rest of the company"; in *Crime and Punishment* Razumikhin [Reasoner] is "reasonable, as his surname clearly shows." [61]

Thus, the devices belonging to the representation within a representation may be applied to the background and its figures both in the pictorial arts and in literature. What takes place here is an enhancement of the semiotic quality of the representation: the description is not a sign of represented reality, as it is in the case of the central figures, but

61. A. Bem, "Lichnye imena u Dostoevskogo" [Personal names in Dostoevsky], *Sborniků vů chest' na prof. L. Miletichů* (Sophia, 1933), pp. 417–423. When Bem notes similar instances of name-giving, he does not relate them to the functions of the characters in the work, although he indicates that they must inevitably have been perceived against the background of poetics of the "realistic" school, representing the "legacy of Gogol which continued a definite tradition." The use of the former tradition appears most of all in the background of a narrative. Valuable material for examples of a similar kind may be found in Bem, "Slovar' lichnykh imen u Dostoevskogo" [Personal designations in Dostoevsky], *O Dostoevskom*, ed. A. Bem, II (Prague, 1933). For example, in *The Humiliated and the Insulted*, Dostoevsky makes one of his heroes, Masloboev, coin such surnames as "Baron Pomoikin" and "Count Butylkin" [Baron Dust-bin and Count Bottle] in a fit of irritation against the aristocrats. See Bem (Sophia, 1933), p. 422. This is another example of the usual appearance of this device in a representation within a representation.

a sign of a sign of this reality. It is a reinforcement of the conventionality of the description.[62] Accordingly, the central figures (the figures in the foreground) are opposed to the secondary figures by the fact that there is a lesser degree of semiotic quality or of conventionality in their description.[63] A lesser degree of semiotic quality is naturally associated with a greater degree of realism (verisimilitude) in the description; the central figures, as opposed to the secondary ones, are less semiotic (conventional) and, accordingly, more lifelike.

In medieval painting, a similar tendency toward the increased conventionality of the background representation and in the functionally less important parts is expressed in the characteristic ornamentalism. Here, we might cite as examples the traditional representation of the "icon hillocks" in the background of the icon, as purely conventional ornaments, or the emphatically ornamental representation of folds of garments in icons [probely] (Plates 17, 18, 19, 20). This heightening of conventionality is particularly obvious in the setting of the icon [oklad] which covers the less important parts of the icon, namely the background and the clothing. This traditional ornament of the Russian icon may be functionally interpreted as a "representation within a representation." [64]

A similar interpretation may be attributed in medieval painting to the forms which are only characteristic of the peripheral part of the representation, namely, forms in a sharp foreshortening and in linear perspective. It would seem that in medieval painting these two forms were considered as conventional, just as now we are inclined to treat strictly

62. A similar phenomenon may be observed in film. Compare the amplification of conventionality by devices of the silent film in the instance of the insertion of a story within a story.

63. B. A. Uspenskii, "O semiotike iskusstva" [On the semiotics of art], *Simpozium po strukturnomu izucheniiu znakovykh sistem* (Moscow, 1962), p. 127, where conventionality is defined in terms of the sign as a reference to the expression, rather than to the content, and the degree of conventionality is determined by the order of the components in the sequence: the sign of a sign of a sign . . . and so forth.

64. The conventional ornament in the margins of the old Russian icon may be interpreted in the same way. Explaining the origins of this decoration, A. I. Anisimov wrote that ancient icons were ornamented in the margins or in the representation of the nimbus, with stones set directly into the ground or into the canvas. "When he lacked these expensive materials, the artist traditionally represented them in paint and color, which then became for him customary attributes in the decoration of the icon." See A. Anisimov, "Domongol'skii period drevnerusskoi ikonopisi" [The pre-Mongolian period in old Russian icon-painting], *Voprosy restavratsii*, II (Moscow, 1928), p. 178. We can see that the conventional ornament here is directly connected with the representation within a representation.

frontal representations and elements of inverse perspective as conventional.[65]

No less typical of the medieval icon and of the medieval miniature is the symbolic representation of the attributes of the background. There, night may appear as a scroll set with stars, and dawn may be represented as a rooster (Plate 21);[66] In the background we may also find allegorical treatments like a river in the form of a stream flowing from a pitcher held by a human figure, or hell represented as a face placed in the background. The perception of this kind of representation implies an additional decoding of meaning on a higher level than the perception of nonsymbolic representations: this phenomenon is analogous to the decoding that takes place in natural language in the formation of phraseological units. Here again a heightening of conventionality with a typical increase in distance between the *signifiant* and the *signifié* is characteristic of the background representation. The conventional background emerges in such instances as an original ideogram.

The conventional representation of scenery by means of simple plaques which described the place of the action (in Shakespearian and pre-Shakespearian theater) may serve as another example of conventional representation of the background. Later canvas stage sets (flats), actually not very different from old conventional stage sets, also possess a high degree of conventionality. The conventionality of the stage set may be seen as deliberately contrasting with the onstage action, enhanc-

---

65. F. I. Buslaev has written that "in ancient Christian painting, the sculptural element dominated"—that is, in the icons were represented, as it were, not the figures themselves, but sculptures of the figures. F. I. Buslaev, "Vizantiiskaia i drevne-russkaia simvolika" [Byzantine and early Russian symbolism], in his book *Istoricheskie ocherki russkoi narodnoi slovesnosti i iskusstva*, II (St. Petersburg, 1910), 204. This is in full agreement with Buslaev's opinion that icons are deliberately conventional art forms— it follows, then, that he can discuss iconographic representation as constructed according to the principle of representation within representation.

Meyerhold, in his experiments with deliberately conventional theatrical production, evidently tried to create something like the inverted perspective on stage. In his memoirs, V. Piast noted that in staging *Calderon* Meyerhold was "bothered by the depth of the stage" and tried to flatten each mise-en-scène of the play. Here is Piast's description of the production: "when he came to the 'crowd' scenes, Meyerhold became inspired by the image of a 'bas-relief.' . . . In order to obtain the effect of the 'bas-relief' immense carpets were involved in the production; they were rolled up and put on the floor in the very back of the stage. When the actors stood on them, they became taller than the ones in front and their shoulders became visible above the heads of those standing in front of them." V. Piast, *Vstrechi* [Encounters] (Moscow, 1929), pp. 171–172. This again is an example of the application of the principle of inverted perspective related to a representation within a representation.

66. See the illustrations in the book *Byliny*, ed. M. Speranskii, I (Moscow, 1916), plate 4, and the remarks of V. N. Shchepkin (p. 441) concerning these illustrations.

ing its realism; here again the background for the central action functions as a "representation within a representation."

Perhaps this dramatic convention, where actor is opposed to scenery (the "representation within a representation"), had some effect on literature and the pictorial arts.[67]

THE UNITY OF THE PRINCIPLES OF REPRESENTATION
IN THE BACKGROUND AND THE FRAME

The unity of the formal devices for the representation of the background and of the frame is characteristic in various forms of art. For example, in older theater, pantomime functions as a background for the action and also often serves as a beginning (for instance, the pantomime introducing *The Murder of Gonzago* in traditional performances of Shakespeare's *Hamlet*).[68] In painting, particularly before the Renaissance, this unity is apparent in the common devices of perspective—of sharp foreshortenings, for example, used for the background and in the periphery of the painting (in opposition to the system of perspective used in the central part of the painting).[69] The same kind of unity may be observed in literary works in the opposition of the external description (characteristic of the background as well as of the frame of the narration) and the internal description.

This similarity of formal devices is by no means accidental. The background and frame belong to the periphery of the artistic text. Accordingly, when we consider a work of art as a closed system, we are justified in expecting, both in the frame and in the background, an external, rather than an internal, point of view. The background of the representation generally serves the same function as the foreground framing. Both are borders of the representation. Both background and foreground frame are in opposition to what takes place in the center of the representation. What is represented behind a central figure might just as easily be imagined as having taken place in front of that same figure—except that it would have hidden the figure. Conversely, what is in fact

---

67. Concerning the influence of the theater on painting, see E. Mâle, *L'art religieux de la fin du moyen âge en France* (Paris, 1908); G. Cohen, "The Influence of the Mysteries on Art," *Gazette des Beaux Arts* (1943); P. Francastel, *La réalité figurative: Eléments structurels de sociologie de l'art* (Paris, 1965), p. 215 ff.; G. R. Kernodle, *From Art to Theater: Form and Convention in the Renaissance* (Chicago, 1945).

68. Concerning the use of pantomime at the beginning of a play, see A. Anikst, 1965, p. 289.

69. See also the breaks in the soil in the foreground typical of ancient painting (expressed by means of caves and cliffs), which correspond in form to the breaks in the mountains in the background (see the "icon hillocks" as a traditionally conventional background of ancient representations).

situated in front of the central subject of a representation is sometimes transferred by the medieval painter to the background of the painting—probably, in part, so as not to hide the central representation (as in the representation of the interior of a building where the exterior of the building in which the action takes place is transferred to the background). In many cases, the background may be understood as a mirror reflection of the imaginary foreground, or as a transparent foreground.

Frequently, the frames are used to set off "a work within a work" (a painting within a painting, a play within a play, a story within a story) and thus the same means are used to designate a frame or a background, although, in principle, the two concepts and their realization are directly opposed. To take an example: if the background of a work is represented using the device of "representation within representation," then this incorporated representation has a greater degree of conventionality in comparison with the central work in which it is incorporated and which frames it. On the other hand, a representation which is placed into another representation may be the central one (at the center of the composition), while the representation which frames it lies on the periphery and plays the role of a frame. In this case the representation which plays the role of the frame is realized as more conventional in comparison with the internal (central) representation which has a higher degree of naturalness.

As a framing device in painting, we can refer to the representation of drawn curtains (in Raphael's *Sistine Madonna,* for instance), or to the frequent representation of windowframes or doorframes, or any other similar exterior motif, in the periphery of a painting.

Framing in theater may be realized by prologues which represent onstage dialogue between spectators and actors before the play actually begins (we may recall here the theatrical prologue to Goethe's *Faust*). In this way the central action is presented as a play within a play.

Finally, in literature, we can refer to the frequent technique of framing a short story by an introductory episode that is not related to the action itself, but into which the short story appears to be inserted (*Thousand and One Nights, The Decameron,* and so forth).

In constructing the frame for a work—in the form of another, complementary work which encloses it—the artist often uses an external point of view. This point of view corresponds to the point of view of the audience or the reader; it is characterized by marked conventionality (ornamentalization), which sets off the uniqueness of the central work.

The degree of conventionality in a work of art fluctuates; these fluctuations may be variously interpreted. A manifestation of conventionality in the description may include an unexpected reference to the code, rather than to the message. For example, Pushkin may refer to a formal device in his poetry:

I vot uzhe treshchat morozy
I serebriatsia sred' polei . . .
(Chitatel' zhdet uzh rifmy *rozy:*
Na, vot voz'mi ee skorei!)
	[The frosts begin to snap, and
	  gleaming
	With silver hoar, the meadows
	  lie . . .
	(The reader waits the rhyme-
	  words: beaming,
	Well, take it, since you are so
	  sly!).][70]

References to the code rather than the message may be exemplified by the convention of addressing the public in the middle of the action of a play (for example, the character of Hans Wurst in medieval comedy). In both cases there is a reference within the text of the narrative to the metalinguistic level which may be conceived as a setting off of the narrative itself.[71]

Thus, we can see that the device of "the work within a work" can be used to represent the frame as well as the background. In both cases, the use of the external point of view is characteristic.

CONCLUDING REMARKS

We have attempted to reveal the unity of the formal devices of composition in literature and in the pictorial arts by presenting some common structural principles of internal organization of the artistic text (in its broad sense). This has proved possible because the literary work and the work of representational art seem to possess the features of a closed system—each work presents a unique microworld, organized according to its own laws and characterized by its own spatial and temporal structure. Further, we have seen that in a literary work and in a work

70. A. S. Pushkin, *Eugene Onegin,* trans. Babette Deutsch, in A. Yarmolinsky, *The Poems, Prose and Plays of Alexander Pushkin* (New York, 1936), p. 199—Trans.

71. "Signs which are used in art are characterized by a different degree of conventionality because of the arbitrary connection between their ordinary usage outside of art and the meaning which they acquire within an artistic system. Art may use as ready-made those signs that have been fabricated in the given society (mythological symbols which have become literary images, etc.), or it may create them anew. . . . Conventional signs, with their distinct differentiation of the plane of content and plane of expression, are conscious of the conventionality of their codes." Iu. Lotman, B. Uspenskii, "Uslovnost' v iskusstve" [Conventionality in art], *Filosofskaia entsiklopediia* V (Moscow, 1970), pp. 287–288—trans.

of representational art, a plurality of authorial positions may be present, entering into different kinds of relational patterns.

In one type of description in a literary work, the authorial position is clearly fixed, and we can consider it as we would consider the position of the artist who paints in the system of direct perspective. In this case, we are justified in posing two important questions: where was the author when he described the events, and how did he learn about the behavior of his characters? In other words, the question which concerns us here has to do with the reader's reliance on the author's view; in the same way we might conjecture about the position of the artist in relation to the event he represents in a painting, from the perspective that he uses in the representation.[72] The representation in direct perspective may be compared to the principle of psychological description from an external viewpoint, with its uses of words of estrangement ("as if," "as it seems," and so on). Description in this instance may be said to be subjective—that is, it makes reference to one or another subjective point of view held by the author, a point of view which is inevitably accidental. In this instance, moreover, the author's knowledge is limited; there are some things he does not know: the inner state of a character in a literary description or, in a perspective representation, that which lies beyond the limits of his horizon. We are speaking here, primarily, about the conscious limitation which the author imposes on his own knowledge, and by means of which he hopes to ensure a greater degree of verisimilitude. It is by virtue of these limitations that the question of the sources of authorial knowledge, about which we have just spoken, is logically justified.

There are a number of cases where the author has particularly emphasized the limitations of his own knowledge. We might recall here the sentence from Gogol's "The Overcoat," discussed earlier, where the author (the narrator), after reporting to us what Akaky Akakievich thought, adds hurriedly: "But perhaps he did not even think this—is it possible to enter into a man's soul and to find out everything that he is thinking?" [73]

Equally significant, in this respect, are the attempts to somehow explain or justify authorial knowledge—and in particular, to motivate the penetration into the mind of the character. This technique is especially characteristic of Dostoevsky, and is illustrated in his foreword to "Krot-

72. See Gukovskii, 1959, p. 201, and also R. Scholes and R. Kellogg, *The Nature of Narrative* (New York, 1966), Chapter 7.

73. See above and also examples from the works of Dostoevsky discussed by Likhachev, 1967, p. 326.

kaya." According to L. Stillman: "In his discussion Dostoevsky uses a fictional stenographer who records the monologue—not an internal monologue, it is true, but a monologue spoken by (and here we have another fiction!) '. . . a hardened hypochondriac, one of those who talk to themselves.' " Stillman continues: "A characteristic trait of Dostoevsky is a concern for motivation, for a formal justification of the speech used to reveal the internal monologue. Hence the extensive dialogues, oral monologues and pseudo-documents: the memoirs, diaries, confessions, letters." [74]

There is, however, another system of description (or representation), in which the question of the sources of the authorial knowledge is disallowed—that is, it is essentially incorrect within the limits of this system. As an example of this, we may refer to the epic and to the representations constructed according to the principles of inverse perspective in pictorial art. An epic poem may end, for example, with the death of all the characters, but we cannot ask how these events came to be known (a natural question in "realistic" literature) without stepping outside the frame of this particular artistic system.[75] In the same way the representation of an object done in inverted perspective is given not through the perception of an individual person, but in its essence. In this case the artist would not allow himself to represent a square object as narrowing towards the horizon line (as prescribed by the rules of linear perspective) just because he happens to see it that way at that particular moment and from that particular position. The artist represents the object as it is and not as it appears to him. There is no question here of the relativity of knowledge and consequently no question of the degree to which the artist may be trusted. The same principle applies to the epic: the stability of epithets in epic works could be considered as a formal characteristic of the description of an object not simply as it appears, but as it really is (not of its appearance, but of its essence).[76]

The concurrence between the principles of representation in the system of inverse perspective and the principles of description in the epic pertains even to the details of description. Thus it is characteristic

---

74. L. N. Shtil'man, "Nabliudeniia nad nekotorymi osobennostiami kompozitsii i stilia v romane Tolstogo *Voina i Mir*" [Observations on some special problems of composition and style in Tolstoy's *War and Peace*], American Contributions to the Fifth International Congress of Slavists (The Hague, 1963), p. 330.

75. In general the fact that you can or cannot ask specific kinds of questions is a feature characterizing an artistic system.

76. The conventionality of such a description may be acknowledged only from the position of some other system of description. Within the frame of the particular system, this kind of description is objective.

of the system of inverse perspective to compress the field of vision: the foliage on the trees may be represented here by only a few leaves, a crowd of people may be represented by a small group of several persons, and so on.[77] A similar device is found in folklore and in old literatures, where the exploits of an army are symbolized in the exploits of a single hero—in the Russian byliny, for example, by Evpaty Kolovrat, or Vsevolod Bui Tur, and so on.[78] We can also refer here to the traditional description of battle in epic literature: the presentation of the battle in the form of a sequence of separate man-to-man combats (for example, in Homer's *Iliad*).[79]

On the other hand, the compression of the field of vision may result in the apparent loss of the bond among the separate objects represented in a painting (when the hand barely touches the object, without actually holding it; or when the legs of moving men collide confusedly).[80] A similar absence of bonding among separate episodes is also possible in literature, primarily because of the special "concentration" of description in each episode (a concentration so strong that each description comes to have its own validity, and the bonds between them fade). This is particularly evident in folklore. We can also see an "uncoordination" in Shakespeare noted by Goethe and compared by him to the use of double lighting in painting. (The use of plural light sources is one of the basic characteristics of the system of inverted perspective.)[81]

The stable epithets of epic are similar to the stable attributes of the old icons. As V. P. Sokolov has shown: "In the same way that the 'tender prince Vladimir, the dear, bright sun' remains 'tender' and 'dear, bright sun' even at the executions, so the saints of the Russian icon do not part, under any circumstances or at any time of the day or night, with their holy garb. The saint always wears his sacred robes, a prince is always

77. See Zhegin, 1970, p. 54.

78. See D. S. Likhachev, *Chelovek v literature Drevnei Rusi* [Man in the literature of old Russia] (Moscow, 1958), pp. 74–75; and P. G. Bogatyrev, *Slovatskie epicheskie rasskazy i liro-epicheskie pesni* [Slovak epic stories and lyric-epic songs] (Moscow, 1963), pp. 28–29.

79. See F. F. Zelinsky for the formulation of the "principle of chronological non-concurrence" in Homer. According to Zelinsky, Homeric action is always developed sequentially, never in a parallel development; that is, two actions never occur simultaneously, but one after the other. See T. Zielinski, "Die Behandlung der gleichzeitigen Ereignisse in antiken Epos," *Philologus*, Supplementband 8 (1899–1900). Compare this with M. Al'tman, "K poetike Gomera" [Towards a poetics of Homer], *Iazyk i literatura*, IV (Leningrad, 1928), p. 48.

80. See Zhegin, 1970, p. 54.

81. See *Razgovory Gete, sobrannye Ekkermanom* [Conversations with Goethe, collected by Eckermann], I (St. Petersburg, 1905), p. 338 ff.

dressed in princely attire, wearing a crown, a soldier in a cloak and armour." [82]

Multiple authorial positions (points of view) are theoretically possible in both kinds of descriptive systems. If we speak about the pictorial arts, the plurality of viewpoints is characteristic in the first place of the system of inverse perspective; however, it can also be found occasionally in modern pictorial art, and at almost all points in the historical evolution of art. In respect to literature, and contrary to some widely-held opinions (that trace the description constructed from a plurality of viewpoints to the beginnings of the realistic social and psychological novel), the use of several different points of view in narration may be noted even in relatively ancient texts.

Thus, the device of parallelism, characteristic of the epics of very different cultures, often indicates the parallel use of several viewpoints. To take a simple example, when the poet says:

Dobryi molodets k senichkam pri-
    vorachival,
Vasilii k teremu prikhazhival—
	[The good fellow was approaching
	    the entry,
	Vasily was coming to the tower
	    house],

he has constructed the description of the same event on two different levels—levels corresponding to two viewpoints (we may say that for some people the hero might be a "good fellow," while to others he might be just "Vasily").

Reference to plural points of view may be seen occasionally in the Irish saga—for example, in the description of the meeting of Cuchulain and Emer in *The Wooing of Emer*. First Emer and her attendants are described as Cuchulain sees them; this allows the narrator to characterize Emer. Cuchulain is then described as Emer and her attendants see him. (He is presented for the most part through the direct speech of one of the attendants, a technique which is typical of epic literature in general.)

The utilization of several opposing points of view may also be observed in old Russian literature: for example, in the sixteenth-century story of the taking of Kazan, where the description combines the opposite points of view of the Russians and the beseiged people of Kazan.[83] We

---

82. V. P. Sokolov, *Iazyk drevnerusskoi ikonopisi: I. Obraznye odezhdy* [The language of the old Russian icon: The Symbolic clothing] (Kazan', 1916), p. 12.

83. See the analysis of this work, from other critical positions, in the works of Likhachev: 1867, pp. 104–107; and "Literaturnyi etiket russkogo srednevekov'ia" [Literary etiquette of the Russian Middle Ages] *Poetics, Poetyka, Poetika,* I (Warsaw, 1961), pp. 646–648.

can note in this connection Bakhtin's remarks on the multiplicity of levels and the polyphonic quality of mystery plays; and on the rudimentary polyphony in Shakespeare, in Rabelais, in Cervantes, and in Grimmelshausen.[84]

In literature, the very possibility of choosing a system of description has its source in everyday speech and narration (we suggested this point earlier). Indeed, the narrator must always choose how to tell a story, whether to reproduce his perceptions of the events sequentially, or to present them in some rearranged form. The rearrangement may be designed to produce a stronger effect, a principle which is used in the detective story: in the beginning of the story the events are arranged in such a way that the audience does not suspect the solution—and then the solution is suddenly presented. Or, on the contrary, it may be designed to produce an objective account of the facts: the narrator does not communicate his own original understanding of the events, considering it at the moment irrelevant—that is, he does not rely only on his position, but tells how everything "in fact" happened, according to his reconstruction.

The two systems of description we have discussed should be considered neither in an evaluative sense nor in an evolutionary context (although the internal point of view is typical of the world view of the Middle Ages,[85] while the external point of view is characteristic of the modern period).[86] Rather, these two systems should be viewed as two basic options between which the author (the narrator or the painter) must choose, and which can coexist in various combinations in the text of the work of art.

---

84. See Bakhtin, 1963, pp. 2–3, 47.

85. The fundamental objectivity in perception and in the representation of the world stems here from the nonacceptance of the arbitrariness of the relation between the sign and the signified, a position which is generally characteristic of the medieval world view.

86. The attention to the method of description (and in particular, to the language of description)—which makes the facts being described depend on the method of their discovery (in other words, attention devoted to the "how" rather than to the "what" of the description)—is indeed characteristic of the modern world view (we might refer here to positivism in philosophy and quantum mechanics in physics).

SELECTED WORKS BY
BORIS USPENSKY

"O semiotike iskusstva" [On semiotics of art], *Simpozium po strukturnomu izucheniiu znakovykh sistem.* Moscow, 1962, pp. 125–129.

"Semiotika u Chestertona" [Semiotics in Chesterton], *Simpozium po strukturnomu izucheniiu znakovykh sistem.* Moscow, 1962, pp. 149–152.

"Gadanie na igral'nykh kartakh, kak semioticheskaia sistema" [Fortune-telling in cards as a semiotic system], *Simpozium po strukturnomu izucheniiu znakovykh sistem.* Moscow, 1962, pp. 83–86 (in conjunction with M. I. Lekomtseva).

"K sisteme peredachi izobrazheniia v russkoi ikonopisi" [Toward a system of transmission of the representation in Russian iconography], *Trudy po znakovym sistemam* II (Uch. Zap. TGU, vyp. 181), Tartu, 1965, pp. 247–257.

Strukturnaia tipologiia iazykov [Structural typology of languages]. Moscow, 1965.

Iazyki Afriki: Voprosy struktury, istorii i tipologii [Languages of Africa: questions of structure, history and typology]. Edited and with Introduction by Uspensky. Moscow, 1966.

"Personologicheskie problemy v lingvisticheskom aspekte" [Personological problems from a linguistic aspect], *Tezisy dokladov vo vtoroi letnei shkole po vtorichnym modeliruiushchim sistemam.* Tartu, 1966, pp. 6–12.

"Struktura khudozhestvennogo teksta i tipologiia kompozitsii" [Structure of the artistic text and the typology of compositions], *Tezisy dokladov vo vtoroi letnei shkole po vtorichnym modeliruiushchim sistemam.* Tartu, 1966, pp. 20–26.

"Problemy lingvisticheskoi tipologii v svete razlicheniia 'govoriashchego' (adresanta) i 'slushaiushchego' (adresata)" [Problems of linguistic typology in terms of the distinction of the speaker (adressor) and listener (addressee)], *To Honor Roman Jakobson, Essays on the Occasion of His Seventieth Birthday.* Vol. 3. The Hague—Paris, 1967, pp. 2087–2108.

"Personologicheskaia klassifikatsiia, kak semioticheskaia problema" [Personological classification as a semiotic problem]. *Trudy po znakovym sistemam* III (Uch. Zap. TGU, vyp. 198), Tartu, 1967, pp. 7–29 (in conjunction with A. M. Piatigorsky).

"P. A. Florenskii i ego rabota 'Obratnaia perspektiva' " [P. A. Florensky and his work "Inverted Perspective"], *Trudy po znakovym sistemam* III (Uch. Zap. TGU, vyp. 198), Tartu, 1967, pp. 378–380 (in conjunction with A. A. Dorogov and V. V. Ivanov).

Arkhaicheskaia sistema tserkovnoslavianskogo proiznosheniia (iz istorii liturgicheskogo proiznosheniia v Rossii), [Archaic system of Old Church Slavic pronunciation (some questions of the history of liturgical pronunciation in Russia)]. Moscow, 1968.

"Les problèmes sémiotiques du style à la lumière de la linguistique," *Information sur les Sciences Sociales* 7, no. 1 (1968): 123–240. Also in *Approaches to Semiotics*, Vol. 4. The Hague, 1971.

Strukturnaia obshchnost' razlichnykh vidov iskusstva na materiale zhivopisi i literatury [Common structural characteristics in different forms of art based on materials from the pictorial arts and literature]. Warsaw, 1968. (Preprint)

"Kety, ikh iazyk, cul'tura, istoriia" [The Kets, their language, culture, and history], *Ketskii sbornik: Lingvistika.* Edited by Uspensky. Moscow, 1968 (in conjunction with V. V. Ivanov and V. N. Toporov).

"Ketskie pesni i drugie teksty" [Ket songs and other texts], *Ketskii sbornik. Mifologiia, etnografiia, teksty.* Edited by Uspensky. Moscow, 1969, pp. 213–226 (in conjunction with V. V. Ivanov, V. N. Toporov, T. N. Moloshnaya, D. M. Segal and T. V. Tsivyan).

"Per l'analisi semiotica delle antiche icone russe," to be published.

"Semioticheskie problemy stilia v lingvisticheskom osviashchenii" [Semiotic problems of style in the light of linguistics] *Trudy po znakovym sistemam,* IV (Uch. Zap. TGU, vyp. 236), Tartu, 1969, pp. 487–501.

Principles of Structural Typology. The Hague—Paris, 1968.

"Vliianie iazyka na religioznoe soznanie" [Influence of language on religious consciousness], *Trudy po znakovym sistemam* IV (Uch. Zap. TGU, vyp. 236), Tartu, 1969, pp. 159–168.

Iz istorii russkikh kanonicheskikh imen (Istoriia udareniia v kanonicheskikh imenakh sobstvennykh v ikh otnoshenii k russkim literaturnym i razgovornym formam) [From the history of Russian canonic names: history of the stress in canonic personal names in their relation to Russian literary and oral forms]. Moscow, 1969.

"Sulla semiotica dell'arte," *I Sistemi di Segni e lo Strutturalismo Sovietico.* Edited by Remo Faccani and Umberto Eco. Milan, 1969, pp. 87–90.

"La cartomanzia come sistema semiotico," *I Sistemi di Segni e lo Strutturalismo Sovietico,* ed. Remo Faccani and Umberto Eco. Milan, 1969, pp. 243–247 (in conjunction with M. I. Lekomceva).

Poetika kompozizii. Struktura khudozhestvennogo teksta i tipologiia kompozitsionnoi formy [A poetics of composition: structure of the artistic text and the typology of a compositional form]. Moscow, 1970.

"K issledovaniiu iazyka drevnei zhivopisi" [Towards a study of the language of ancient pictorial art]. Introduction to: L. F. Zhegin, *Iazyk zhivopisnogo proizvedeniia. Uslovnost' drevnego iskusstva.* Moscow, 1970, pp. 4–34.

"Uslovnost' v iskusstve" [Conventionality in art], *Filosofskaia entsiklopediia.* Vol. 5. Moscow, 1970, pp. 287–288 (in conjunction with Yury M. Lotman).

" 'Grammaticheskaia pravil'nost' i poeticheskaia metafora" ["Grammatical correctness" and the poetic metaphor], *Tezisy dokladov IV letnei shkoly po vtorichnym modeliruiushchim sistemam 17–24 avgusta 1970 g.* Tartu, 1970, pp. 123–126.

"Struktura khudozhestvennogo teksta i tekstologiia (nekotorye voprosy peredachi priamoi rechi v *Voine i mire* Tolstogo)" [Structure of the poetic text and textology; some questions pertaining to the transmission of direct speech in *War and Peace* by Tolstoy], *Poetika i stilistika russkoi literatury. Sbornik pamiati V. V. Vinogradova.* Leningrad, 1971, pp. 219–230.

"O semiotike ikony" [On the semiotics of the icon], *Trudy po znakovym sistemam* V (Uch. Zap. TGU, vyp. 284), Tartu, 1971, pp. 178–222.

"O semioticheskom mekhanizme kul'tury" [On the semiotic mechanism of culture], *Trudy po znakovym sistemam* V (Uch. Zap. TGU, vyp. 284), Tartu, 1971, pp. 144–166 (in conjunction with Yury M. Lotman).

"Mena imen v Rossii v istoricheskoi i semioticheskoi perspektive (k rabote A. M. Selishcheva 'Smena familii i lichnykh imen')" [Name changing in Russia in historical and semiotic perspective (concerning A. M. Selishchev's work "Changes in family and personal names")], *Trudy po znakovym sistemam* V (Uch. Zap. TGU, vyp. 284), Tartu, 1971, pp. 481–492.

"Poétique de la composition. Point de vue: le problème de la dénomination. L'alternance des points de vue interne et externe en tant que marque du cadre dans une oeuvre littéraire," *Poétique* 9 (1972): 124–134.

"Structural Isomorphism of Verbal and Visual Art," *Poetics,* (in press).

"Mif—imia—kul'tura" [Myth—name—culture], *Trudy po znakovym sistemam* VI, (in press) (in conjunction with Yury M. Lotman).

INDEX

Address, forms of, 23–25 and n.
Alberti, Leon Battista, 135
Anecdote, 11 n., 127
Architecture, 2
Art: plastic, 2 n., Japanese, 145 n., Egyptian, 158 and n., Mayan, 158, still life, 159 n. *See also* Art, pictorial
Art, pictorial: temporal sequence in, 77–78 and n., plates 3, 4; placing of figures, 124; opposition of internal and external viewpoints, 134–135; Assyrian, 135 and Plate 5; Renaissance, 135; importance and function of the frame in, 140–141, 166; organization of microspaces in, 154, 155, Plate 8; and backgrounds in medieval painting, 163–164, Plate 21. *See also* Background; Frame of artistic text; Perspective; Periphery
Artistic text, 5, 139 n.; forcible violation of, 138–139; compound nature of, 151–155. *See also* Frame of artistic text
Author: as evaluator, 8, 13; shifts in position of, 17–21; and points of view in naming, 26–27; influence of, on speech of a character, 41–45; internal and external positions of, and speech of characters, 50–56; spatial attachment to a character, 58–59; and grammar, 69–75; positions of, in narration, 87–89 (external and internal), 89–94 (sequential alternation), 95–97 (simultaneous); as invisible observer, 130–131; retrospective position of, 133. *See also* Knowledge, author's; Narrator; Point(s) of view; Speech
Avvakum, *Life of the Archpriest Avvakum*, 16, 44–45, 68–69, 72, 125

Background: principles of representation,

155–165; in medieval painting, 156; and microspaces in Renaissance art, 156–157, Plate 13; in ancient painting, 157–158; as decoration, 157 and n., 158; as a picture within a picture, 157, 158, 159, plates 14, 15, 16; conventional representation of characters, 163, in ornamentalism, 163, in perspective, 163–164 and n., in symbols, 164, of scenery, 164–165; and frame, unity of representation, 165–167
Bakhtin, M. M., 3 n., 5 n., 8 n., 10–11, 15, 19 n., 132 n., 133 and n., 151, 172
Behavior: means of describing, on psychological plane, 83–87; motivations for character's, 120–121
Bely (Belyĭ), Andrey, 72 n., 109 n.
Bem, A., 162 n.
Benoit, A., 158
Bird's-eye viewpoint, 63–65, 156
Bonds among objects or episodes, lack of, 170
Botticelli, S., *Adoration of the Magi*, 12 n., Plate 1
Brothers Karamazov, The (Dostoevsky), 12, 103, 112, 162; and phraseological plane, 26–27; and spatial and temporal planes, 58, 67–69; and psychological plane, 85 n., 87, 91, 96–97, 105; internal and external description of characters in, 92–95; combined points of view in, 133–134
Bulgakov, Mikhail A., *The Master and Margarita*, 79, 131
Bunin, Ivan A.: "Natalie," 88; "The Grammar of Love," 148

Center of a representation and viewpoints, 145
Characters: and ideological plane, 8, 9,

177

Icherzählung (first-person narration), 19, 68–69; transformation of, 88, 90–91, 97
Icon hillocks, 163, 165 n., plates 17, 18
Icons, Russian, 158, 170–171; ornamentation of, 163 and n., plates 17, 18, 19, 20
Ideology (evaluation), plane of, 6, 8–16; and temporal perspective, 69; substituted viewpoint, 119; and phraseological plane, 102–104; and psychological plane, 104–105; and the described object, 123–124; and irony, 126; and opposition of internal and external viewpoints, 131–132; and combined points of view, 133; and the framing of a narrative, 151
Illumination. *See* Lighting
Introduction of a character, 22, 27 n.
Irony, creation of, 103, 125–126
Ivan the Terrible, 24

Kafka, Franz, *Metamorphosis*, 160
Kaverin, V., *Two Captains*, 91
Khlebnikov, V., 72
Knowledge, author's: and psychological viewpoint, 98–99; conscious limitation of, 168; attempts to justify, 168–169; unquestioned sources of, 169–170

Language(s): juxtaposition of, in speech, 53, 54; synthesis of, 53; and the object described. *See also* Speech, French, use of
langue, 36 and n., 40
Lermontov, Mikhail Y., *A Hero of Our Times*, 9–10
Leskov, Nikolai S., 19 and n.; "A Lady Macbeth of the Mtsensk District," 69–71, 74–75, 147
Likhachev, D. S., 68–69, 123, 149
Lighting, 2; sources, 96, 135, 154; double, 108, 170
Literature: and point of view, 5; naming as a construction device in, 25–27; translation into visual media, 78–79; frames of a work in, 146–151, 166; microdescriptions in, 154–155; background figures ("extras"), behavior of, 159–161, naming of, 161–162; mobile and stationary characters in, 161
London, Jack, "Love of Life," 149
Lotman, Yury M., 9 n., 12 n., 16, 63, 78–79
Luke, Gospel of, 149

Mandelshtam, O. E., 78 n.

Melnikov-Perchersky, 121, 123
Memory, 77
Miracle, compositional function of, 146–147
Mirror images, 143–145
Monologue, internal, 43. *See also* Narrated monologue; *skaz*
Montage, 3, 5, 62
Movements: sequential, 60–62; of author's spatial position, 60–63; representation of, in pictorial arts, 62; of observer, 62–63

Names and naming: and points of view, 20–31; in ordinary speech, 20–21 and n.; in journalistic writing, 21–22; of characters, 121–122, 161–162; as a framing device, 152. *See also* Epistolary prose; Napoleon Bonaparte
Napoleon Bonaparte, naming of: by press, 21–22; in *War and Peace*, 27–32
Narrated monologue, 18, 41–43, 52, 55, 110
Narration, "consistent," 89
Narrator: role of, in *War and Peace*, 109–117; perception of, 111–112; types of, in literature, 111 n.; temporal position of, 113 and n.; "panchronic" and synchronic, 113–114; knowledge of, 115–116; first-person, function as a frame, 147
Neoclassicism, 12 and n.
Nicknames, 20–21, 27
Niedersicht. See Perspective, "sharply converging"

Observer, viewpoint of, 18, 21, 115. *See also* Point(s) of view, external

Painting. *See* Art, pictorial
Pantomime, 165
Paralinguistic phenomena, 41
Parallelism, 171
parole, 36 and n., 40
Perceiver, function of, as a frame, 147 and n., Plate 7
Perception, 77, 112 and n.
Periphery of artistic text, 143, 156 and n., 159, 165–166
Perspective, 57, 165; direct (linear), 2 and n., 135 and n., 168; inverted, 2, 80, 135–136, 169–170, 171, examples, 142, 143, 145; double, in a narrative, 67; "sharply converging" (*Niedersicht*), 143, examples,